THE PRINCIPLES AND PRACTICE

*of*

# HEALTH EVANGELISM

## SECOND EDITION

ELVIN ADAMS, MD, MPH

# THE PRINCIPLES AND PRACTICE OF HEALTH EVANGELISM
## SECOND EDITION

*iUniverse books may be ordered through booksellers or by contacting:*

*iUniverse*
*1663 Liberty Drive*
*Bloomington, IN 47403*
*www.iuniverse.com*
*844-349-9409*

*ISBN: 978-1-6632-3590-9 (sc)*
*ISBN: 978-1-6632-3591-6 (e)*

*Print information available on the last page.*

*iUniverse rev. date: 02/14/2022*

# Contents

# Foreword

It would be difficult to exaggerate the impact the first reading of this book by Dr. Elvin Adams had on changing my perspective on what constitutes "health evangelism." At the time, I was the Health Ministries coordinator for a new church plant and thought we were doing just fine in that department.

We held monthly Dinner with the Doctor programs where physicians in the community lectured while the attendees enjoyed a free plant-based meal. We encouraged church members to attend to make friends with the community and considered this good friendship evangelism. We did some cooking schools as well, hoping to encourage further healthy habits and solidify those friendships.

Then my pastor, Chris Anderson, read this book and handed it to me telling me, "we need to do this…"

The profound concepts shared by Dr. Adams completely changed my view of what true health evangelism encompasses. We changed the way we presented our monthly programs and added many weekly programs as well. They all strove to follow the simple principles found in this book. And results followed.

It seems to me that there are problems within the end-time remnant church. Isaiah 58 and Revelation 3 outline many of these. Here are a few: satisfaction with knowledge without passion to share, lack of personal transformation resulting from following truth, lack of friends who aren't already familiar with said truths, and inability/lack of experience sharing.

This book outlines the antidote for all these. It is health evangelism, true medical missionary work. And it is vital for every member of the remnant church to take hold of this work at this time in earth's history.

Dr. Adams expertly shares principles as well as personal anecdotes demonstrating the foundation and practical applications of true health evangelism. Without undue focus on the problems, he presents the solutions. His long experience in public health warns of potential pitfalls and solutions to avoid them.

In summary, Principles and Practice of Health Evangelism is a lifechanging volume. Health evangelism is the work for this time. The "principles" are here clearly outlined, logically developed, and a pleasure to read. It is my hope that everyone reading will take the next step and "practice" what is contained in this important book.

Eric Nelson, MD

# Preface to First Edition

It was more than 10 years ago that I wrote "The Handbook of Health Evangelism." Since then, I have had more experience doing health evangelism. My ideas have been refined and expanded.

I have developed new tools for evaluating health evangelism programs to see if they accurately meet the definition. I also foresee the impact health evangelism, rightly conducted, can have on church growth and retention of new members

The health concepts first delivered to the Seventh-day Adventist church more than 150 years ago have been verified by the Adventist Health Studies of the past 60 years. Larger studies of secular populations have expanded this knowledge of healthful living far beyond our investigative capabilities.

Gifted doctors and scientists have written books and developed health programs that have caught the interest of many in the public. Healthful living has become popular with millions, but these movements are most often not led by Seventh-day Adventists.

This book is a challenge to all Seventh-day Adventist health professionals, church administrators, and church members to take up the cause of health evangelism. Health evangelism brings new levels of health to individuals and creates a closer walk with God. Health evangelism brings people to the church and keeps them in the church.

Who am I to write this book? Listing my credentials seems like bragging and unchristian on the face of it. But here in Texas there is a saying that "It ain't bragging if it is true." So, here is a listing of my educational and life experiences that I bring to the writing of this book.

I was born a fifth-generation Seventh-day Adventist. (Admittedly, this has no merit with God). I was raised in a two-parent home of college educated parents who served as missionaries in Japan, Korea, and Jamaica and were employees of the church in one capacity or another their entire lives.

I attended Seventh-day Adventist elementary and secondary schools in the mission field. My senior high school year I attended and graduated from Andrews Academy in Berrien Springs, Michigan. My major field of study in college was chemistry. I graduated from Washington Adventist University in Takoma Park, Maryland.

My wife and I have been married over 50 years and have raised three daughters who are successful in their chosen professions.

My medical training was at Loma Linda University School of Medicine. I completed a general rotating internship at the Washington Adventist Hospital. I also completed a residency in internal medicine at the Loma Linda Medical Center. I am board certified as a specialist in internal medicine by the American Board of Internal Medicine and continue to participate in the Maintenance of Certification program of the Board.

I received a Master of Public Health degree from the Bloomberg School of Public Health of Johns Hopkins University in Baltimore Maryland.

I served my country as a Lt. Commander in the U.S. Public Health Service during the Viet Nam war. I was appointed the Medical Staff Director of the National Clearinghouse on Smoking and Health. It was my privilege to author, contribute to, and review many of the U.S. Surgeon General's reports on the harmful effects of tobacco use in its various forms.

I have been employed by Adventist Hospitals. I have been affiliated with the self-supporting hospitals and I have been in private medical practice. I have had or still have licenses to practice in California, Maryland, North Carolina, and Texas.

In the field of Public Health, I have served as Medical Director and Local Health Authority in multiple county jurisdictions. I have been certified multiple times as a specialist in HIV/AIDS by the American Academy of HIV Medicine.

Within the Seventh-day Adventist church structure, I have served as the Health Ministries Director at the conference level. For a period of three years, I was an Associate Health Director of the General Conference Department of Health Ministries.

In the local church, I have served as Sabbath School teacher, deacon, elder, grounds & maintenance worker, and Director of Health Ministries. More recently, I have been involved in the radio and television ministry of the Crowley Seventh-day Adventist church in Crowley, Texas.

Health evangelism has been a constant interest of mine throughout the decades. I created the Best Weigh nutrition and weight management program in 1974 and have conducted it hundreds of times in churches across this country. Best Weigh has received some international attention and has been conducted in Great Britton and Australia.

I have authored hundreds of articles, presentations, and several scientific publications in peer reviewed scientific journals. My larger books include, "Jesus Was Thin, So You Can Be Thin Too," and "The Handbook of Health Evangelism."

My single-minded focus has been church-based health evangelism. The local church is the Christian's home. Too many health education programs contain useful scientific information but don't lead people to Christ or fellowship in the local church.

People don't have the power to change. God provides the power to change. This power is imparted by the Holy Spirit, through the merits of our Lord and Savior Jesus Christ. Too often this is the missing element in health programming. Information, insight, education, and example are all too weak to change a sinner into a saint.

We must come to see that all things are possible through Jesus Christ who clearly stated that "Without Me you can do nothing." **John 15:5 (NKJV)** Jesus saves your mind, soul, and body.

This book is written to focus your attention on how to conduct health evangelism in a soul winning way utilizing the resources in the local church. Read and with God's help make it happen in your local church.

# Preface to the Second Edition

The first edition of this book was well received by many who are dedicated to the concepts of health evangelism.

Health evangelism is a sleeping giant in the Seventh-day Adventist Church. The greatest opportunity before us today is a meaningful response to the global pandemic of obesity. Obesity is the root cause of dozens of diseases that result in disability and death.

There are many preventive approaches to the obesity crisis. There are dozens of new diet books every year. There are prescription medications, surgical approaches, commercial programs, special foods, and a variety of supplements. Nothing is working. Obesity is getting worse and worse in the United States and around the world.

Obese Sabbath keepers squeeze into pews from week to week with the assurance that they are worshiping on the right day, but at the same time abandoning the nutritional and exercise counsel given us 150 years ago. Something must change!

Do we have a God who can change us or not? Salvation is not just for the "soul." The good news in health evangelism is that Jesus can work with you to successfully change you, not just for eternity but right now. We must show our neighbors that we have the key to long-term success. Come to our church. Join us who are struggling with you. We will show you how to eat and how to exercise. We will share precious promises from the Bible. We will pray with you and for you.

We will cry with you when you fail. We will pray for ourselves, and you that we may do better tomorrow. We will hold on to you.

Health evangelism can be applied to any of the ills that affect the public. There are dozens of health programs that need the evangelist modifications to make them what health evangelism should be.

Today we live in a data driven society. Health evangelism has no growth chart, no check list of milestones reached. It is buried in the titles of a thousand administrators who have a half dozen other titles as well. They have no budget, and no administrative staff to assist them. There is no definition of what kinds of data is needed and no system to collect and analyze the effectiveness of health evangelism. Perhaps it really is dead and not just sleeping.

In the past five years numerous suggestions for major and minor edits to this book have been suggested by my readers. This edition has been carefully copy edited by several friends but especially Dr. Eric Nelson of Hixon, TN.

May God use this tool to awaken, energize, and mobilize health evangelism in this sick and failing world. God will bless us if we do His work in His way.

# 1

# What is Health Evangelism?

HEALTH EVANGELISM IS THE GOOD NEWS THAT JESUS MAKES PEOPLE healthier. Health evangelism is Christ-centered evangelism integrated with a health program. The health component of health evangelism contains information regarding the risks associated with unhealthy living and provides behavior change strategies designed to correct bad habits and addictions.

> *Health evangelism is the good news that Jesus makes people healthier.*

The evangelistic component of health evangelism introduces people to Jesus. Jesus provides the power to change. Lasting behavior change is impossible for many people who rely on their own efforts, but a relationship with Jesus transforms the life. This is true in the physical as well as the spiritual realm.

Many people who previously didn't know Jesus will identify a health evangelism program as the start of their Christian experience. Many who already have a religious background will find a deeper and intensely practical relationship with Jesus as they learn to trust Him for daily behavior change.

> *Health programs that fail to present Jesus are not real health evangelism programs.*

Health programs that fail to present Jesus are not really health evangelism programs. They fail to present Jesus as the source of power for both immediate and lasting behavior change. Traditional evangelistic meetings that fail to advocate behavior changes that lead to improved health, and fail to connect behavior change with Jesus, lack a practical component. Such evangelistic series proclaim a theoretical religion that resides only in the mind of the hearer.

Many health programs are primarily secular in nature. They point a person to the adverse consequences of a risky behavior and advocate specific behavior changes to promote or recover health. The information is usually scientifically sound but fails to change many lives. Many health programs are also commercial ventures—businesses of behavior change driven by a profit motive.

Most health programs are not designed to be overtly evangelistic. Secular health programs do not become health evangelism programs just because they are conducted by church members or are conducted in a Seventh-day Adventist church.

Some secular health programs conducted by churches are called "friendship" evangelism. How sad that a person can come to a Seventh-day Adventist church, meet Seventh-day Adventist people, learn some health information but not learn of Jesus who can provide the power to change. What kind of friendship is that?

Health programs measure certain variables that document a person's starting health status. These same questions or tests are usually measured again at the end of a program. This "before and after" process measures the changes that have taken place during a program and are a measure of the effectiveness of a program. Common health variables include blood sugar, cholesterol, blood pressure, weight, body mass index, etc.

Evangelistic meetings measure attendance at meetings and ultimately baptisms. Evangelistic meetings often have a health talk at the beginning or the end of an evangelistic lecture. Health topics tacked onto evangelistic meetings do not constitute health evangelism.

Health evangelism is overt evangelistic activity inserted into a health program. Valid health evangelism introduces individuals to Jesus as the one who has the power to change lives. In health evangelism a person is introduced to the Bible as the primary source of knowledge about Jesus. The Bible has many examples of the help that Jesus provided those who were seeking better health.

---

*In health evangelism a person is taught how to pray.*

---

In health evangelism a person is taught how to pray. Prayer is the way a person contacts Jesus. By prayer a person can ask for help, a person can express gratitude for success, and a person can enjoy fellowship with Jesus.

Health evangelism programs provide an opportunity for a person to daily contact a Seventh-day Adventist helper for encouragement. Church members provide social and spiritual support. Church members can also share their own experiences with Jesus. They can pray with those who are struggling to change. They can form friendships.

Health evangelism programs conducted in Seventh-day Adventist churches provide an opportunity for the community to become familiar with the church facility. From the parking lot to the restrooms, people become familiar with the layout of the church. The public comes to feel at home in your church environment. This is also evangelistic.

I have found that many Seventh-day Adventist health professionals are reluctant to insert spiritual content into health programs. Perhaps they feel the public would be offended by talking about Jesus. They feel that the public comes for health information, not to learn about Jesus. Unfortunately, health information by itself does not change behavior. Jesus provides the power for sustained healthful living.

Some Seventh-day Adventist health professionals are not skilled at communicating spiritual messages, others may not have experienced Jesus in their own lives and have not learned how essential Jesus is to successful healthful living.

Evangelists have not helped the situation much either. The constant question posed to those conducting health programs is, "Where are the baptisms?" This question looks at the end of the process and does not recognize the multiple steps that precede baptism. Health evangelism helps prepare people for baptism by leading them through the several steps that precede baptism.

Perhaps the biggest reason we are not doing more health evangelism is because we have not been doing it up to this point and we really do not know how to do it. On the scientific side, health evangelism of the type advocated here has not been studied. We would do more health evangelism if we had proof that health evangelism is more effective in changing behaviors than traditional behavior change models.

Fortunately, some data confirming the validity of health evangelism have become available. (See Chapter 16 on the Best Weigh nutrition and weight management program.)

This book summarizes my experience in what works and does not work. If you are a pastor, layperson or health professional, interested in the health message of the Seventh-day Adventist church and how to share this with others, this book is for you. I hope and pray that you will put these principles to work. God will bless you.

In my practice of health evangelism, I have been inspired most by the healing ministry of our Lord and Savior Jesus Christ who spent more time healing than in preaching. I have been inspired by the picture of health evangelism outlined in Isaiah 58 and certain key passages in the Spirit of Prophecy.

The quotation that most intrigues me is: "I wish to tell you that soon there will be no work done in ministerial lines but medical missionary work..." Counsels on Health 533. This brief passage tells me that medical missionary work will one day eclipse all the evangelistic approaches that ministers are now using.

This passage could mean that the overt spiritual part of the church's work will become so prohibited that a subtler secondary way of doing pastoral work, in the guise of health evangelism, will be the only course open for outreach. This would be a sort of "second-best but it will have to do" type of development.

I believe the church will eventually discover that medical missionary work is a superior form of evangelism. Evangelistic efforts characterized by traditional doctrinal presentations appear to work well in some parts of the world, but are much less effective in the United States, western Europe, Australia, and Japan.

If it is true that soon there will be no work done in ministerial lines but medical missionary work, we should be exploring ways of maximizing the effectiveness of health evangelism now. We should be experimenting with medical missionary work. We should work at it until it can be demonstrated that health evangelism is a tool that surpasses the effectiveness of traditional evangelistic approaches.

When the superior effectiveness of well designed and well-practiced health evangelism is demonstrated, we will switch over to the better way of doing things. I hope this happens soon so the work can be done and we can go home to Heaven.

Conversely, health evangelism should NOT be the venue for the introduction of many of the distinctive doctrines of the Seventh-day Adventist church. A health evangelism program can be used to introduce at least 10 of the 28 fundamental beliefs. These are the doctrines that are focused behavior change and directly affect health issues.

The presentation of the Sabbath, the sanctuary doctrine, the state of the dead and other testing truths can be introduced later on as interest develops and questions arise. In a health evangelism program, the spiritual emphasis should be on how God through Jesus helps a person breaks habits, addictions, and effects lasting behavior change.

Here is a second quotation from the Spirit of Prophecy that has challenged me.

> "Again and again I have been instructed that the medical missionary work is to bear the same relation to the work of the third angel's message that the arm and hand bear to the body. Under the direction of the divine Head they are to work unitedly in preparing the way for the coming of Christ. The right arm of the body of truth is to be constantly active, constantly at work, and God will strengthen it. But it is not to be made the body. At the same time the body is not to say to the arm: "I have no need of thee." The body has need of the arm in order to do active, aggressive work. Both have their appointed work, and each will suffer great loss if worked independently of the other." ***Testimonies for the Church Volume Six, 288.***

This vision of health evangelism just hasn't happened. Some among us see a fulfillment of this statement in the Adventist Health System. The plain truth is that, in the United States, the hospitals operated by the Seventh-day Adventist church are not efficient evangelistic tools for the church. There is no meaningful connection between hospitals and church evangelist activities.

Church officials at administrative levels sit on the boards of hospitals, but this fact alone does not make hospitals particularly Christian or Adventist. Exposure to Christian or unique Seventh-day Adventist principles during a hospital stay are brief or non-existent. Former hospital patients are not flocking in significant numbers to evangelistic meetings or seeking membership in Seventh-day Adventist churches.

One prominent hospital administrator told me. "When the finances get tight, something has to go, and it is going to be health education and preventive medicine" Adventist hospitals haven't been the soul winning right arm they were envisioned to be. Our hospitals are largely staffed with well-trained, non-Adventist, physicians and nurses and provide a level of health care that is comparable to what is available at other secular hospitals in the community.

It is my contention that the right arm of the message has been severed from the body and is functioning independently. Both the body and the arm have suffered great loss by having worked independently of each other.

The quote from Spirit of Prophecy which most clearly points out where health evangelism should be done and who should be doing it is:

> "We have come to a time when every member of the church should take hold of medical missionary work.... Everywhere people are perishing for lack of a knowledge of the truths that have been committed to us. The members of the church are in need of an awakening, that they may realize their responsibility to impart these truths." ***Welfare Ministry, p. 138***

Here the root of our current problem is outlined. We haven't been doing health evangelism in the right place or with the right people. The institution in which health evangelism is to occur is the local church. The home of health evangelism is not to be in hospitals, schools, public auditoriums, or lifestyle centers, but the local church.

This quotation also indicates who is to do health evangelism. Every member of the church should take hold of medical missionary work. There is a role for pastors, doctors, dentists, nurses, therapists, counselors and others, but every church member needs to be involved with health evangelism as well.

Part of the problem is that some Seventh-day Adventist health professionals have tried to organize and conduct health evangelism programs independent of the church and church members. These programs have been conducted in public venues for the public at large. These programs are held at an arm's length from the local church.

Most of the time this limits church member support to contributing some money, sitting in the audience or praying for the program's success. Health evangelism conducted in this way fails to create an interface between the church and the public and between church members and the public. This approach may be economically viable but does little to advance the Lord's work.

There is a better way to attract people in the community. Our neighbors will value our church more if we learn to do health evangelism in the right way. Health evangelism removes prejudice that exists against the church.

> "Much of the prejudice that prevents the truth of the third angel's message from reaching the hearts of the people might be removed if more attention were given to health reform. When people become interested in this subject, the way is often prepared for the entrance of other truths. If they see that we are intelligent with regard to health, they will be more ready to believe that we are sound in Bible doctrines." ***Counsels on Health, p. 452***

I hope we as a people will learn to do health evangelism in the right way. Let's follow the counsel that has been given us. Let us design and conduct programs that will utilize church members, be conducted in the local church and be aggressively evangelistic.

As you read, I pray God will impress your mind with the importance of health evangelism. I hope you will be inspired to implement health evangelism in your local church and that the third angel's message will be completed in your community due to your efforts and the efforts of your fellow church members.

# 2

# Christ's Method Alone

HERE IS ONE OF THE MOST QUOTED REFERENCES REGARDING HEALTH evangelism from the writings of Ellen G. White.

> "Christ's method alone will give true success in reaching the people. The Saviour mingled with men as one who desired their good. He showed His sympathy for them, ministered to their needs, and won their confidence. Then He bade them, 'Follow Me.'" *Ministry of Healing 143*

In my opinion this quotation is often misused and misunderstood by those conducting health programs for the church. This quote is frequently used to justify the implementation of purely secular health activities.

This quotation lists several steps in the process leading to the spiritual invitation "Follow Me." First there is "mingling" with people. This is not a careless, unconcerned mingling, but a mingling that desires a person's good. The obvious purpose for conducting health work is to make people's lives better—to improve their health.

The next step is showing sympathy. This involves a caring, empathetic attitude. This is conveyed with body language, facial expression, and kind words. People should be able to sense that we are genuinely concerned about their health and welfare.

The third step is to minister to a person's needs. This is can take days, months, or even years. Once a person's needs have been addressed—then we can bid them follow Christ.

On the surface this passage appears to justify a work for people that is primarily secular to begin with and then moves toward the spiritual. This approach starts out with just health information and ends up—assuming all goes well—with a spiritual emphasis.

This approach—except for the spiritual emphasis at the end—also rather exactly matches the approach of all health improvement programs offered to the public by secular governments and private organizations. Seventh-day Adventist health practitioners who subscribe to the secular approach first are essentially duplicating the health services provided by all other secular health entities. Unless you get to the "follow Me" part you are no different than anyone else.

Those who derive a "secular-to-spiritual" continuum from this passage fail to understand Christ's method, fail to understand the primacy of the spiritual approach, and also fail to consider the context. Look at a few lines from the chapter from which this passage was taken.

Luke worked with Paul. They were a medical missionary team. Eventually, Paul left Luke in Philippi where Luke conducted healing and preaching by himself for several years. In this chapter, the relationship between healing and the gospel first occurs in this paragraph.

> "Physical healing is bound up with the gospel commission. In the work of the gospel, teaching and healing are never to be separated." ***Ministry of Healing 140***

Here there is no sequence from physical to spiritual. Teaching the gospel and healing are never to be separated.

In this next paragraph the current human condition is outlined. People are longing for a power to give them mastery over sin, a power that will give health and life and peace. This comes from Jesus. This needs to be put right up front in the health message. "Jesus can change you."

> "Everywhere there are hearts crying out for something which they have not. They long for a power that will give them mastery over sin, a power that will deliver them from the bondage of evil, a power that will give health and life and peace. Many who once knew the power of God's word have dwelt where there is no recognition of God, and they long for the divine presence." *Ministry of Healing 143*

In the sentence immediately preceding our opening quote is this sentence.

> "A great work of reform is demanded, and it is only through the grace of Christ that the work of restoration, physical, mental, and spiritual, can be accomplished." *Ministry of Healing 143*

---

*It is only through the grace of Christ that the work of restoration, physical, mental, and spiritual, can be accomplished."*

---

The grace of Christ is where the power is. Get to it up front. Do not tack it on at the end.

> "If less time were given to sermonizing, and more time were spent in personal ministry, greater results would be seen. The poor are to be relieved, the sick cared for, the sorrowing and the bereaved comforted, the ignorant instructed, the inexperienced counseled. We are to weep with those that weep, and rejoice with those that rejoice. Accompanied by the power of persuasion, the power of prayer, the power of the love of God, this work will not, cannot, be without fruit." *Ministry of Healing 143*

This is the thought immediately after our opening quote. It initially reads as if it could be secular work. Relieving the poor, caring for the sick, bringing comfort, instruction, and counsel. But notice the last sentence in the paragraph. All the above activities are to be accompanied by the power of prayer, and the power of the love of God. There is no secular work here. We are to pray on all occasions and point to Jesus on all occasions. Look at the very next paragraph.

> "We should ever remember that the object of the medical missionary work is to point sin-sick men and women to the Man of Calvary, who takes away the sin of the world. By beholding Him, they will be changed into His likeness. We are to encourage the sick and suffering to look to Jesus and live. Let the workers keep Christ, the Great Physician, constantly before those to whom disease of body and soul has brought discouragement. Point them to the One who can heal both physical and spiritual disease. Tell them of the One who is touched with the feeling of their infirmities. Encourage them to place themselves in the care of Him who gave His life to make it possible for them to have life eternal. Talk of His love; tell of His power to save." ***Ministry of Healing 144***

---

*Pointing people to Jesus is the primary object of health evangelism.*

---

Pointing to Jesus is the primary object of medical missionary work. Forgiveness of sin is a central goal of medical missionary work. People will not be permanently changed until they behold Jesus. Christ the Great Physician should be constantly held up before those for whom we are working. We are to tell them that Jesus is touched with the feeling of their infirmities. We are to encourage them to put themselves in the care of Jesus. We are to talk of His love; and to tell of His power to save. There is no secular sequence here.

Look at this paragraph on the next page of Ministry of Healing.

> "Many have no faith in God and have lost confidence in man. But they appreciate acts of sympathy and helpfulness. As they see one with no inducement of earthly praise or compensation come into their homes, ministering to the sick, feeding the hungry, clothing the naked, comforting the sad, and tenderly pointing all to Him of whose love and pity the human worker is but the messenger--as they see this, their hearts are touched. Gratitude springs up. Faith is kindled. They see that God cares for them, and they are prepared to listen as His word is opened." ***Ministry of Healing 145***

Here are a lot of home health activities. This paragraph encourages us to minister to the sick, feed the hungry, clothe the naked, and comfort the sad. But notice that we are to tenderly point all to Him whose love and pity the human worker is but the messenger.

True health evangelists are to point everyone they work for to Jesus all the time. There is no secular preamble. If you do not speak of Jesus, you are not a health evangelist. If you do not pray with your subjects, you are not a health evangelist. If you do not open scripture to all, you are not a health evangelist.

Some will reject you if you take a spiritual approach to your healing efforts. Some do not want to hear about Jesus. Some do not want the Bible. Some do not want prayer. For those who reject you, care can be received from a secular medical center or secular health department nearby.

There is no scientific health information you possess that is so unique to you that no one else has it. Jesus and His power to change and to save is really the only unique message you possess. To the extent that you leave Jesus to a later hour—just to that extent you have failed as a health evangelist.

Here is another quote that very specifically tells us what Christ's method was. Each work of healing was improved by implanting the divine principles of his love. This is how we are to work. Each opportunity to educate or heal is an opportunity to point to Jesus.

> "[Jesus] went about doing good, teaching the ignorant, and healing the sick. His work did not stop with an exhibition of his power over disease. He made each work of healing an occasion of implanting in the heart the divine principles of his love and benevolence. Thus his followers are to work." *Review and Herald, May 2, 1912*

Perhaps the clearest and most concise counsel regarding the relationship between the gospel ministry and health ministry is this.

> "By the ministry of the word the gospel is preached; by medical missionary work the gospel is practiced. The gospel is bound up with medical missionary work. Neither is to stand alone, bound up in itself. The workers in each are to labor unselfishly and unitedly, striving to save sinners." *Vol. 13 Manuscript Releases, 303*

This point can also be confirmed by approaching it from the opposite point of view as well. The curious crowd that followed Jesus occasionally pried him with questions that were not relevant to salvation. Today they would be questions about the mysteries of space, medicine, or science. Jesus who made it all, could have explained it all. But Jesus never answered a single question that wasn't related to salvation.

> "The curiosity that led them to come to Him with prying questions He did not gratify. All such questionings He made the occasion for solemn, earnest, vital appeals. To those who were so eager to pluck from the tree of knowledge, He offered the fruit of the tree of life. They found every avenue closed except the way that leads to God. Every fountain was sealed save the fountain

of eternal life." ***Counsels to Parents, Teachers, and Students 386***

The goal of health evangelism is not good health but the salvation of sinners. Health evangelism should focus exclusively on how Jesus can provide power to change your life now and for eternity. Anything less than this is to miss the mark.

# 3

# Without Me You Can Do Nothing

Jesus said, "I am the vine, you are the branches. He who abides in Me, and I in him, bears much fruit; for without Me you can do nothing. **John 15:5(NKJV)**

How slow we are to believe these words of Jesus, "Without Me you can do nothing." You want to be able to do something on your own. You wake up every morning. You shower, eat breakfast, and take up the duties of life. You bring home a paycheck and pay your bills. You probably live in a safe neighborhood. The children are yours. You go to church, and you keep your house and yard looking nice. You are a pretty good person and seriously wish the rest of the world would settle down.

The truth is that when you woke up this morning that was a gift from Jesus. The food you ate for breakfast was a gift from Jesus. Your job was a gift from Jesus. Your paycheck was a gift from Jesus. The peace in your neighborhood is a gift from Jesus. Your children are a gift from Jesus. Everything you have, everything you are, and everything you do is a gift from Jesus.

Until you recognize Jesus as the source of your life, all that you are, and all that you have and your only hope in this life and the next, you will lose it all forever on the day you die.

One of our greatest errors is to subdivide the human experience into the spiritual life, the mental life, and the physical life. These are artificial distinctions that do not really exist. It is convenient to confine Jesus to the spiritual life—that is why you go to church. That done, the rest of your life is yours.

The truth is your spiritual, mental, and physical life is all part of the same you. All the dimensions of life are integrated in you. You are a single, live being created by God with multiple combined aspects that cannot be separated.

Consider again Jesus statement that "Without Me you can do nothing." This truth has profound implications for health evangelism. Gospel workers are quick to point to Jesus as the source of salvation. In contrast, Health workers too often advocate improving yourself, by yourself, following established steps of behavior change recommended by secular authorities.

Unfortunately, the established steps of behavior change, though perhaps an accurate description of how change occurs, don't work for many people. This truth is demonstrated nicely by the current obesity epidemic.

Every week there is a new book on dieting and weight loss. Each book has a unique diet. There are special foods, a special sequence in eating foods, super foods, juices, smoothies, and teas. There are dozens of commercial weight loss programs. Surgeons are willing to alter your anatomy to force you to eat less or to alter your digestive system in such a way that you can no longer absorb nutrients from the diet you eat. Each book, each special food, each surgical approach has a success story attached to it. Someone did it and was successful. All these approaches to control weight work for a few people, but do not work very long for most people.

The world is getting fatter and fatter. There is not a single nation in the world where obesity is becoming less and less. There is no people group anywhere in the world that is successful in controlling the human appetite for food.

The basic truth is just what Jesus said, "Without Me you can do nothing." This simple statement is the truth. We are a nation of obese people who are looking for that one book, diet, program, or surgery that will make us what we want to be.

> *"I can do all things through Christ who strengthens me."*
> *Philippians 4:13*

Jesus is the champion of appetite control. With Jesus' help, every obese person can be successful in losing weight. The Bible says, "I can do all things through Christ who strengthens me." **Philippians 4:13(NKJV)** Without Jesus you can do nothing. With Jesus you can do anything and everything necessary for this life and the next.

Health evangelists are not doing Christ's work in this world unless the programs they conduct start with the basic truth that without Jesus there is no long-term success. With Christ there can be permanent victory over every habit and addiction.

All things are possible through the power that Jesus provides. For this reason, the help of Jesus should be incorporated into the established steps of behavior change. A health evangelist who doesn't introduce Jesus as the most powerful and effective agent of behavior change is just another secular health educator.

# 4

# Raising the Dead

---

WHO ARE THE CLIENTS AND PATIENTS WHO COME TO HEALTH evangelism programs for help with their habits and addictions? They are often seen as people who formed bad health practices at an early age. We see people as being trapped in a harmful environment. Often, there has been abuse as a child or an adult. Others never learned the right way to live. All who come to health programs present special challenges and unique educational opportunities.

I have found it helpful in my health ministry to apply the Biblical diagnosis to those who come for help. The correct diagnosis is that they are, DEAD, DEVILISH, DISOBEDIENT, and DEPRAVED. This is not my particular prejudice, for the diagnosis is made by the Bible.

> And you He made alive, who were dead in trespasses and sins, in which you once walked according to the course of this world, according to the prince of the power of the air, the spirit who now works in the sons of disobedience, among whom also we all once conducted ourselves in the lusts of our flesh, fulfilling the desires of the flesh and of the mind, and were by nature children of wrath, just as the others. **Ephesians 2:1-3 (NKJV)**

Those who come to health programs are not just uneducated, sick, trapped, or addicted—they are DEAD. The Bible says that they are "dead in trespasses and sins. Grasping this fundamental truth about human nature makes all the difference in the approach we take in trying to help a person.

Education is thought to be the key to behavior change. A person can unlearn bad behaviors and through education learn new healthful behaviors. Education consists in enlightening a person as to the harmful effects of current behaviors and sharing the scientific evidence that a change in behavior will result in better health. Unfortunately, education is totally worthless if a person is DEAD. A person who is dead will have to be brought to life before education will be effective.

Setting a good example is thought to be important in helping people change. If they can see that you are living the right way and you are healthy and happy, they will be more likely to copy your good example and be motivated to live right. Setting a good example is totally irrelevant if the person you are trying to help is DEAD.

Likewise, encouragement doesn't help the dead. We like to coach those who are struggling with a bad habit. We say, "Keep it up," "You can make it," and "Hang in there." Unfortunately, encouragement doesn't help those who are DEAD.

In desperate cases we remove a person from a toxic environment and place them where they can be transformed, far away from the negative influences at home or work. Lifestyle Centers were designed for this purpose. But a new environment will not help those who are DEAD. So, education, example, encouragement and environment are not useful tools in trying to reform people who are dead.

The Bible further adds to the diagnosis of death the fact that people are controlled by the devil, "walking…according to the prince of the power of the air". Transforming the life of a person controlled by the devil is an impossible accomplishment by human effort alone. You may make positive changes for a while, but if the devil is in control of your life, the prospect for permanent change in behavior is bleak. The Bible says that those with a harmful lifestyle are "walking according to the course of this world, according to the prince of the power of the air." This is the devil. People with bad habits cannot control themselves because their lives are directed by the devil.

The Bible also diagnoses people as "the sons of disobedience." People cannot do what they are told to do. They disobey the laws of health. They disobey common sense. They disobey their doctor's advice. They disobey their spouse's advice.

The pubic that comes to a health program may look like washed, well clothed, and decent people but the Bible says that they are depraved. The text above says, "we all once conducted ourselves in the lusts of our flesh, fulfilling the desires of the flesh and of the mind, and were by nature children of wrath, just as the others."

Depraved people follow the "desires of the flesh." They cannot say no to food. They cannot say no to cigarettes. They cannot say no to alcohol. They are trapped—slaves to their perverted and depraved desires.

The solution to the problem is provided in the next verses in Ephesians.

> But God, who is rich in mercy, because of His great love with which He loved us, even when we were dead in trespasses, made us alive together with Christ (by grace you have been saved), and raised us up together, and made us sit together in the heavenly places in Christ Jesus, that in the ages to come He might show the exceeding riches of His grace in His kindness toward us in Christ Jesus. For by grace you have been saved through faith, and that not of yourselves; it is the gift of God, not of works, lest anyone should boast. For we are His workmanship, created in Christ Jesus for good works, which God prepared beforehand that we should walk in them. **Ephesians 2:4-10 (NKJV)**

*God can make all things right once again.*

God can make all things right once again. Not because we are worthy but because of his great mercy and because of his great love for us. God makes us alive with Christ. We are not saved by our own efforts because if we were we would take credit for our accomplishments. But God has the power to recreate us with the ability to do what is right.

This is the heart of traditional evangelism, and it is the heart of health evangelism. Jesus saves us from our sins. Jesus saves us from our bad eating habits. Jesus saves us from tobacco and alcohol. We are cheating the public out of the most wonderful news regarding their bad habits if we keep this good news from them.

If we see the people who come to a health evangelism program as being dead, it will help us realize the critical importance of introducing them to Christ who can raise the dead and give them new life.

# 5

# Where Are the Baptisms?

OVER THE YEARS OF CONDUCTING HEALTH EVANGELISM PROGRAMS I have repeatedly been asked, "Where are the baptisms?" This is a fair question. Pastors and church administrators are interested in numbers that indicate church growth. A person is counted as an authentic member of the church once baptism has taken place. What is the relationship between health evangelism and baptisms? Should you expect baptisms from health evangelism programs?

Conventional health education programs are not designed to be evangelistic. Many health education programs are conducted by church members in an entirely secular manner in a secular setting. It is not to be expected that these programs would be evangelistic or result in baptisms. These more secular programs are rightly accused of creating "healthy sinners."

Other health education programs have been integrated in some way with traditional evangelistic efforts. In some cases a Five-day Plan to Stop Smoking was held just before an evangelistic crusade in the hopes that the reformed smokers would stay for the doctrinal presentations once they stopped smoking. This never worked very well.

At other times a health segment was included in an evangelistic crusade. A "health nugget" would come before the real meat of the program. This format sometimes increased the crowds, and reformed health habits but there was only a marginal increase in baptisms.

Over time, most evangelists, not seeing any particular benefit from health education, abandoned the combination of the health message with evangelistic efforts. With the gradual secularization of the church membership at many levels, the whole health message of the church has been abandoned by many church members, and even some pastors, and church administrators.

The problem is not with health evangelism as much as it is with traditional evangelism. What worked well 100 years ago, is no longer effective in drawing crowds into the church. In developed countries where traditional evangelistic crusades have been shown to be less effective now compared with the past, new strategies need to be considered. I believe it is time to take a fresh look at health evangelism.

## Friendship Evangelism

Health evangelism programs, rightly conducted, will lead to baptisms and will elevate the reputation of a church in the community. Health evangelism programs, organized along the lines suggested in this book will make many friends in the community and go a long way toward preparing people for baptism and full church membership.

A survey of recent converts to the church in North America identified various reasons a person joined a church. These are the data.

| | | |
|---|---|---|
| 1. Friends | 79% |
| 2. Pastor | 6% |
| 3. Sabbath School | 5% |
| 4. Programs | 3% |
| 5. Special need | 2% |
| 6. Visitation | 1% |
| 7. Crusade | 1% |

The most important influence in a person joining a church is the presence of personal friends in the congregation. Health evangelism programs, when conducted correctly, create friendships between the public and church members. Health evangelism programs should be designed to create an active, meaningful, interface between church members and individuals in the community.

Soul saving friendships can be built in small groups that meet each session of a health evangelism program. Lasting friendships with men and women from the community have been formed in every health evangelism program I have conducted. From these friendships new church members are acquired.

Traditional evangelistic efforts are usually conducted by a charismatic preacher who carries the burden of presenting truth, pretty much by himself. Usually, there are no small groups and no meaningful interface between church members and the public who come to these large meetings. This method of evangelism fails to create friendships between church members and the public who attend these meetings.

In traditional evangelistic efforts, if local church members are involved, they are usually relegated to the role of helping to swell the audience, pray for the meetings, or perhaps usher and take up an offering. There is no specific activity in traditional evangelistic meetings designed for individuals from the public to create friendships with church members. This is one of the reasons why so many new members leave the church shortly after the meetings are past. They simply do not have any friends in the church they have just joined. The evangelist is gone to another city. The new church member just got baptized into a church of total strangers.

Newly baptized church members are more likely to stay if they have at least one good friend in the church. Health evangelism programs featuring small group interactions between the public and church members creates one-on-one relationships and sustains them. Solid, lasting friendships are formed. Baptisms resulting from health evangelism programs where friendships are made, are much more likely to stay in the church than baptisms resulting from traditional evangelistic activities.

Health evangelism programs will prepare community people to be exposed to more traditional evangelistic meetings at some subsequent time. Health evangelism and traditional evangelistic meetings should not be piggy backed one on the other but each should be conducted often enough that those who are ready for indoctrination can avail themselves of a traditional evangelistic crusade.

What I have found works best is for health evangelism programs to be offered on a regular, continuing basis on one track and traditional evangelistic efforts at regular intervals on another track. The purpose of each track is clear. The health evangelism track is health oriented but creates firm friendships with church members and introduces a person to God as the agent of behavior change in the daily life. The traditional evangelistic crusade track is for the purpose of broadening the spiritual understanding and experience of an individual along doctrinal lines. This prepares a person for full membership in the church.

## Baptism: Event or Process?

Baptisms are events that can be easily measured and are carefully counted. The effectiveness of a pastor's ministry is often equated with the number of baptisms that are produced by their ministry. But counting baptisms alone is a bit near sighted because it ignores the long process that leads up to baptism and also ignores the process of discipling that should follow.

Becoming a Christian is not just an isolated event but a process. Baptism is a single point along a continuum. We put too much emphasis on baptism and tend to ignore the processes that come before and after. There are many measurable points in the process leading to baptism. Health evangelism programs lead people through many of these initial steps.

Those who conduct health evangelism programs should measure these intermediate steps that lead to baptism. When this is done, the value of health evangelism will be demonstrated. What are some of these intermediate steps?

**Step 1. An interest in something you do in your church.** What does your church do? Sabbath services are probably the most notable thing your church does. Frankly, services in your church will not be of much interest to anyone who goes to their own church on a regular basis.

Health evangelism will make your church more attractive because few churches do anything for the health of the community. If your church regularly helped people stop smoking, lose weight, reverse diabetes or hypertension or other chronic lifestyle related disease, that would make your church more attractive to those struggling with these problems.

The more health evangelism activities you conduct, the more interest the community will have in your church. This would simply be a social gospel if your help was solely physical or mental in nature. Each of your community activities should point to Jesus as the agent of lasting behavior change in the human life. When you do this, then you are conducting true health evangelism.

The very first step in a person becoming a member of your church is developing an interest in something you do in your church. So, start doing something. Do it often, do it well, and do it regularly. The community will flock to your church.

**Step 2. Come to your church.** This is another obvious step in becoming a church member. Health evangelism programs help people take this step if your health evangelism program is conducted in the local church. When a person comes to a health evangelism program in your church they must get directions, drive to your church, find a parking spot, find the right entrance, come through the door, and say "hello" to someone. It is much less threatening for a person in the community to come to your church for a health evangelism program on a week night than to come to regular religious services on the weekend.

If you provide specific help for a specific health problem at your church, the community will come. At some time in the future, when they have made friends with church members, they will find it much easier to come to your church for religious services because, they know how to get to your church, where to park, which door to come through, they will recognize people and will even know where the restrooms are located.

This step toward baptism is as easy to measure as baptisms. Keeping statistics on the number of non-church member visits to your church will be a measure of the effectiveness of your health evangelism program. These numbers will help pastors and church administrators see the value of health evangelism programs.

Count every visit by every non-church member every time they step through your door. If 20 non-church members attend a 5-Day Plan to Stop smoking for 5 nights that equals 100 non-church member visits to your church. This can simply be called the "non-Adventist person visit" or NAPV.

**Step 3. Become friends with church members.** Most health education programs provide accurate health and medical information, but have been poor at providing personal contact with church members. I believe that health evangelism programs should be designed to maximize the interface between church members and the public. This is the one factor that will change them from being primarily informational to being interactive and evangelistic.

Each church member who helps with your health evangelism program should be assigned to 3-4 community participants. Sufficient time should be created in the health evangelism program for church members to interact with the individuals from the community. Give church members real but simple work to do. Let them review the high points of the night's lecture. Let them ask individuals what they personally have decided to do in their own lives as a result of the lecture.

Give the church members time to get some feedback from the participants in small groups. Let them listen to their struggles and hardships. Teach them to have a sympathetic ear. Teach them to be nonjudgmental. Teach them to be friends. This is not hard for church members to learn or to do. This type of friendship activity is not at all like giving formal Bible studies. Give church members a list of questions to ask and teach them to listen and be sympathetic. This is how friendships are formed.

This is a step toward baptism that can be measured. Count each church member contact with a non-church member as a friendship interaction. This is another step toward baptism that results from health evangelism programs. Contact could be by phone, text, email, or in person. Each interaction of this type should be counted and entered into your program's database.

**Step 4. Develop or strengthen a relationship with God.** This is probably the most important step in any health evangelism program. If you become a church member without taking this step, you are a Christian only in name. Church membership is equated with developing a personal relationship with God. Where and when does this relationship with God occur? Baptism is the public step that indicates that an individual has made a full commitment to Jesus, but baptism doesn't make it happen.

Health evangelism programs are an ideal setting in which a person can to get to know Jesus. People come to health evangelism programs because they have a behavioral problem that needs to be changed. The program provides information your audience needs to know to make changes in how they live. You provide individual counseling and friendship through your church members, but the audience needs more.

In every health evangelism program there should be simple, specific information on how Jesus helps people change behavior. This evangelistic approach should be very specific and narrowly focused on the behavioral problem the participant is trying to overcome. Many will find that Jesus is an ever present help in time of need in a health evangelism program, but only if you design it that way.

Information about Jesus, with an opportunity to apply His help to a specific problem, puts problem-specific evangelism into health education and creates a health evangelism program. If people find that God helps them in tangible ways in a health evangelism program, they will be much more inclined to join your church once they have been introduced to the distinctive doctrines.

This step toward baptism can be measured but is a bit more difficult. In your questionnaire following the health evangelism program, and in each of the follow-up visits you can ask people what their relationship with Jesus is with respect to the problem they were trying to overcome. Many will confess that they have a new or deeper relationship with Jesus as a result of your health evangelism program. They will share that they never would have been successful in changing their behavior unless they had received God's help.

This is one more step in the process leading to baptism. We shouldn't baptize anyone who doesn't have an experimental relationship with Jesus. Too often we baptize people who intellectually give assent to a body of doctrines but who have no real experience of God's power in their lives.

**Step 5. Change certain behaviors.** Obviously, health evangelism programs are about changing the way you live. Many health destroying habits and addictions can be changed in a health evangelism program. A healthier lifestyle free from addictions is another step toward baptism and it is quite easy to measure.

**Step 6. Accept Distinctive Doctrines.** This is the last step in the process before baptism. To be a church member in regular standing, it is necessary to accept the distinctive doctrines of the church. Learning the distinctive doctrines is not a function of health evangelism except for the doctrines dealing with healthful living.

**Step 7. Baptism.** At last, a person joins the church by baptism. We all rejoice! This is the main goal of the church. The church is to proclaim the gospel of Jesus Christ and to baptize those who believe on His name.

Is it fair to ask those who conduct health evangelism programs, "Where are the baptisms?" Not really. The question reveals an ignorance of the processes that leads to baptism. Such a question reveals a lack of appreciation for the ways in which health evangelism prepares people for baptism. Of the seven steps leading to baptism I have outlined above, health evangelism leads people through the first five. That should be good enough.Health evangelism is only the right hand of the gospel not the whole gospel. Health evangelism opens doors, makes friends, and gives people an experimental relationship with Jesus but it does not fully indoctrinate them or directly result in baptisms.

Health evangelism can be understood as being "problem specific" evangelism. You can be "saved" spiritually in a health evangelism program, but it is "getting saved" over just one behavioral problem, not all of life's problems. We all started our journey toward God at some point. Health evangelism can be the starting point for many. A rudimentary experience with God, developed in overcoming a specific health problem, can over time and spiritual growth lead to a fuller experience.

Your church should hold health evangelism programs that are designed and conducted in the way that will guide people along the steps leading to baptism. Do not say that health evangelism programs are not evangelistic. Health evangelism is focused evangelism that helps people deal with specific addictions and habits.

I had one lady who came from a secular background, but experimenting with prayer she successfully quit smoking with God's help. In asking her about her success she said, "This is a model of behavior change that I can now apply to other problem areas in my life." That would be the process of "sanctification" in more traditional theological terms. She had learned that God had helped her with one problem and she was now ready to expand her experience with God and overcome in other areas as well.

Exactly when and how a person comes to God is a mystery to us who do His work. We are wise if we realize there are many ways people can initiate a relationship with God. We need to recognize that every human necessity is an opportunity to introduce a person to God who helps with every need.

# 6

# Motivation for Health Evangelism

MOTIVATION IS THE UNDERLYING DRIVE THAT PUSHES AN INDIVIDUAL toward accomplishments. The motives of traditional evangelists are obvious. Their drive is to save souls for the kingdom of God. In the Seventh-day Adventist church they are usually on a salary with a conference.

They are dedicated to their craft. They may have expensive props and sophisticated multi-media equipment, but the primary purpose is the communication of God's saving love to those who don't know Him. Evangelists may be eloquent but are rarely egotistical. They are driven less by financial profit and are more satisfied to see acquisitions to the local church membership—and then they move on.

Health professionals present a mixed bag of motivations. Some are truly dedicated to restoring the sick to good health regardless of how much money they make. Others recognizing their ability to generate wealth focus more on the business aspects of medical practice and put profits over healing.

Some health educators primarily seek fame and fortune. There are many who often unwittingly fit this category. They have a scientifically sound health program that correctly educates about some aspect of healthful living. They often travel from church to church carrying their unique piece of scientific truth and conducting programs for church members or the public. They never become widely known. Their program is rarely adopted or promoted through church channels. They join ASI or Outpost Ministries but represent many talented people who help represent what Mrs. White calls "a strange medley of disorganized atoms." **Counsels on Health 514**

A few achieve a measure of recognition, but most don't. Health evangelism creates opportunities for the salvation of souls, communication of life changing health principles from the field of science, and the opportunity to make money through the private ownership of health programs.

Some health evangelists felt that science alone should carry the day. To these people accurate knowledge educates and provides sufficient motivation for behavior change. Spiritual matters belong in some subsequent endeavor. These practitioners are still looking for an effective bridge between science and evangelism. To these health educators the science is the bait and evangelism is the hook.

Those who accept this concept of health evangelism feel that playing the evangelistic card too early reveals our bias toward the spiritual. The label they give to their initial exclusive focus on science without a spiritual component is "disinterested service" or "friendship evangelism."

The thought being that we are to provide health programs without regard to our interest in people joining the church. Why bother someone about spiritual matters when all they wanted to do is stop smoking? The following quotes from Spirit of Prophecy are used to support this position.

> "In your care of the sick, act tenderly, kindly, faithfully, that you may have a converting influence upon them. You have need of the grace of Christ in order to properly represent the service of Christ. And as you present the grace of truth in true disinterested service, angels will be present to sustain you. The Comforter will be with you to fulfill the promise of the Saviour, «Lo, I am with you alway, even unto the end of the world.» **Medical Ministry, p. 196**

I recall one outstanding example of mistaken disinterested service. I met a Seven-day Adventist doctor who enthusiastically conducted dozens of 5-Day Plans to Stop Smoking. He had more than 15,000 smokers attend his programs over the years, and he bragged to me, "Not one of them ever knew I was a Seventh-day Adventist."

What was his problem? Was he embarrassed to be a Seventh-day Adventist? Did he feel that his spiritual identity would diminish his effectiveness? Did he feel he could do a better job at changing behavior than Jesus could?

Disinterested service doesn't mean that we act without regard to the spiritual needs of people. Disinterested service means we do not perform acts of charity for selfish purposes, personal gain or recognition. Some would say that inserting an evangelistic component in a health education program represents a selfish purpose but this is not the case.

The passage above specifically mentions that disinterested service may result in a "converting influence," we are to present the "grace of truth." Presenting spiritual matters is not a selfish matter. It is a matter of eternal importance and should be free of any personal wishes for recognition and not mixed with desire for enrichment or personal gain.

> "The Lord sees and understands, and He will use you, despite your weakness, if you offer your talent as a consecrated gift to His service; for in active, disinterested service the weak become strong and enjoy His precious commendation. The joy of the Lord is an element of strength. If you are faithful, the peace that passeth all understanding will be your reward in this life, and in the future life you will enter into the joy of your Lord. *Christian Service, p. 101.*

In this quotation we see that even though we may be weak, as we dedicate our skills to His service, free from selfish purposes for things like personal gain or recognition, the Lord strengthens us to do His service.

In the following quotation, disinterested service is seen to include such things as praying with people, reading to them from the Bible, and speaking with them of the Saviour. This is specifically with regard to the control of appetite behavior. So, there is no place for excluding God as the agent of behavior change in the name of conducting health programs with "disinterested service."

> "In almost every community there are large numbers who do not listen to the preaching of God's word or attend any religious service. If they are reached by the gospel, it must be carried to their homes. Often the relief of their physical needs is the only avenue by which they can be approached. Missionary nurses who care for the sick and relieve the distress of the poor will find many opportunities to pray with them, to read to them from God's word, and to speak of the Saviour. They can pray with and for the helpless ones who have not strength of will to control the appetites that passion has degraded. They can bring a ray of hope into the lives of the defeated and disheartened. Their unselfish love, manifested in acts of disinterested kindness, will make it easier for the suffering ones to believe in the love of Christ." *Messages to Young People, p. 223*

Next we see that disinterested service includes denying self to do good for others, devoting all we have to the service of Christ and not laying up treasures for ourselves on earth and by avoiding the love of money. Nothing is said about leaving a spiritual message out of our efforts.

> "Those who deny self to do others good, and who devote themselves and all they have to Christ's service, will realize the happiness which the selfish man seeks for in vain. Said our Saviour: «Whosoever he be of you that forsaketh not all that he hath, he cannot be My disciple.» Charity «seeketh not her own.» This is the fruit of that disinterested love and benevolence which characterized

the life of Christ. The law of God in our hearts will bring our own interests in subordination to high and eternal considerations. We are enjoined by Christ to seek first the kingdom of God and His righteousness. This is our first and highest duty. Our Master expressly warned His servants not to lay up treasures upon the earth; for in so doing their hearts would be upon earthly rather than heavenly things. Here is where many poor souls have made shipwreck of faith. They have gone directly contrary to the express injunction of our Lord, and have allowed the love of money to become the ruling passion of their lives. They are intemperate in their efforts to acquire means. They are as much intoxicated with their insane desire for riches as is the inebriate with his liquor." *Vol. 3 Testimonies for the Church, 397-398.*

A compelling example of disinterested service is recounted in the interaction of Elisha with Naaman the leper. The details of the story from 2 Kings 5 are familiar. The cure of Naaman's leprosy after dipping seven times in the Jordan River immediately changed his feeling from rage and fury to thankfulness and beyond that it resulted in a change of theological belief. His cure convinced him that the God of Elisha is the God of the whole earth. It turned him from a worshipper of Rimmon into a worshipper of Jehovah. He must proclaim this. He must let the prophet know what is in his heart.

Great wealth was offered to Elisha that could have been used to advance the work of God in Israel, but he refused to take any reward. Naaman was thus taught that Jehovah was his true Healer, the prophet the mere instrument, and that it was to Jehovah that his gratitude, his thanks, and his offerings were due.

Elisha had to show that "the gift of God could not be purchased with money;" (Acts 8:20) he had to impress it on Naaman, that Jehovah was a God not like other gods, and that his prophets were men not like other men. He had to teach the doctrine of free grace.

If we would benefit others, our own hearts must be right with God. There must be no doubt about our sincerity, no uncertainty about our motives. We see how little Elisha thought of self. He had a great opportunity, and he used it well. He had a strong temptation presented to him, and he resisted it. It is a splendid instance of disinterested service, a splendid illustration of the power of Divine grace.

> *To the extent that health evangelism promotes the individual conducting the program, just to that extent it is robbing God of the recognition due Him.*

To the extent that health evangelism promotes or enriches the individual or organization sponsoring the health evangelism activity, just to that extent it is robbing God of the thankfulness and recognition due Him.

It is often necessary to meet the temporal necessities of the individuals we help. We may need to provide clothing, food or shelter. But in the process, we should look for the opportunity to speak of virtue and the love of Christ. Disinterested service will not purposely leave out opportunities to speak a word for God.

«Thy neighbor as thyself,»--the question arises, «Who is my neighbor?» The Saviour's reply is found in the parable of the good Samaritan, which teaches us that any human being who needs our sympathy and our kind offices, is our neighbor. The suffering and destitute of all classes are our neighbors; and when their wants are brought to our knowledge it is our duty to relieve them as far as possible. A principle is brought out in this parable that it would be well for the followers of Christ to adopt. First meet the temporal necessities of the needy, and relieve their physical wants and sufferings, and you will then find an open avenue to the heart, where you may plant the good seeds of virtue and religion." *Advent Review and Sabbath Herald, 01-18-1887.*

The church has been asked to provide services of a humanitarian nature in developing countries. At times contracts with governments prohibit any active proselytizing. The name of Jesus can not be named, prayers can not be offered and spiritual meetings can not be held. It is my opinion that sinking resources into such operations doesn't represent disinterested service.

In circumstances where proclaiming the gospel is specifically prohibited, when we agree to limit our efforts to secular activities, we are no better than any other worldly enterprise that provides physical services. If we feel constrained or are contractually constrained from speaking freely about God, when circumstances warrant and opportunity occurs, we should avoid those opportunities and let others carry on that work.

Evangelism is the work of the church in all of its institutional settings. The health work should never be an exception. Health ministry in all forms should be designed to be evangelistic. Evangelistic opportunities should be maximized. Questions need to be asked at every juncture. "Will this element increase or decrease the evangelistic potential of this enterprise?"

# 7

# Spiritual Conversion and Health Evangelism

IN THE SEVENTH-DAY ADVENTIST CHURCH CANDIDATES ARE NOT baptized until they profess to understand and believe all the fundamental beliefs of the church. Sometimes a person is baptized who is not fully exposed to the «health message.»

Despite occasional loosening of some criteria for baptism, there are a lot of doctrinal hoops for a person to jump through to become eligible for baptism. This has a way of working against health evangelism. For example, if a previously secular person quits smoking with God's help and has a new relationship with Jesus, there is no way for this to be formally recognized by the church. In reality, this person was «converted» or «saved» at a stop smoking clinic. This person found Jesus and their life was turned around. This person's newfound trust in Christ is not recognized; he is not welcomed into the fellowship of believers or considered a serious candidate for baptism.

In a health evangelism program, it is possible to have a conversion experience. Your life is completely turned around when you trust God to make a change in your life. You are far from being doctrinally mature, but the salvific step you took should be recognized in some way by the church. You should be welcomed into the fellowship of the saved.

This conversion experience can occur over any single aspect of life that needs changing with the power of God. When you first trust God to save you from a bad habit or addiction, your life is turned around and changed. Once you have experienced the power of God in your life you are interested to learn what else God can do for you.

Divine deliverance from one bad habit creates the possibility that God can do even more for you. God will help you with all of your bad habits. Once your life is turned around on one point, you are on the road to Christian maturity.

Those who accept Christ to change their lives should be recognized for having been converted. They are baby Christians. They have sipped the milk of the Word. Some act of recognition that this step has taken place needs to be developed. In New Testament times such a person would likely be baptized in recognition of a new life begun.

The best example of this from the Bible is the healing of the demoniac found three of the four gospels. Jesus was asked to leave the country by the alarmed population who had lost their livelihood in the drowning of 2000 pigs in the sea of Galilee. As he and the disciples were entering the boat to depart the demoniacs begged to join Jesus and the disciples.

These heathen men were healed and wanted to learn more from Jesus, but Jesus told him to "Return to your own house, and tell what great things God has done for you." And he went his way and proclaimed throughout the whole city what great things Jesus had done for him. Luke 8:39 (NKJV)

This is health evangelism. The demoniac knew nothing about the sabbath, the sacrificial system, the sanctuary, or the state of the dead. He had only one message. "I once was lost, but now I am found. I was a slave of demons, but now I am free. I was dead but now I am alive. Jesus saves. Jesus saves."

A health message without Jesus is message without hope or meaning. It points to the change needing to be made but fails to provide the power necessary for a permanent change.

If a health program is conducted in an evangelistic way, people will come to Jesus and be converted by trusting Jesus to change their lives. Having one's life changed by Jesus can occur with any problem a person has. For many people, obesity and gluttony are besetting sins from which they need to be liberated. Jesus can do this for them. They can be saved at a health evangelistic weight management program such as Best Weigh.

The church needs to develop meaningful ways to recognize the conversion experience of an individual who is "saved" in a health evangelism program. Doctrinal maturity can be achieved over time with additional study.

Health reform and salvation are closely connected. It is a mistake to educate and inform people about health and expect them to make lasting changes in their behavior within their own power. A few can do this, but most cannot. Most will never change unless they have an experience with Jesus Christ.

> "The light God has given on health reform is for our salvation and the salvation of the world ... Let the poor have the gospel of health preached unto them from a practical point of view." ***Testimony Studies on Diet and Foods 193***

Health reform is not to be considered just a salvation from disease or symptoms, but salvation from slavery to the habits that trap us in unhealthful behaviors. This kind of salvation only comes from Jesus. We tend to limit our concept of health reform to the physical or mental arena of life and place the salvation experience into a mystical spiritual arena. But Jesus is needed in all facets of life. Health evangelism needs to be fully infused with the gospel.

> "The gospel is to be bound up with the principles of true health reform. The gospel and the medical missionary work are to advance together. Christianity is to be brought into the practical life." ***Vol. 6 Testimonies 379***

The primary purpose of health evangelism is to introduce people to Jesus.

> "We should ever remember that the object of the medical missionary work is to point sin-sick men and women to the Man of Calvary, who takes away the sin of the world. By beholding Him, they will be changed into His likeness. We are to encourage the sick and suffering to look to Jesus and live". **Counsels on Diet and Food 458**

Some program directors feel that health information presented to the public should be more of a scientific nature and not so much from the Bible. A main point of this book is that the Bible should be used much more in health evangelism programs. If lessons from the Bible are not used in your health program it really isn't a health evangelism program.

> "The principles of health reform are found in the Word of God. The gospel of health is to be firmly linked with the ministry of the Word. It is the Lord's design that the restoring influence of health reform shall be a part of the last great effort to proclaim the gospel message." **Medical Ministry 259**

*Health evangelism is all about the gospel. Jesus saves people from bad habits and slavery to addictions.*

Health evangelism is all about the gospel. Jesus saves people from bad habits and slavery to addictions.

# 8

# Types of Programs

This is a review of a few types of programs or settings in which health education is currently practiced within or loosely affiliated with the Seventh-day Adventist Church. There are a variety of formats and settings with strengths and weaknesses associated with each approach. Each is considered to be evangelistic but not one of them is successfully attracting significant numbers of interests or converts to the Seventh-day Adventist church. These are presented as a gallery of failures begging for a more effective approach to health evangelism.

## Local Church-based Programs

Health evangelism programs have occasionally been conducted in the local church. The next chapter deals with the advantages and desirability of working in the local church. The denomination has more churches than any other type of institution. Church buildings stand empty most of the time. This creates an ideal setting for health evangelism.

Church-based programs have included smoking cessation programs, weight management programs, depression recovery, nutrition courses, and cooking schools to mention just a few. The programs do not offer a cure to the sick as much as they minister to the "worried well" who have harmful habits and behaviors that will destroy their health if not corrected.

It was generally accepted that these programs constituted health evangelism and that subsequent attendance at traditional evangelistic services or regular church attendance would naturally flow from conducting health programs in the church. This didn't happen. The local church is still an ideal candidate site for conducting health evangelism, but a different approach is needed as will be discussed in a future chapter.

Some health programs are not appropriate for a local church setting. Drug rehabilitation should probably not be done in the local church. Drug addicts often need to be institutionalized to kick the habit. Drug addicts need frequent monitoring and support services for an extended period of time. Drug addicts are usually highly manipulative people who lie and steal to support their habits. Church members are not equipped to recognize or handle these behaviors and can be taken in by drug addicts. The local church might hold a prevention or maintenance program for recovering addicts but not a drug detoxification program.

The same is probably true for alcoholism as well. The church might sponsor an Alcoholics Anonymous program but leave acute detoxification to hospitals. If your church does sponsor an AA meeting, I believe it should be a nonsmoking meeting where coffee; tea and caffeine drinks are not provided or allowed.

Some churches have sponsored medical clinics for the medically indigent. I have volunteered at and been involved in organizing several medical clinics for indigent members of the community. Clinics do require a high level of security to protect prescription medication that may be kept on the premises. Clinics require the services of physicians and nurses. Clinical services constitute the practice of medicine and open the local church, Conference, Union, and Division with ascending liability. When a successful model of church-based clinics is developed, the spiritual needs of patients will need to be addressed. Clinic patients should have access to spiritual counseling and prayer provided by dedicated Christian staff. There should also be access to spiritual literature, Bible Studies, and invitations to local church services.

### Resources for the Local Church

There are many health education resources available for local churches from the North American Division of Seventh-day Adventists. These are catalogued at the website http://www.nadhealthministries.org. A variety of programs, books, pamphlets, and supplies on health are available for free or a nominal cost.

The world headquarters of the Seventh-day Adventist church also operates a website that has an abundance of health promotional materials. This is at http://www.healthministries.com. Here you will find health evangelism programs, books, articles, useful links, newsletters and a schedule of church sponsored health conventions.

All the health materials available at the above sites contain scientifically sound health information. Few of the materials are optimized for soul winning. It will take some of the creativity suggested in this book to change a health program into a health evangelism program when you use these materials.

## Hospital-based Health evangelism

Early in the 20th century the quality of medical care was beginning to improve and become more rational and scientific in approach. The Seventh-day Adventist church operated many small and some larger health care institutions which were usually called a Sanitarium.

The Sanitarium was an institution where clients and patients came for an extended period of time. They were fed a healthful diet and educated on how to eat to preserve health. They were exposed to exercise regimens and a variety of baths and hydrotherapy treatments.

The services were health promoting, educational, and provided in a semi-resort setting. Spiritual services were a regular part of the daily routine. Clients were usually wealthy and paid cash for their care. Some beds were reserved for those with more modest means who could not pay.

At the same time those with more serious illnesses were also seen. Surgery, diagnostic laboratory, and X-ray services were developed and provided.

Throughout the past 100 years gradual changes occurred in the Adventist health care model. The sanitarium model was gradually abandoned by the church. Hospitals were modeled after secular institutions. The diet, exercise, educational, and spiritual components died as the sanitarium model was abandoned.

Most hospitals today do not do much in the way of health education or health evangelism. In the past some Adventist operated hospitals conducted smoking cessation programs. The very first 5-Day Plan to Stop Smoking program I ever helped conduct was with Elder A. C. Marple, chaplain of the Washington Adventist Hospital. This was in the late 1960's and smoking cessations clinics in those days were well attended. We had 40-60 participants attending every monthly session in a hospital conference room.

This 5-Day Plan to Stop Smoking at the Washington Adventist Hospital helped the hospital's reputation in the community. Elder Marple made the program slightly evangelistic by referring to help that was available from God but no specifics or "how to" instructions were given.

The disadvantage of the hospital-based program was that there was no connection with the local church. There were no church members to be buddies with those who were trying to quit. Elder Marple wasn't a pastor of a congregation. There was no follow-up. In short, there was no way to connect smokers with a local church for continued spiritual growth.

Health education programs in hospitals today are limited to rehabilitation services for specific conditions. There is diabetic education concerning home blood sugar testing and details of the diabetic diet. There is cardiac rehabilitation for those who have had a heart attack. This includes dietary recommendations and a graduated exercise program under controlled and monitored conditions. This helps define the limits within which a cardiac patient can work or exercise.

Some hospitals have pulmonary rehabilitation programs for those with emphysema or chronic bronchitis who have stopped smoking but need continued lung treatments and breathing exercises. Smoking education and cessation advice is also provided by many hospitals.

A few hospitals provide grief recovery for spouses and family members after losing a loved one. All of these activities are especially suited for hospitals. The spiritual dimensions of these health problems are not usually addressed, and the educators are often not members of the Seventh-day Adventist church.

Hospitals have conducted a variety of health education programs but in times of tight budgets it is usually the education programs for patients that first get cut. There are many opportunities for health evangelism in the hospital setting but these have not been systematically developed or encouraged.

Occasionally, an Adventist operated hospital has a patient who joins the church and is baptized because of someone's ministry. An occasional baptism, however, doesn't justify the church operating a hospital. Hospitals are multimillion-dollar enterprises supported by hundreds or thousands of highly trained people most of whom are not usually Seventh-day Adventist. One or two baptisms a year represents a poor return on investment.

*Hospitals are not cost-effective health evangelistic tools.*

Hospitals are not cost-effective health evangelistic tools. Do not get me wrong, hospitals provide highly technical, medical and surgical services for persons in their immediate community, but a hospital's evangelistic contribution to the church is quite limited and diminishing.

There is no practical way to insert local churches or church members into the business of a hospital. A couple of hospitals in the Adventist Health System utilize local church members as "community chaplains" to visit and comfort the sick. Many other Adventist operated hospitals are reluctant have any affiliation with local Seventh-day Adventist churches. They are "community" hospitals that are simply managed by Seventh-day Adventists. In practice, most hospitals effectively keep the church at an arm's length, away from day-to-day operations.

Additionally, there is a trend among some Adventist operated hospitals to join or become affiliated with larger, entirely secular health care systems. Often a 51% or larger share of control is relinquished to the management team of a larger hospital. These arrangements are designed to bring about financial stability and ensure the continued viability of the Adventist operated hospital. When such arrangements are made, the spiritual emphasis unique to Seventh-day Adventists is often relinquished. Such hospitals survive financially but are less useful in the Lord's work. Again the "No margin, no mission" philosophy prevails.

The Florida Hospital system is the largest Seventh-day Adventist Hospital on the east coast located in Orlando Florida. The staff has developed a faith-based lifestyle program called CREATION which is an acronym for the eight steps for better health. The curriculum can be taken by an individual or presented to the public through the local church. The materials are scientifically accurate, biblically based, colorfully presented, and available in a variety of formats including a format for Vacation Bible School. A local college is using these materials on their student body to promote healthful choices. These resources can be reviewed and purchased at http://www.creationhealth.com.

## Mega-Health Events

"Your Pathway to Health" is an organization that conducts massive two or three-day health screening and treatment events once or twice a year in major cities around the United States. These events are conducted in very large facilities. Services are provided by hundreds of volunteer health professionals. Thousands of patients receive free medical, dental, and ancillary health services. These events are conducted a few days or weeks before major evangelistic meetings are conducted in the city.

The scope of services provided include general medical evaluations, minor surgery services, Podiatry, physical therapy, women's health services, mental health evaluations, dental care, vision assessments, legal counsel, X-ray's, and clinical laboratory services. Patients receive triage at entry to the facility and are directed to the stations where they most need help.

Results of tests and follow-up activities are often provided at local Seventh-day Adventist churches. The desire is that contact with local churches and church members will prompt participation in local health programs or Bible studies.

Serious health problems have been identified by "Your Pathway to Health" and timely referrals have been made. Lives have been saved. Large events create a high level of visibility for the Seventh-day Adventist church and much positive publicity has been generated by the "Your Pathway to Health" events.

The overall health impact on an individual attending "Your Pathway to Health" is about the same as if a person was to receive a onetime free examination and diagnostic testing in an emergency room or doc-in-a-box. For the patient, this free service is simply a single point in time. Referral to specialists and continuing care falls back on the expensive fee-for-service or managed health care system locally available.

The overall evangelistic impact on an individual attending "Your Pathway to Heath" depends on the spiritual receptivity of the patient and the Christian experience of the provider (many of whom are not Seventh-day Adventists.) An additional point of spiritual contact can occur when the patient goes to get results at the local Seventh-day Adventist church. For follow-up, the patient is going to an unfamiliar place to have a onetime meeting with an unfamiliar person. Under such circumstances, it is unlikely that the interaction will progress beyond conventional formalities.

The "Your Pathway to Health" suffers from growing pains typical of any new organization. Basic organization, training of volunteers, establishing more meaningful follow-up, and clear lines of communication all need to be improved. Significant chaos is always evident when an organization works with local volunteers who have never participated in an effort like this before. A onetime event is always much more about publicity and visibility than it is about enduring relationships or continuity of health care.

## Lifestyle Centers

Lifestyle centers are trying to maintain the Sanitarium model of care abandoned by the hospital system during the previous century. Lifestyle centers provide a basic level of diagnosis and treatment of a few medical conditions, but their primary function is health education and rehabilitation. Lifestyle centers focus on modification of risk factors for disease. The inpatient portions of these programs can last from seven to 28 days.

In the United States, every lifestyle center is self-supporting. They are not owned or operated by the Seventh-day Adventist church. These institutions are conservative in religious orientation and health practice.

Lifestyle centers provide a vegetarian and often a vegan diet. Meals consist of tastefully prepared but often dishes unfamiliar to their clients. Recipes are shared and food preparation is practiced under the watchful eye of the nutrition staff.

Rigorous exercise regimens are pursued daily. These programs are adjusted for age and medical condition. Great improvements in exercise distance and endurance are accomplished. New habits are formed.

These live-in programs often have a physical therapy component with steam baths, hot and cold contrasting showers, fomentations, and massage therapy. Soreness in the muscles is relieved.

Clients are exposed to strong spiritual influences. Every staff member freely speaks of spiritual things. There are morning and evening worship services. The Sabbath is devoted to preaching, study, and conversations on spiritual topics.

The administrations of these institutions are guided by the Spirit of Prophecy counsel regarding the establishment of Sanitariums. These small institutions are also felt by many to more closely approximate what Seventh-day Adventist health institutions were meant to be, in contrast to the community hospital model. Most of these institutions are members of an umbrella organization called Outpost Ministries. There are over 200 member organizations. These can be accessed at outpostcenters.org.

## Lifestyle Centers and the Local Church

There are fundamental problems with lifestyle centers. These independent ministries cannot be faulted for being separate from the administrative structure of the Seventh-day Adventist church, but they are to be faulted for divorcing themselves from local Seventh-day Adventist churches.

---

*The local church is the Christian's home, not the lifestyle center.*

---

The local church is the Christian's home, not the lifestyle center. Not one of these institutions has designed or implemented a system for creating connections between their clients and the local Seventh-day Adventist church in the home community from which their clients come. In this aspect in particular, lifestyle centers have failed to maximize the evangelistic potential of their health programs.

Lifestyle centers largely ignore local churches. There are some important reasons for this. Local Seventh-day Adventist churches are largely filled with intemperate people who need to know and practice the health message better than they do. Members of the local church would be a bad example to returning clients who have learned healthful living practices at a local lifestyle center. These may be the facts, but do not constitute good enough reasons for leaving the local churches out of the picture.

Certain lifestyle centers are large enough to have a church right on their property. This further isolates the institution from the local community of churches. A church on campus provides a good reason for staff, students, and clients to stay away from other churches since they can worship right on the lifestyle center premises.

Lifestyle centers should assume the responsibility for reforming the lives of church members and help bring up the quality of life in the local church. At a minimum, lifestyle centers should identify key members, in every church, who are living the health message. These key members would make wonderful contacts for the clients of lifestyle centers who return home and need someone at the local level to help them maintain their newfound health behaviors.

Let me propose a mechanism for accomplishing this goal. Lifestyle centers should insert a local church in the process of enrolling new clients. They could refer all inquiries to the closest local Seventh-day Adventist church in the prospective client's home community.

A friendly church member, living in the town where prospective clients live, can come over to their house and explain the various programs available at the lifestyle center. The church member can complete the enrollment forms. These forms can be faxed or mailed to the central office of the lifestyle center. The local church member can then communicate a confirmed appointment back to the prospective client.

When the local church is inserted into the program of the lifestyle center in this way, prospective clients have taken some very important evangelistic steps. They have met someone in their own hometown who goes to the Seventh-day Adventist church. They have made a friend.

This friend will help them get into the lifestyle center. This friend will be there when they come home from the lifestyle center.

The local Seventh-day Adventist church member can also help clients adhere to the newly acquired health habits. The church member is only a call away and should be available 24 hours a day to offer practical, moral and spiritual support.

The local Seventh-day Adventist church member can also be available to conduct periodic follow-up surveys for the lifestyle center. This will provide the lifestyle center with much needed, long term effectiveness data that will justify the work it does. Additionally, some of the administrative burden is cast onto a volunteer system saving the lifestyle center some money.

## Setting up Local Church Affiliations

Lifestyle centers should promote their services in local Seventh-day Adventist churches. Every weekend they should be in some church promoting healthful living. Jesus is returning to take to heaven a church that is free from every spot and wrinkle. We have too many spots and wrinkles, too much indulgence of appetite, too much indolence and lack of physical activity.

Every Seventh-day Adventist church within driving distance of a lifestyle center should be regularly visited by someone from the center. Health programs should be conducted in local churches. At the same time church members can be identified who may be willing to be affiliated with the lifestyle center. Review the lifestyle of church members who volunteer for service. If found acceptable, give them a credential--perhaps a badge, a laminated card, a plaque, or a letter. Give them promotional materials, and application forms for the lifestyle center.

This should be a voluntary system. Perhaps some incentives could be built in. The church member might be able to spend a weekend now and then or participate in a short course at the lifestyle center.

What a blessing to the local church would result from this affiliation with a lifestyle center. Church members would learn to live better lives and would relate to community people who attended the live-in programs. Church members would have a reason to call on graduates of these programs. They would regularly meet with them and help them live healthfully. The local church can provide Bible studies to those who are interested. New church members will come from this affiliation. The local church is the Christian's home—not the lifestyle center.

Lifestyle centers should think about good health but they should think first and foremost as to how to get people into the kingdom of God and become members of some local Seventh-day Adventist church.

## Boarding Schools and Health Evangelism

Some of the lifestyle centers have schools attached to them. Weimar Institute has a college. Hartland Institute in Virginia has a school program as do some other institutions. In some cases, these schools are recognized by the state or church but in most instances, there is no official accreditation. This is not especially bad. The students receive a basic education with an emphasis on healthful living and Christian principles. Much of what I have said about the local church applies to these schools as well. Many of these students have come apart from local churches that are lukewarm and lacking in evangelistic activity. These students should turn around and embrace the churches they just left and help make them evangelistic centers in their local communities.

## Vegetarian Restaurants

There have been some successful vegetarian restaurants operated by Seventh-day Adventist individuals or self-supporting institutions. These restaurants provide healthful food attractively prepared. These restaurants often have an educational component with literature on healthful living and classes to help people learn how to prepare healthful vegetarian meals.

Ways should be explored to make these institutions more evangelistic. There should be ways to tie a restaurant to a local church. Programs sponsored by the restaurant should not only be conducted at the restaurant but at a local Seventh-day Adventist church as well. The goal of the restaurant should be to win souls for the kingdom of God and get people to worship in a local Seventh-day Adventist church.

## Adventist Community Services

Adventist Community Services (ACS) is an organization dedicated to disaster relief. When there is a tornado, flood or other natural disaster, the ACS vans are there, and local church members help with distribution of clothes, blankets, and food. ACS is useful, but the evangelistic potential of these activities is quite small. Local church members are not encouraged to maintain any meaningful and potentially evangelistic contact with those they help.

## ADRA

Adventist Development and Relief Agency, (ADRA) receives some financial support from the church but most of the budget comes from direct grants from various foundations and governments around the world. ADRA handles huge amounts of money, food, clothing, and relief supplies. ADRA is involved with thousands of different projects in hundreds of countries. ADRA is wonderful.

However, ADRA is not overtly evangelistic. The credit for the work ADRA does is often given to the donor organization or nation. The name Seventh-day Adventist is often not identified in the work ADRA does. By downplaying ADRA's affiliation with the church they have gained support of the world. If your analysis of the success of ADRA is measured by effort, it is simply wonderful. If analysis of success is measured by progress toward the goals of the church, the success would be considerably less.

The church should not be involved in doing the world's relief work; particularly if the church's name is withheld in the effort. There are almost no mechanisms for connecting recipients of ADRA's help with local Seventh-day Adventist Churches.

The most available, most important, and least utilized institution for health ministries within the Seventh-day Adventist denomination is the local church. It stands empty; its members occupied with the cares of the world and idle with respect to health evangelism.

## Private Entrepreneurs

### Life Long Health

A few Seventh-day Adventists have become very successful capitalizing on Seventh-day Adventist health principles. One such example is Don Hall of Life Long Health. He has developed health assessment tools that are widely used in industry. He has developed and marketed a variety of health education programs including "Eight Weeks to Wellness," "Weight Management for Life," and "Fitness for Life." His materials are available at myllh.org.

The scientific information in Don Hall's material is scientifically sound and attractively presented but is entirely secular in approach. Considerable adaptation would be necessary for his programs to become health evangelism programs. There are no links to Seventh-day Adventist websites on his lengthy page of links to health information sites.

## CHIP

Another example of a privately developed program is the Coronary Health Improvement Project (CHIP) developed by Hans Diehl, DrHSc, MPH, FACN. CHIP is an intense program that runs four nights a week for a month and relies on a series of video presentations. It is often conducted in Seventh-day Adventist churches. The cost is several hundred dollars per participant. The health information provided is accurate and up to date. Lives are changed for the better.

CHIP was sold to Seventh-day Adventist sanitarium/hospital system in Australia and the CHIP now stands for The Complete Health Improvement Program. This program is essentially secular in nature. There is no reference to scripture, no interface with church members, no prayer, and no information on how God changes behavior.

## Health Expo

Another privately developed program that has gained a global reputation is the Health Expo Program. This is a screening program to identify habits adverse to good health. It has a simple health age appraisal tool. Guests then rotate through stations where counseling can be given on how to improve health. There are colorful banners placed at each station. This program is presented to the public in public places and at times at a local Seventh-day Adventist church. The program is finished in one day. Evangelistic potential is limited. The attractive materials are available at http://www.healthexpobanners.com.

These are three examples of health education materials developed by private Seventh-day Adventist entrepreneurs. There are dozens more not listed here. The problem as I see it is that the information provided though excellent is generally available online and in dozens of formats. There is nothing unique or special about the information provided in these programs.

The fact that a Seventh-day Adventist developed a health program doesn't make it evangelistic or particularly useful for the church. Secular programs conducted in the church are still secular programs. If people come to your church and don't learn about the Creator of the universe who can reach down and change your life you have wasted their time and they are less likely to return.

We must be intentional in our outreach. We must understand what health evangelism is. It is more than useful health information.

## Adventist Medical Evangelism Network (AMEN)

AMEN is a professional organization composed primarily of Seventh-day Adventist physicians, dentists, and optometrists whose mission is to team with pastors and church members, uniting the church to restore Christ's ministry of healing to the world. The focus is on training Seventh-day Adventist health professionals to be effective medical evangelists. AMEN primarily works to apply practical, spiritual approaches in a clinical practice context not in a local church setting.

AMEN is an independent ministry that supports the mission of the Seventh-day Adventist Church; however, it is not part of, affiliated with, or endorsed by the Seventh-day Adventist church.

# 9

# Organizing a Health Evangelism Program

## Groundwork

IF YOU ARE EXCITED ABOUT HEALTH EVANGELISM AND WISH TO develop this type of outreach at your local church, start discussing with others in the congregation and see if an interest develops. Consider sharing this book with others to create a shared vision for health evangelism. Explore health evangelism with the pastor. Have they ever conducted or participated in a health evangelism program? When was the last time? What role did they have? What was the result? Was the experience positive or negative? Would the pastoral staff be interested in having a health evangelism program in the present location? Would they help by giving a talk each session of the program? Would the pastor help promote the program in the church? The answers to all these questions are important before beginning to organize your health evangelism program.

If the pastor is supportive, consider approaching additional local church leaders to see if they would be supportive as well. Have a chat with the head elder, head deacon and deaconess. Talk with health professionals in the church. Have any of them ever taken part in a health evangelism program? Are they willing to help? Will they be able to give one or more talks during the program? Consider if church board approval is needed prior to moving forward.

Lastly, and I do not put as much emphasis on this as many do, find out what will be received favorably by the community. Some feel it important to do a "needs assessment" of the community. If you do a door-to-door survey in any community, you will find smokers, sedentary people, overweight people, alcoholics, and people who need stress reduction.

> *Your community is filled with people who need whatever program you can offer.*

If you have the time to do a community survey, please do one, but do not look upon surveys as being particularly important. Pick an established health evangelism program, or design one of your own, and offer it to the public. Your community is filled with people who need whatever program you can offer. A health survey might identify potential participants you can specifically invite to your program once it is organized.

After conducting the same program over and over a few times, your reputation will be such that no further advertising will be necessary, and all your meetings will be crowded. Just choose something, get started and do it. The public will come.

## Announcing the Health Evangelism Program to the Church

It is usually most effective to make the announcement of your upcoming health evangelism program during a church service. It is helpful if the sermon that week focuses on healthful living and commitment to serving those in need. Ask church members to commit themselves to helping in the health evangelism program.

At the end of the sermon, ask for a show of hands of those who are willing to support the upcoming health evangelism program. Announce the time and place for the first organizational meeting. Follow this up with church-wide email invites/announcements and personal phone calls/reminders and/or text messages.

Now begins the "Gideon process." Of all those who raised their hands at church, only a few will show up for the first organizational meeting. Once the details of the program are laid out, only a few of those who came to learn about the program will find that it will fit their schedule. As preparation continues from week to week, before your program begins, additional church members will drop out.

Do not be discouraged by the attrition of church members. It is much better to lose these volunteers from your program before it starts, than to lose them during the program. Any loss of church member helpers during the program is tragic. It leaves gaps in coverage of small groups and creates the impression of disorganization and even a "not caring" attitude on the part of the church.

I learned this lesson in a dramatic way early in my practice of health evangelism. I had the mistaken idea that church members were anxious to interface with the public. I though all I had to do was to create the opportunity for fellowship and church members would enthusiastically engage with the public who came for help.

The setting was a 5-Day Plan to stop smoking held in the gymnasium of the church school adjacent to the church. Two church members were located at each table where several smokers who wanted to quit were assigned. I provided the church members with no training and no materials. They were merely given the opportunity to be "buddies" with the smokers who wanted to quit.

On the second night several of the church member helpers were missing. By the third night no church members showed up to help. I hastily called a meeting at my home for the church members who were supposed to be buddies to find out what the problem was.

In answer to my inquiry a spokesperson for the group said, "You are the expert doctor. People come to hear you. They don't need us." I suddenly realized that church members need to be trained to be helpers. This doesn't come naturally to them.

I was the subject expert, but church members were the interface with the participants. From then on, I trained all volunteers and received commitments from them that they would participate and help those who came to each program.

## The First Organizational Meeting

Order is the first law of Heaven. Any task undertaken by the church should be appropriately organized with a careful distribution of labor. It is helpful to schedule the organizational meeting on the same night as the proposed program. This will automatically identify any scheduling conflicts among volunteers.

At the first organizational meeting about half the time should be spent in spiritual preparation. Have a short spiritual talk, perhaps relating to behavior change. This can be followed by a season of prayer. The last half of the meeting is spent on an overview of the proposed program. This is where you get down to the "nuts and bolts" details.

- Overview of program organization
  - Time, location, outline of nightly program
- Finalize dates for program
- List job descriptions
- Make plans for advertising
- Identify number of small group helpers

The number of small group leaders identified will give you an upper limit on how many participants can be registered for the program. If ten small group leaders are identified, this will give you five small groups. Limit enrollment to 6 community participants per small group. This would limit registration to the first 30-36 interests who call.

It's helpful to have people preregister for a program by calling in their reservations or registering online. If the initial response is poor, additional advertising can be done before the program begins. After two or three identical health evangelism programs have been conducted, little advertising will be necessary. Word of mouth from previous participants will quickly fill all available slots.

The most important part of preparing church members to help in any program is their own spiritual preparation. I like to have church members read a passage in the Spirit of Prophecy before coming to each training session. A good first assignment is the chapter, "In Contact With Others" from Ministry of Healing pages 483-496. Reading assignments for church members may include the following:

1. "In Contact With Others," Ministry of Healing 483-496.
2. "Helping the Tempted," Ministry of Healing 161-169.
3. "Working for the Intemperate" Ministry of Healing 171-182.
4. "Help in Daily Living" Ministry of Healing 469-482.
5. "He Ordained Twelve" Desire of Ages 290-297.
6. "Give Ye Them to eat" Desire of Ages 364-371.
7. "The First Evangelists" Desire of Ages 349-358.
8. "Duty to Preserve Health" Counsels on Health. 563, 566.
9. "True Motive in Service" Mount of Blessing, 79, 101.
10. "Medical Evangelism" Counsels on Health 503-508.
11. "Religion and Health" Counsels on Health 28-31.

There are hundreds of texts from the Holy Bible that can be assigned for study as well.

These reading assignments are not designed to provide technical or scientific training for the church members. These passages spiritually prepare church members for ministry.

Church members usually have better health habits than those who are coming for help. Church members quite naturally have a superiority complex about their own lifestyle and at times are a bit critical and condescending toward those who come for help.

To encourage empathy, ask church members as they read the assigned passage to identify that portion of their reading that gave them the most instruction or correction. They can share their findings with others at the next organizational meeting. It is heartwarming to see church members confess their hard heartedness and unforgiving attitude as these defects are identified by the reading they do.

Prayer is important in preparation. Prayer should be made for the Holy Spirit to identify people in the community who particularly need your program. The Holy Spirit can bring advertising to their attention. The Holy Spirit creates within the mind and heart a sincere desire to change. The Holy Spirit will bring to your program just those who will be benefitted by what you are offering.

> "It is true that men sometimes become ashamed of their sinful ways, and give up some of their evil habits, before they are conscious that they are being drawn to Christ. But whenever they make an effort to reform, from a sincere desire to do right, it is the power of Christ that is drawing them. An influence of which they are unconscious works upon the soul, and the conscience is quickened, and the outward life is amended." ***Steps to Christ 27***

Prayer also prepares members to participate in the program. Prayer gives your helpers a burden for souls. It creates a desire to be of service. Prayer softens words and attitudes. Prayer makes your helpers the attractive, loving assistants your attendees will need.

After the spiritual preparation of your church members is done for the evening, it is time to look at the program in fine detail. I list all the jobs that are needed to do the program effectively. Each job description should be presented and discussed. Church members who feel they can do a specific job can volunteer for that job. Keep track of who volunteers for what. In some cases, certain particularly well qualified individuals might be asked to help with certain positions to avoid unqualified individuals from volunteering.

Gradually, the roster of jobs is filled. In a large church some larger jobs can be further subdivided so everyone will have something to do. In smaller churches it may be necessary for one church member to do several jobs.

It will usually take three weeks of preparation to get all jobs assigned and a team to be built. I want to reemphasize that about half the preparation session should be spent in spiritual preparation. With careful preparation, when the program begins, you will have a united group of helpers who will be anxious to help those who come for help.

## Church Members and Small Groups

The key element of every successful health evangelism program is small groups. No matter who developed the health program you are using, and no matter how it was designed to be conducted, it is important to modify the program so that participants spend a substantial amount of time in small groups.

Small group activities should take from one third to one half of your program time. It is in small groups that specific problems are identified. It is in small groups that victories are shared. It is in small groups that the success of the program is realized.

Small groups should be led by church members. There should be a minimum of two church members assigned to each small group and ideally no more than six participants.

This feature of health evangelism is so important that I limit the number of community participants who can attend a program based on the number of small group leaders I have been able to recruit. If I have five small groups lead by 10 church members, I will then limit enrollment for this session to 30-36 community participants.

If there are more people who want to come to your health evangelism program than you can accommodate in the current program, take down their names and numbers. Use these individuals as the nucleus for your next program. Alternatively, you can present the problem to the church to recruit additional church members to lead small groups. Do not enlarge the size of each small group to accommodate all who were interested in attending the program. If a small group gets too large, communication within the group becomes limited and the intimate dynamic is lost.

> *The purpose of small groups is to create an environment where sharing can occur.*

The purpose of small groups is to create an environment where sharing can occur. The bigger the group, the poorer the group dynamic. You should only allow as many participants to come to your program as you have the personnel available to give them individual attention.

I have been an observer at several large health evangelism programs. These were conducted by skilled communicators who were highly educated health professionals. The speakers were appreciated and were rewarded by appropriate applause. These programs lacked the one-on-one personal attention that could have been provided in small groups. I feel that these large group programs had very limited long-term impact on the lives of those who attended.

The primary interface with the health program participant should be the church member. Church members often have the same weaknesses and struggles as the ones who are coming for help. This is okay. Church members will struggle right along with the participants. Your helpers will frequently have more success than those who have come for help. We tend to shape up when we know that people are watching us.

In asking for volunteers to be small group leaders it is important to keep follow-up activities in mind as well. Church members are needed every day of the program and after the program to conduct follow-up activities. Thorough follow-up will take as much time as conducting the program. Follow-up should continue at quarterly intervals for a whole year.

# Materials

This is a list of the materials and documents you should obtain or develop yourself to be able to conduct a health evangelism program properly. If time is taken to carefully develop materials that are not commercially available, it will greatly simplify conducting future programs. These materials will be useful if you export your health evangelism program to other churches in your area.

1. 1. Director's Manual.
   a. How to organize and conduct a program.
   b. Job descriptions
   c. Spiritual assignments
2. Helpers Guide
3. Participants Workbook
4. All forms needed to conduct a program
5. Promotion Kit containing all advertising materials
6. Educational handouts

# Director's Manual

If you are not fortunate enough to get a director's manual with the program you are conducting, it will be useful to make one up as you go along. It should have documentation of everything you do. It should contain samples of all the materials you need to conduct a program.

The director's manual will contain a job description for every activity involved in the program. This will give the program director the overview of how to organize and conduct the program.

The job description for each task should be copied and distributed to the church members who volunteer for each job. With written job descriptions, there will be no confusion about who has which assignment. If the program you are conducting doesn't have job descriptions, it would be good to compose them during the organizational meetings.

The director's manual will have all the spiritual assignments that are to be made for the helpers during their training. Selections have been suggested above.

The director's manual should contain a copy of the Helpers Guide, Participants Workbook, data management pieces, educational handouts, multimedia presentations and any other materials that are used in conducting your program.

## Helpers Guide

The Helpers Guide is a manual used by the helpers in your program. (I like to call the church members simply "helpers." Using the term "Coach" implies someone who knows more about the problem than you do and who really isn't in the struggle with you.) The church members who are helpers are obviously mentors, but I do not use the words: counselor, adviser, instructor, partner, guide, or mentor as they imply a position of superiority. It may be true that your helpers are healthier, smarter, and closer to God than many who come for help, but it is never good to have a superiority complex when doing health evangelism.

The Helpers Guide will contain all the materials needed to facilitate small groups. It will include a copy of the Participant's Workbook. Group leaders will help the participants complete the Workbook assignments.

Include in the Helpers Guide materials on conducting small groups. Include material on being a good listener and how to lead out in small groups. Include tips on how to deal with outspoken group members and how to draw out discussion from quieter group members.

The Helpers Guide is a place where each group leader can keep personal information about the members of his or her small group. Start with a list of each of the participants. Include their addresses and phone numbers. Encourage helpers and participants to keep in touch with each other frequently throughout the entire program.

Group leaders need to identify the best times to contact participants. Are texts or phone calls preferred? Give each participant your contact information. Indicate the best times for them to text/call you. Participants should be encouraged to initiate contact, but if a group leader doesn't hear from a participant, it is appropriate to call and see how things are going.

If the relationship between group leaders and participants progresses beyond phone calls, then so much the better. In every group there will be special friendships formed. Sometimes a participant and a group leader will share a common hobby or interest. They will make time to visit with one another and share experiences. They may meet for lunch at a restaurant or at one another's houses.

The Holy Spirit will help direct in the assignments of participants to the small group in which they will receive the most help. In one 5-Day Plan I conducted, a smoker was linked with church member, George. They had been assigned to each other by the person registering people. As they got to know each other on the first night of the program, they found that they worked in the same building but on different floors.

What a help George was to that smoker who was trying to quit. George and the smoker would eat lunch together. They would walk around the building to get some fresh air. George was called several times a day when the ex-smoker would have a craving for a cigarette. In short order these two became special friends.

God must have arranged for George and this participant to be in the same small group. This was God's blessing the program and making it more effective. This pairing was not an accident, coincidence, or random event. It is an example of how God works to make a program effective when it is conducted in a way He can especially bless.

## Participants Workbook

The Participant's Workbook can be just an empty folder with pockets to keep handout materials. If there are going to be a lot of handouts it will be better to provide inexpensive three ring notebooks in which to keep material. Be sure to 3-hole punch your handouts before the program so they will fit into the notebook without additional fuss on the part of the participants.

The handouts that go into the Workbook are distributed at each session of the program. Handouts may include copies of the health lectures, copies of supplemental materials used during the program, the quizzes and exercises that are conducted in small groups. Keep progress records in the workbook as well. Weight loss charts should be kept there for reference in a weight management program.

A fully developed program will have colorful multi-page handouts for each session of the program. These should be purchased in advance or printed, collated, and punched before each program.

## Forms

Forms needed to conduct a program include registration forms, exit questionnaires, and progress cards. A registration form asks for basic demographic data. Obtain contact information which will be helpful for the group leaders to use in contacting participants. Determine health issues that may limit participation in exercise programs. Determine a person's religious affiliation. Ask about the frequency of private prayer and Bible study.

An exit questionnaire given at the last session will document changes that have occurred in knowledge and practices during the program. Exclude the demographic data collected the first night. Include the same questions you asked the first night regarding health habits, Bible study, prayer, etc. This exit questionnaire should also be used as a follow-up questionnaire to be used at intervals over a year to document continued behavior change or a relapse.

A Progress Card can be used to document a person's daily adherence to various program elements. The participant should turn in completed Progress Cards from week to week and receive a new blank one at each session. As a supplement to the paper Progress Card, you may have these forms online for persons to fill out at home from day to day.

Additional forms you develop might include name tags for helpers and participants to wear. You might create decorative labels for the Director's Manual, Workbook, and Helper's Guide as well. You can make signs with arrows to direct people to their respective small groups. You might have tent shaped signs on each table to identify which small group meets there.

## Promotion Kit

The Promotion Kit should contain the advertising pieces you developed to promote your program. Keep copies of letters sent to doctor's offices, articles written for the local papers, advertising you placed in local papers, scripts used on the radio or TV, and form letters you sent to participants who took part in other programs. Copies of posters, banners, brochures, and handouts should be catalogued and kept in the Director's Manual. This will be helpful when you repeat the program.

## Educational Handout Materials

In every program there will be some supplemental materials that come to your attention. These may be duplicated and handed out to participants. These materials may include recipes, copies of articles, or handouts of lecture materials. Copies of these handouts or a record of where they are located online need to be kept.

# 10

## Program Format

---

### Do One Thing Well

HOW OFTEN SHOULD A HEALTH EVANGELISM PROGRAM BE CONDUCTED? What days of the week are best? After this program what should we do next? These are all important questions.

Many times, health evangelism programs have been scheduled to complement traditional evangelistic endeavors. Pastors and evangelists have conducted health evangelism programs as a prelude to traditional evangelistic meetings. I have seen for example, a 5-Day Plan to Stop Smoking attached to the front end of a 6-week evangelistic series. I have participated in an evangelistic series where the first 10 minutes of each evening's presentation was a "health nugget."

Several other variations have been tried over the decades. Very simply, none of these formats have particularly enhanced evangelistic outcomes. Today the health message is often presented in a single evangelistic lecture. So, what does work? How should health evangelism program be conducted?

Health evangelism programs should stand on their own. They should be designed to be evangelistic in their own right. It is not particularly desirable or undesirable for health evangelism programs to be directly connected to other more traditional doctrinal evangelistic programs.

It is desirable for a church to become skilled in conducting health evangelism. This requires a church to conduct the same health evangelism program over and over again. Not just once or twice, but on a regularly scheduled basis. Not for just one year, but year after year. There are many advantages of doing things this way.

Continuous programming of the same health evangelism program builds a core of dedicated church members, who become skilled in doing this work. They quickly learn the ropes of organization. When it is time to do the next program very little effort is necessary to get things started once again. Everyone knows who does what and when to do it. There may be a new helper or two to orient to the program, but the program runs smoothly with dedicated "permanent" volunteer staff.

Additionally, when the same health evangelism program is conducted repeatedly, church members become skilled in relating to people who come for behavior change. Church members quickly learn all the excuses people offer for lack of compliance with the program. They learn the traps that befall those who are struggling with bad habits. Church members become skilled counselors.

More importantly, church members learn to pray for those who are struggling to break the bonds of sin and live better, healthier lives. They can become spiritual guides to those who need someone to place their hands in the hand of a loving Savior who helps them break bad habits.

None of these advantages can be achieved by doing a health evangelism program just once or twice and then going on to something else. Learn to do one thing well.

An additional advantage in doing just one health evangelism program repeatedly is that the community comes to rely on your church for help with one specific health problem. If you conduct a weight control program, those who have been successful will encourage their obese neighbors to, "Go down to the Seventh-day Adventist church. They help people with weight problems."

A good reputation is the result of consistency and reliability. We are known as Seventh-day Adventists because we go to church every Sabbath. We will be established as health evangelists when we consistently offer lifesaving health programming on a regular, dependable, basis.

---

*A good reputation is the result of consistency and reliability*

---

A program offered continuously and consistently will find a valued place in the spectrum of health services available in your community.

Another benefit of doing one program well is the networking that results. Other community agencies will start referring clients to your health evangelism program. Case workers dispensing food stamps to obese persons may advise their clients to enroll in your weight management program. The longer you operate the same health evangelism program in a community the more referrals you will receive from other agencies.

These voluntary and governmental agencies will be comfortable referring clients to your health evangelism program because your program has a life of its own and is not obviously or directly connected with traditional evangelistic efforts. This doesn't mean you cannot conduct traditional evangelistic meetings in the same church in which you do health evangelism, but they should run on parallel tracks, not on an obvious sequential track.

Agencies will prefer to refer clients to your health evangelism program because your program is a low-cost effort run by volunteers. What I am saying is that the American Heart Association would rather refer an overweight client to your weight management program because you are both voluntary organizations. The Heart Association is not going to create business for Weight Watchers, Overeaters Anonymous, TOPS, or any other for profit, commercial organization.

The current national climate in the United States is such that "faith-based" initiatives are looked upon favorably. A church that offers behavior change programs of various types will be a valued community resource.

An equally important part of networking is for you to learn the services offered by other agencies in your community. You will have occasion to refer people with various needs to other organizations that can provide help to your clients.

It has been my experience that most churches will do a health program just once. In the Texas Conference I had the opportunity to officially promote the Best Weigh nutrition and weight management program around the conference. I promoted Best Weigh at pastor's meetings and in regional meetings with pastors. At the start, interest in Best Weigh was high. In the first year 15 churches around the Conference conducted Best Weigh programs.

All the pastors reported that Best Weigh was an effective program. In every program many were able to achieve their weight loss goals. Usually there was one person who would lose 30 pounds or more during the ten weeks of the program.

Church members were involved with Best Weigh who had never been involved in church activities before. More non-Adventists attended the program than had attended other programs in recent history of the church. The pastors were uniformly positive about the impact of Best Weigh on the church and the community.

Even with so many churches involved and with such positive results, only two churches, conducted more than one Best Weigh program. All other churches called it quits after conducting just one.

One church's experience in Mesquite, Texas is particularly instructive. At the first Best Weigh program they had 30 non-Adventist's attend. The church had invested $1500 in advertising. For their second Best Weigh the church scaled back the advertising to just $300. The results were better than at first as over 50 non-Adventists came out. For the third Best Weigh the advertising was done for the church by the local school district. The school system enclosed Best Weigh announcements in letters to parents. Again, Best Weigh attendance was up, over 50 non-Adventists attended the third Best Weigh program. No money at all was invested in advertising.

The lesson to be learned is that as you repeatedly offer the same health evangelism program, the more popular the program becomes. It will take less effort and expense to attract the public. Several Bible study interests were raised from each Best Weigh program in this church. Sadly, with a change in pastors the Best Weigh Programs in this church ceased.

## Sequencing and Bridging

There have been a variety of attempts to create a bridge between health programs and evangelistic programs. Available health programs are largely secular in design and evangelistic programs are overtly spiritual. When there is no significant spiritual emphasis in the health program the transition to evangelistic meetings is abrupt, difficult, and not usually effective.

It was common in the 1970's for hundreds of people to come to the 5-Day Plan to Stop Smoking but only a few would stay for the follow-up evangelistic programs. Many minds have tried to develop a successful transition between secular and spiritual programs. Nothing has been found that works very well.

One model that was developed envisioned a whole series of programs starting with a secular program dealing with health issues followed by a psychological program dealing with stress or depression. and finally coming around to spiritual evangelistic meetings. This scheme never worked successfully. When differing programs are all lined up in a row a different people attend each program. Continued attendance of your original crowd tapers off rapidly.

If you do just one program, the audience will be composed of those who want help with the one specific behavioral problem that program addresses. To be sure, we all have multiple problems but who is to say what we should work on next? Who are we to say that you will be best benefitted if you attend program A and then proceed to program B, followed by programs C, D and ending up with E, which stands for evangelism? I think the A-B-C-D-E approach is doomed to failure.

Do not get me wrong. I believe that many churches, especially larger ones, can offer several different kinds of health evangelism programs during the church year. It is my opinion that these programs should all be on independent parallel tracks. I illustrate the concept this way.

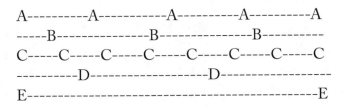

```
A---------A-----------A----------A---------A
-----B--------------B--------------B----------
C-----C-----C-----C-----C-----C-----C-----C
---------D------------------D----------------
E-------------------------------------------E
```

A stop smoking program should be followed by another stop smoking program. The dates for the next stop smoking program should be set before the current program is finished. You should have the brochures printed that list all the stop smoking programs you are going to conduct for the whole year.

When a person successfully completes a smoking cessation program, he or she is most interested in when the next smoking cessation program is going to be held. Ex-smokers have relatives and friends who need your services, and they will recommend your stop smoking program to friends and associates.

It is appropriate to advertise all the various programs you offer at your church in every program you conduct. All smokers who come to quit should know that there is a cooking school, a weight loss program, exercise programs and, yes, evangelistic meetings available.

Some who just quit smoking will need a weight control program while others are ready to start an exercise program. A few will be ready for an evangelistic program. If you are operating continuous programing on parallel tracts the choice as to what to do next is up to the participant. No one will feel any pressure to attend one program or another. People like to have options. They want and appreciate the availability of choices.

The Holy Spirit prompts us to work on our habits sequentially, but in a sequence that differs from person to person. If your church offers a variety of behavioral change programs, it is likely that the Holy Spirit will prompt a person who overcame one problem to attend another one of your programs. Sequencing is an individual matter that should be under the control of the Spirit working on a person's life and not the wishes of the evangelist or health programmer.

When the sequencing is A -- B -- C -- D -- Evangelism, the participant soon learns that your church doesn't offer health programs on a regular and dependable basis to serve the continuing health needs of the community but only as a prelude to traditional evangelism. I have heard evangelists repeatedly use the bait and hook analogy. The health program is the bait, and the doctrinal presentations are the hooks.

I reject this analogy and the entire thought process behind it. I feel that health programs should be evangelistic in and of themselves. Participants who are enslaved by some life destroying habit should be pointed to Jesus as the agent of real and lasting change in the human life. Health evangelism rightly conducted is the bait and the hook. Let me emphasize this by asking, "If a person's life wasn't changed by God in your health program, why should a person have any interest in your doctrinal discussions?" However, those who have had a taste of God's power in their lives as they overcome a bad habit, are those who will hunger and thirst for more. This thought is more fully developed in another chapter.

## Duration of a Program

How long should a health evangelism program run? How many times a week should you meet? The 5-Day Plan to Stop Smoking was great because it ran five days and was over with. You could wedge it in between weekends. There was a one-week investment of time and then you were through. Unfortunately, quitting smoking is a process that is usually not completed in just 5 days.

It would have been nice to study the optimum time required to achieve lasting success when quitting smoking and then design a program to best fit the needs of smokers. The ideal duration of a smoking cessation program hasn't been determined exactly. I have observed smoking cessation programs of varying duration.

On the short side, I have seen an all-day-long, 8–12-hour, marathon smoking cessation program. The hope was that you could quit smoking in just one day. On the long end, there was SmokeEnders, a program that lasted several weeks. What is best? No one knows.

There are several issues to consider in determining the duration of a health evangelism program. Perhaps most important is, how long can you run a program that people will still attend? We would like to think that the public is very interested in health information and is willing to spend as much time as necessary to be properly educated and to get one's habits changed.

This just isn't true. Some programs need to be nightly for a few nights. I believe that smoking cessation fits in this category. The cravings are intense for just a few days and attending meetings daily can help keep you from relapsing. Other programs should be drawn out and conducted at a slower pace over a much longer time.

For many health evangelism programs, conducting meetings just once a week is ideal. The less frequent the meetings, the longer the program will need to run. Do not overdo it. I have seen intense nutrition programs run four nights a week for a month. The material presented was excellent and the speaker was captivating, but it was an overload for the public and for the church members as well. This program might have been better supported by the public and local church members if it ran one night a week for three or four months rather than 16 sessions crammed into just one month. Some churches offer a health program just one session per month but keep it up on a year around basis.

After you decide what is best for the participants who are going to come to your program, it is best to consult with your church members and determine just how much time they are willing to devote to your program. If you plan to have small groups hosted by church members, it is important to find out just how often church members are willing to meet and for how many weeks.

In my experience, you get the most help from individual church members when the program is offered on a one session a week basis. If you conduct the same program with the same volunteers two or three nights a week the help will be strained and will begin to drop out or fail to volunteer for your next program

As a rule, it is wise to avoid weekend days and nights unless you have a one session program such as a health fair, in which case a weekend day might work out well. The duration and frequency of health evangelism programming requires an analysis of what is ideal for the public and then secondarily adapted to the willingness of your church member volunteers.

# 11

# Program Location

HEALTH EVANGELISM PROGRAMS HAVE BEEN CONDUCTED IN A VARIETY of settings. Success depends to a large degree on the venue you choose. In my estimation, the ideal location for conducting health evangelism programs is in the local church. There are many advantages to using the local church. But the most important reason is outlined here:

> "The church is God's appointed agency for the salvation of men. It was organized for service, and its mission is to carry the gospel to the world. From the beginning it has been God's plan that through His church shall be reflected to the world His fullness and His sufficiency. The members of the church, those whom He has called out of darkness into His marvelous light, are to show forth His glory. The church is the repository of the riches of the grace of Christ; and through the church will eventually be made manifest, even to "the principalities and powers in heavenly places," the final and full display of the love of God. Ephesians 3:10."
> *Acts of the Apostles, 9*

The local church is the Christian's home. The local church holds a congregation of saints. The local church has dedicated people who know the Lord. The local church has people with the gifts of service and compassion who know how to speak a word of encouragement, advice, support, and comfort for those who are struggling to overcome a harmful habit or addiction. You do not have these resources in any other setting.

Jesus valued the local church so highly that when Saul on the road to Damascus inquired, "What do You want me to do?" **Acts 9:6 (NKJV)** did not give Saul any personal instruction regarding his life work but directed him to the local church.

"Jesus gave sanction to the authority of His organized church and placed Saul in connection with His appointed agencies on earth. Christ had now a church as His representative on earth, and to it belonged the work of directing the repentant sinner in the way of life…

> "Jesus is the friend of sinners, and His heart is touched with their woe. He has all power, both in heaven and on earth; but He respects the means that He has ordained for the enlightenment and salvation of men; He directs sinners to the church, which He has made a channel of light to the world.
>
> "When, in the midst of his blind error and prejudice, Saul was given a revelation of the Christ whom he was persecuting, he was placed in direct communication with the church which is the light of the world. In this case Ananias represents Christ, and also represents Christ's ministers upon the earth, who are appointed to act in His stead. In Christ's stead Ananias touches the eyes of Saul, that they may receive sight. In Christ's stead he places his hands upon him, and, as he prays in Christ's name, Saul receives the Holy Ghost. All is done in the name and by the authority of Christ. Christ is the fountain; the church is the channel of communication."
> *Acts of the Apostles, 122*

The church has developed many modalities for spreading the gospel to the world, but there is only one place the Christian can call home, and that is the local church. Health evangelism needs a home base. Health evangelism needs a sponsoring institution. It should be the local church.

Health evangelism also needs a personal interface with those struggling to overcome habits and addictions. These should be local church members who themselves have experienced the healing power of Jesus in their lives. Health evangelism is more than information about healthful living, it is power of God unto salvation from the health destroying snares of the Devil.

Here is one more illustration from Scripture to drive this point home. Cornelius, a Roman officer, was an honest seeker for truth. In answer to his prayers an angel was sent to give him instruction regarding salvation. Instead of the angel who came directly from the presence of Jesus sharing the truth about Jesus, heaven, and eternal life with Cornelius, the angel directed Cornelius to send for Simon Peter. The angel said,"

> "Send men to Joppa, and call for one Simon." Thus God gave evidence of His regard for the gospel ministry and for His organized church. The angel was not commissioned to tell Cornelius the story of the cross. A man subject, even as the centurion himself, to human frailties and temptations, was to be the one to tell him of the crucified and risen Saviour.

> "As His representatives among men, God does not choose angels who have never fallen, but human beings, men of like passions with those they seek to save. Christ took humanity that He might reach humanity. A divine-human Saviour was needed to bring salvation to the world. And to men and women has been committed the sacred trust of making known "the unsearchable riches of Christ." Ephesians 3:8.

> "In His wisdom the Lord brings those who are seeking for truth into touch with fellow beings who know the truth. It is the plan of Heaven that those who have

received light shall impart it to those in darkness. Humanity, drawing its efficiency from the great Source of wisdom, is made the instrumentality, the working agency, through which the gospel exercises its transforming power on mind and heart." *Acts of the Apostles 134*

Another advantage to using the local church: the building is empty and unused except for a few hours a week. The local church building is designed for group meetings. The sanctuary can be used for a large audience. Smaller health evangelism programs might be conducted in the fellowship hall or can be held in Sabbath School rooms. So, whether you plan big or small programs, the church can hold your crowd.

The price is also right. It is your church. You shouldn't have to pay any rent to conduct a series of meetings there. Renting facilities elsewhere can be expensive. There will be a huge cost advantage to using your own local church for health evangelism.

Another big advantage of conducting health evangelism programs in your local church is that the Seventh-day Adventist church will get the visibility and credit for the program. The more you do for your community from the home base of your local church, the better the reputation your church will have. Ideally, your church reputation should advance to the point where anyone with any problem will first think of your Seventh-day Adventist church as the place to go for help.

Ownership is a big problem with health evangelism programs. Local church members need to realize that health evangelism is their program. Conducting health evangelism activities in the local church creates this ownership. Anything sponsored by and conducted in your local Seventh-day Adventist church is your program.

Health evangelism programs conducted away from the church will be perceived as only belonging to those few who are organizing and conducting the program. Church members will usually be neutral about such programs. To create a feeling of ownership on the part of church members, health evangelism program must be conducted in the local church.

Worse things can happen. If a health evangelism program is conducted off site, it is sometimes perceived in a negative light. The former Philadelphia Lifestyle Center is just such a case in point. It was a centrally situated old mansion located on a beautiful, wooded, five-acre estate in downtown Philadelphia. It was staffed by Dr. Vincent Gardner and his wife. There was very little support from anyone else.

The Lifestyle Center was conceived to be a cooperative effort of all the churches in the Philadelphia area. Programs for the public were conducted there on a regular basis. Church members from local churches provided some staff and program support. This effort struggled for a few years and eventually failed due to lack of consistent support from local churches.

I talked with a few of the local pastors about the situation. Pastors uniformly saw this health evangelism effort in a negative light. As their church members became involved in the Lifestyle Center, they were seen less and less in the local church. This had the effect of siphoning off talent from the local church.

Pastors were unhappy because their best and most active members were dividing their time between activities in the local church and the Lifestyle Center. This meant a net drain on the resources of each church involved. Pastors were against it.

This is an illustration of the ownership principle. If health evangelism programs had been conducted in local churches, the pastors might have been happier. They would see the church building used for community work. They would see non-Adventists coming to the Adventist Church on a regular basis. Pastors would see church members coming out to support "their" own programs. The pastors would have seen evangelistic possibilities in health evangelism.

Ownership of programs will only come about if programs are conducted in the local church with participation of local church members. You fail to establish ownership when health evangelism is conducted in outside settings.

## Is Using the Local Church a Barrier for the Public?

Conducting health evangelism programs in the local church is not threatening for non-church members during "off hours" when regularly scheduled religious services are not scheduled. It is one thing to invite your neighbor to come to church on Sabbath or to a full set of evangelistic meetings and quite another to invite your neighbor to a cooking class or weight control program during the week.

> *Conducting health evangelism programs in the local church during "off hours" is not threatening to your neighbors.*

Your neighbors might be reluctant to come to your church if they know they are going to be indoctrinated. They will be less reluctant to come to your church for a program designed help them with health problems. Your neighbors are much more likely to go to your church for a health program than they are to go there for spiritual services.

Neighbors are also a curious lot. While coming to your church for a health evangelism program, they will want to look the facilities over. This should be welcomed. If your program is not being conducted in the sanctuary, you should have the sanctuary lights on low, perhaps the temperature adjusted to a comfortable level to encourage lingering a bit longer in the place of worship. It is nice to arrange for someone to be practicing the organ or playing the piano at the time of your meetings so that your participants can hear strains of music that will be familiar to them or at least create the comforting atmosphere expected in church.

When the time comes to invite your neighbors to church for spiritual services, it will be easier if they have already been there, if they have sat in the pews, heard sweet music, and have looked through your hymnal.

*The best reason to conduct health evangelism programs in the local church is because it is the Christian's home*

The best reason to conduct health evangelism programs in the local church is because it is the Christian's home. We are in the business of bringing people home. Let's get our neighbors and friends there as soon as possible. If they come to the church for a health evangelism program, they are almost home. If they come back time after time for a health program, they gradually become comfortable attending your church for non-Sabbath services. For these people, it will be a painless transition to come back again on the Sabbath to worship with you.

Finally, Churches provide an ideal location for conducting health evangelism because of the sheer number of churches available for such purposes. The church operates more than 50,000 churches in about 200 countries. Health evangelism may be conducted elaborately in some large churches and in a humbler way in small churches, but with so many churches available, it seems the primary setting for health evangelism should be the local church.

This is not to say that health evangelism should never be conducted in a high school auditorium, hospital conference room or in Lifestyle Centers, I am just saying that all such activity will be limited in scope and influence. If we want health evangelism to reach millions, it must be conducted in local churches.

Of course, there are some disadvantages to conducting health evangelism programs in the local church. These problems are real but do not present an insurmountable barrier to the success of health evangelism. In several cases, the problems represent unique situations where health evangelism can correct the problem thus improving the situation of the local church.

One significant problem has to do with the basic reputation of some churches. In some communities, there is considerable hostility against Seventh-day Adventists. Under these circumstances it might seem that conducting health evangelism programs in some other setting would be preferable to conducting programs in the local church building.

Perhaps the Seventh-day Adventist church in your community has a poor reputation because you have never consistently offered any services that the community found to be of any value. The only way to change your standing is to begin to offer some service to the community that will be valued by the community.

Another objection to conducting health evangelism programs in the local church has to do with the location of the church. Some churches are on back streets, off the beaten path or in an undesirable neighborhood. These undesirable features are used as an argument to conduct health evangelism programs in a more favorable location. Even this objection is easy to overcome.

My first full-time health evangelism assignment was at the Seventh-day Adventist church in Towson Maryland. The church was not attractive. The "sanctuary" was in the basement of the parsonage and would comfortably seat about 90 people in the padded stackable chairs that took the place of pews. The church was located on a back road.

The pastor suggested we hold the program in a local school auditorium which was more conveniently located and would avoid identification with Seventh-day Adventists. I wanted to utilize church members and draw attention to our local church, so I insisted we use the church. The pastor appeared to be insightful as only 12 smokers showed up for our first program.

Our next 5-Day plan was scheduled just one month later. The pastor was even more insistent that we conduct the program at a local school auditorium, but I resisted. At the second 5-Day Plan we had just over 30 smokers attend.

The third 5-Day plan conducted in that little church basement off the beaten path brought out 90 smokers who wanted to quit. The reputation of the church had changed. It was a source of valuable help for the community despite its unfavorable location.

All our programs from that time forward were well attended. If your plan is to conduct only one health evangelism program, and you want to maximize the number of those who attend, you should conduct your program in the most public place possible. However, this will not have lasting impact on the reputation of the local Seventh-day Adventist church.

It may be slower, but it is a surer way to success if you conduct your health evangelism in the local church no matter how remote or isolated the location. It will take several programs to change your reputation in the community, but the change will come. The word will get out. "If you want help go to the Seventh-day Adventist church. They really help people."

Some churches are in a physically rundown condition. You may be embarrassed by the shabby condition of your church. This makes you reluctant to conduct any public meetings there. The prospect of inviting the public to your church creates the perfect reason to fix up the place. God's house doesn't need to be fancy, but it should be clean and neat.

The size of the church building may also be a concern. You could service a larger crowd in a larger facility. Here is an error. There will be a further development of this concept later, but you do not want to invite more people to your program than you can come close to. If your church is small and you only have a few members, you do not really want a large turn out to a health evangelism program.

Much of the effectiveness of health evangelism comes from the one-on-one relationships that are formed between members and the public. A large turnout in a large facility serviced by only a few church members would defeat this purpose. The size of the facility used for health evangelism purposes should match the number of those who are available to help.

In short, small churches should plan on small programs for small groups until their numbers grow to the point where the whole church is ready to move to a larger facility. Big programs conducted by a few people that lack opportunities for one-on-one interactions have a net negative effect on the reputation of the Seventh-day Adventist church.

## Spirit of Prophecy Quotations on the Local Church.

The following testimonies from the pen of Ellen G. White recommended conducting health evangelism activities in every church in the land. Mrs. White suggests that the local church is the key institution for health evangelism.

The following quotation envisions a church educational effort that trains church members to provide both spiritual and health services for the community. A wide variety of activities are outlined in just a few sentences.

> "Every church should be a training school for Christian workers. Its members should be taught how to give Bible readings, how to conduct and teach Sabbath-school classes, how best to help the poor and to care for the sick, how to work for the unconverted. There should be schools of health, cooking schools, and classes in various lines of Christian help work. There should not only be teaching, but actual work under experienced instructors. Let the teachers lead the way in working among the people, and others, uniting with them, will learn from their example. One example is worth more than many precepts." *The Ministry of Healing, p. 149.*

> Mrs. White had a vision of the far-reaching influence of health evangelism. She saw it operating from the churches in "every place" and in "every city" staffed by "church members."

"The medical missionary work is growing in importance, and claims the attention of the churches. It is a part of the gospel message, and must receive recognition. It is the heaven-ordained means of finding entrance to the hearts of people. It is the duty of our church members in every place to follow the instruction of the Great Teacher. The gospel message is to be preached in every city; for this is in accordance with the example of Christ and His disciples. Medical missionaries are to seek patiently and earnestly to reach the higher classes. If this work is faithfully done, professional men will become trained evangelists." *Medical Ministry, 241.*

"The Lord gave me light that in every place where a church was established, medical missionary work was to be done. But there was in the Battle Creek church a great deal of selfishness. Those at the very heart of the work indulged their own wishes in a way that dishonored God. Dr. Kellogg was not sustained in the health reform work, the importance of which had been kept before the church for thirty years. This work was hindered because of the feelings and prejudices of some in Battle Creek who were not disposed to conform their course of action to the Lord of God regarding health reform principles." *Battle Creek Letters, p 11.*

The following quotation is very sobering because the problems created by conducting health work in venues other than the church have resulted in the very digressions from our primary purpose that were foretold. Today, health evangelism is not well organized. Health evangelism today is a strange assortment of efforts in a variety of settings. There is no unified vision. There is no consistency or clarity in the message proclaimed.

"The medical missionary work should be a part of the work of every church in our land. Disconnected from the church, it would soon become a strange medley of disorganized atoms. It would consume, but not produce. Instead of acting as God's helping hand to forward His truth, it would sap the life and force from the church and weaken the message. Conducted independently, it would not only consume talent and means needed in other lines, but in the very work of helping the helpless apart from the ministry of the word, it would place men where they would scoff at Bible truth." ***Counsels on Health, 514.***

The local church is an ideal home base for health evangelism. There are many local churches, they are designed for group meetings, they are empty most of the time, they have a membership available to staff health evangelism programs, Christ pointed inquirers to the local church, and we have Spirit of Prophecy counsel that health evangelism should be found in every local church. It is time we see the obvious and get to work in the local church.

# 12

# Conducting a Health Evangelism Program

You have decided to conduct a health evangelism program. You have promoted it in the church, recruited volunteers, and organized everyone and everything. Now it is opening night. It is time to start your program.

The following program format has worked well for me. I have used it for cooking schools, weight control programs, smoking cessation programs and exercise programs. Your program should contain the following program elements.

## Registration

On the first night of the program have all your staff at the church an hour early. This will allow for early completion of the set-up. It is important to be completely ready when the first participants show up. On the first night of any program, a few individuals will show up 30-45 minutes early.

On the first night, you should have greeters out in the parking area. This will assure the participants that they have come to the right place and your attendants can help with the parking. Attendants can point out the correct door to enter for registration. If the parking lot isn't well-lit, the parking attendants should have flashlights to provide some light.

Greeters should be at the front door to warmly welcome people. They should use the name of the program repeatedly so participants will know they are at the right place. Signs or posters about the program should be placed in the lobby and at registration tables to provide additional reassurance that the participants are where they want to be.

Register people in the lobby. You will need a table where you hand out registration forms to be filled out. You will need one or two additional tables where people can sit to fill out the registration forms. Have pens at every table. It will take longer than you think for people to complete the paperwork.

---

*It will take longer than you think for people to complete the paperwork.*

---

If you are charging a registration fee for the program, there should be another table where people can pay, and you can make change for those who bring big bills. Some health evangelists never charge for the programs they conduct. I find no fault with this. On the other hand, paying something to attend a program helps establish its value and credibility with people.

At times, skeptical or wary participants will ask if they can attend your program for a session or two before they pay to see whether or not this program will benefit them. You should always agree to this. The object of the program is to help people—not to make money.

It also works out well to have a group or family discount. This will encourage friends and family to come together. They will think they have a real bargain if two can get in for the price of one or three can get in for the price of two.

If anyone is hesitant to provide the information requested on your registration form, you can instruct them to leave blank the items they are uncomfortable disclosing. You can tell them that all participants are a part of a scientific study to evaluate the effectiveness of the program and the information collected will be kept confidential. The data collected are only used to tabulate trends and measure effectiveness. Identifying information is never disclosed to any outside party.

It avoids confusion later if small groups are formed at the time of registration. Have a separate sheet of lined paper for each small group. As participants turn in their completed registration forms, assign each participant to one of the small groups. Write each name on one of the group forms. Each participant should also be given the number of the group to which they are assigned. You can write a person's group number on the workbook or in "Group Number" square on a Progress Card.

Husbands and wives may want to be assigned to the same group but in my experience couples do better if they are in separate groups. A group of friends may all want to be in the same group as well. With a glance at the group composition sheets you will be able to know how many are in each group. You can make adjustments to group size as the people register.

At registration, hand out the Participant's Workbook. It will be empty except for the first night's worksheets. Or you can just hand out an empty folder and tell the participants that they will receive the first night's materials in their small group. Remember to record each person's small group number somewhere on the workbook or Progress Card so each participant will know where to go when you break out into small groups.

Give everyone a name tag to wear. These tags will be particularly useful in small groups. Those conducting the program should wear name tags as well. Participants should wear nametags for a three or four sessions. By then everyone will know each other, and nametags become less important. Church members who are helping in the program should also wear their nametags for at least the first four sessions.

Next, direct those who have registered to the room where the main lecture is to be held. You may hold a small program with few registrants in a Sabbath School classroom. For a larger group a fellowship hall is good. You may even use the sanctuary for your program if it is the best room for the size of crowd you have.

Some have objected to using the sanctuary for health evangelism activities supposing it should be reserved for worship services. The sanctuary has always been used for traditional evangelistic meetings when these services have been conducted at the church. Health evangelism is just as evangelistic as traditional evangelism except you are starting with a focus on physical behaviors rather than on the spiritual.

It seems to me that when a health program speaks of the power for change provided by our Lord, we speak of the power of prayer, and prescribe scripture reading that the sanctuary is an acceptable venue for conducting the program especially if it is the only suitable room in your church complex.

Any PA system or Audio-visual equipment should be set-up well before the first participant comes into the auditorium to sit down. It is appropriate to have some classical or light music playing. It breaks the silence before the program begins and provides a cover for whispered conversations.

## Welcome

Start your program on time. This honors those who planned ahead and came on time. You can make an exception to this rule at your first session. Registration always takes longer than expected and there are some who come late.

When it is time to begin, the master of ceremonies should stride purposefully to the podium and stand there until he or she has everyone's attention. In a strong voice, welcome everyone to the program. The master of ceremonies should repeat the name of the program several times during his remarks. This will reassure everyone that they are in the right place.

I like to have one of the church members be the master of ceremonies. A church member usually works out better than a minister or the health professional. A church member can also talk up the program without it appearing to boast.

During the welcoming remarks, outline what is going to take place during the first session and give an overview of the entire program. Remind the audience how long the program will last in terms of weeks and the time you expect to dismiss each night. On the first night, point out the location of restrooms.

Now it is time for the introductions. Introduce the health professionals who are there and mention the part they have in the program. Introduce the pastor. Introduce the small group concept and point out the tables or rooms where the small groups will meet. Have the helpers and small group leaders stand so the participants can see the dedicated staff that is bringing this program to them.

Acknowledge the help of all who have a part in conducting the program. In this way the audience will see that this isn't a commercial program put on by one or two individuals for the purpose of financial gain, but a voluntary effort of a substantial number of church members. This program is a service of love for the community.

It would be good to reassure those who paid a registration fee that the funds raised do not go to support the local church. Church members are volunteers. The funds raised support community programming at various levels and to purchase materials necessary to conduct the program. It should be stressed that no one is being compensated in any way for participating in the program. All are volunteers. This will raise the credibility of what you are doing in the eyes of the audience.

# The Health Lecture

Introduce the first speaker and get started. Although, we do not want to boast or conduct programs in our own strength it is important for the public to know that your health evangelism program is credible and is conducted by qualified individuals. At each introduction, take time to briefly state the professional qualifications of your speakers and their experience.

The first speaker should present the medical or scientific portion of your program. It might be a medical doctor speaking about lung disease, cancer, or heart disease at a smoking cessation program. It might be a dietician at a weight control program or cooking school. As far as possible, use help available in your own congregation.

If there are no health professionals in your church, the presentations can be done by lay persons who have studied the topic and can speak with some confidence. For one or more sessions you might invite a health professional who is not a member of your church to speak. This should be someone who has respect in the community and one whom you know is sympathetic to the objectives of your program.

# The Pastor's Part

Introduce the pastor. Mention the pastor's qualifications and the pastoral services available at the church. It is appropriate to indicate when he preaches. Invite any who want to, to come to regular church services.

The pastor should speak about how to obtain God's help with behavior change. I have been to health evangelism programs where the pastor spoke and managed to squeeze into his remarks three or four of the distinctive doctrines of the Seventh-day Adventist church. I believe this is wrong. Your health evangelism program is about the behavior changes needed to improve health, not distinctive doctrines. Health evangelism is problem specific evangelism not broad-spectrum evangelism. The pastor should stick to behavior change from a Christian/Biblical perspective.

There are many books on psychology describing the steps involved in behavior change. The principles in these books correctly describe the mental and behavior steps one goes through in changing behavior, but these books do not have the ability to impart the power to accomplish behavior change. Behavior change books are a map showing where you need to go, but they don't give you a car to get there.

Lasting behavior change comes from God. The pastor knows God and should speak to how God helps people bring about lasting change in their lives.

Will people be offended by this? Some will, but most will not. If the pastor focuses on how God helps with the specific problem at hand, no one will leave the program. Most of your participants have tried to change their behavior many times, in the past, and have failed. They are at a place where they are willing to listen to any angle (including God's help) if there is even a remote chance that it will work for them now.

If participants object to the spiritual material in the program, offer to refund their registration fee and wish them well. In most communities there are many Godless self-help programs. If a participant at your weight control program is offended that you suggest that God will help them lose weight, let them go to Weight Watchers, TOPS, Overeaters Anonymous, Jenny Craig or a dozen other secular weight control programs where God is never mentioned.

If a participant at your smoking cessation program is offended that you point to God as the One who can help them overcome the addiction to smoking, refer them to the American Cancer Society, American Heart Association, The American Lung Association, local hospital, or health insurance company where they can receive help in quitting smoking the Godless way.

Where is the addict to learn that God will help them? They should be able to learn this at a Seventh-day Adventist church. We hate to see anyone turn away from the church to seek help elsewhere, but there are hundreds of Godless, self-help programs for these people to go to and enroll in. Where are the programs that point to God as the Help for human helplessness? Health evangelism programs that introduce people to God as the helper for every problem should be found in every Seventh-day Adventist church in the world.

If the pastor is supportive of your health evangelism program but unable or unwilling to speak on behavior change, others can be chosen to do this part. This behavior change through God's help is the evangelistic key to success in your program. It should not be omitted under any circumstances. This spiritual emphasis is equally as effective coming from the pastor, a health professional, or any layperson who has experienced God's help in overcoming some habit.

## Demonstrations

If your health evangelism program has demonstrations of some type put them on just before you dismiss to small groups. Food demonstrations are useful in weight management programs and in cooking schools. Smoking Sam is a useful demonstration at smoking cessation programs. Showing the correct type of clothing and shoes for an exercise class are appropriate.

## Small Groups

The small group activity is most effective at the end of the program. Between ½ and 1/3 of program time should be spent in small groups. At the first session, when it is time for small groups, it is best to have the small group leaders stand and hold up the number for the group they are going to facilitate. If the tables are in the same room as the lecture, they can be clearly labeled so there is no confusion about where each group is to meet.

If you are utilizing rooms elsewhere in your church for small groups, those rooms should be clearly marked, and maps should be distributed so it will be easy for everyone to find their way to their assigned group. Small group leaders should be dismissed first so they can lead the way to their locations and be there to welcome group members as they come in.

At the first session, each group leader should have a copy of the small group compositions forms that were developed during registration. This will tell the small group leaders how many to expect in their group and their names. There may be some shifting of group composition on the first night. People who come meet others they know and want to change groups to be with acquaintances. All this shifting is acceptable. Group composition lists will need to be changed to reflect the adjustments that were made; it is important to have accurate records.

Everyone in each small group should have name tags. The first order of business is introductions all around. Exchange names, background, interests, and hobbies. The object is to make the group feel comfortable, to break the ice, and to give a feeling of informality.

Goals are good to discuss. What does each person want to get out of this program? What have they tried before? How far did they get in previous tries? Be as specific as possible. In a weight control program, ask how much weight each participant wants to lose during the 10 weeks of the program? These goals are written down in the participant's workbook.

The main discussion in each small group should center on the behavior changes recommended by the health professional in the evening's lecture. For instance, if the health professional suggested eating less sugar, small group members would discuss where the most sugar is in their diet. Once the source of excess sugar is identified, small group members should be encouraged to make specific commitments to reduce their sugar intake during the coming week. These commitments to behavior change should be recorded in the workbook.

One participant might decide to eliminate drinking sweetened soft drinks. Another might decide to switch to diet sodas. For another, it might be eating fewer deserts–perhaps limiting deserts to just one serving a week. In small groups you individualize the prescription that was given in a general way in the health lecture.

You can be creative and develop additional handouts on the subject of that session. This material can be distributed in small groups for participants to study at home. Occasionally there can be a quiz over the evening's topic. Once everyone has completed the quiz, the helpers can provide the answers. This can be the focal point for additional group discussion.

Helpers should offer their availability to help with any problems that might come up during the time between programs. They should distribute their day and evening contact information and indicate the best times and methods of contact. In the current era, texting is frequently easier than calling. Participants should be encouraged to contact their small group leaders if they are having problems of any kind. It is also appropriate for helpers to contact their small group members at least once during the week just to keep in contact with them and to encourage them to come back to the next session.

Helpers will sometimes have occasion for further socialization with group members outside of small group time at the church. All this extra, unofficial, contact is encouraged. Church members have gone shopping with group members. Others have met after work and gone to a restaurant together. The options for socialization are unlimited. Lasting friendships are formed from these informal contacts.

This is the interface the church needs with its community; church members becoming friends with non-church members. This will often prove to be more evangelistic than preaching. Most people join the church because they have friends in the church. Small groups are where these friendships are formed.

---

*Most people join the church because they have friends in the church. Small groups are where these friendships are formed.*

---

Ideally the health professional and pastor should remain at church during the small group sessions. They may want to join a different small group from week to week. They may want to circulate from group to group. They should be available to clarify points and answer specific questions that may be beyond the knowledge of the small group leader. Knowing this additional help is available will encourage many church members to volunteer as small group leaders. They will never be caught in a situation where they will not be able to get an answer. Someone will always be available to help them should the need arise.

---

*Small group leaders do not need to be experts.*

---

Small group leaders do not need to be experts. Their role is to facilitate discussion. The topic is the evening's lectures. There are handouts that cover the topic in detail. Quizzes and workbook activities will facilitate group discussion. Be sure the helpers have the answers to any quizzes you use, along with an explanation of the answers.

Dismiss the program for the night from the small groups. Groups will break up at slightly different times and the evening's program will gradually dissolve away.

## After Glow (Post Program Assessment)

Immediately after the last small group has been dismissed, call the helpers and small group leaders together for an assessment of the evening's program. There are several tasks to take care of.

Review activities that occurred in small groups. There will be stories of victory and overcoming which will cheer the hearts of all. Success needs to be shared. There will be special problems that certain participants are having. These difficulties should be recognized, and special efforts made to help those participants who are struggling.

There should be a season of prayer. Thank God for the successes that have occurred. Ask for God's special blessing on those who are having difficulty.

There should be an accounting of those participants who did not attend the evening's meeting. Some will be known to have valid reasons for not attending, while others will just not be accounted for. Small group leaders should take the responsibility of contacting individuals from their small group who did not attend. Find out if there was a problem.

If absent participants are not planning on coming back, they should be let go without too much fuss. It will be useful to see if they want to be notified of future programs; if so, retain them on your contact list. If they are not interested in any further contact with your church, it is the courteous thing to do to remove their names from your contact list.

This entire "after glow" process should be limited to about 15 minutes. Helpers will be anxious to get home and prolonging this session will discourage future participation by church members if it is carried on too long.

It takes time and effort to organize and conduct a health evangelism program in this way. This design maximizes the evangelistic potential of a health program.

# 13

# Finding the Right Personnel

---

WHO ARE THE PEOPLE WHO SHOULD BE CONDUCTING HEALTH evangelism programs? What is the personnel mix you need for a successful program? The 5-Day Plan to Stop Smoking was designed to be conducted by a doctor and minister team. In some places these programs were conducted by other health professionals and even by laymen. Let's look at personnel issues in conducting health evangelism programs.

## The Minister

It is natural to assume that a health evangelism program conducted in the local church would utilize the services of the local pastor. There is a role for your pastor in health evangelism, but I believe the pastor's role should not be central to the program.

The pastor is a busy person. It is not necessary or desirable for the pastor to personally conduct every program at the church. Health evangelism programs should be conducted by church members. Pastors have many responsibilities that occupy their time. If your pastor is particularly busy, but still generally supportive of health evangelism programs, give your pastor a break and structure your health evangelism program so the pastor has only a small but important involvement.

Over the course of years, pastors tend to come and go. If health evangelism programs are too dependent on the pastor, an established program might die if the pastor moves away. It is better to have health evangelism programs established, conducted, and maintained by church members. In this way there will be more stability of your programs if the pastor moves on to other assignments.

Then again, some pastors do not live the health message. Pastors, who are overweight, do not exercise regularly, openly drink coffee or tea will tend to have a negative influence on health evangelism. Programs. Under these circumstances, it might be wise not to conduct any health evangelism programs in your church until the situation is more favorable.

At times, pastors become jealous of the success church members are having in doing health evangelism programs. When this occurs, a subtle antagonism will develop toward you, your committee, or the health evangelism program itself. The pastor may consistently come to your program late or boycott a meeting or two.

The pastor may suggest interrupting an established cycle of health evangelism programs so he may conduct some other program he is more interested in. If this should happen to you, it will be better for you to quit doing health evangelism for a while. If the problem persists and health evangelism activities are suppressed for a prolonged period, you might consider transferring your health evangelism activities to another church that will be more receptive.

Under no circumstances should you insist on conducting health evangelism in your church if you sense any negativity on the part of the Pastor. I learned this lesson the hard way. I was a full-time health evangelist for a local Seventh-day Adventist Church in Maryland. The pastor of the church, with whom I thought I was going to work, was transferred to another Conference the same week I arrived at the church.

The conference assigned a newly baptized, and not yet ordained pastor, to work with me in the church. This was this pastor's very first church assignment and it was my first church as well. We attempted to blend our ministries in that little church, but it didn't really work out well at all. I tried to schedule times for the pastor and me to study and to pray together but the appointments weren't kept. There were many excuses.

I had an office and medical examination room at the church. I am a medical doctor and spent my days working at the church. The pastor spent his days visiting the sick in the hospital. It was role reversal.

We conducted a variety of health evangelism activities in the church on a continuous basis. I planned a speaking part for the pastor in every 5-Day Plan, every cooking school, every weight control program and every exercise program I conducted.

The pastor failed to see the evangelistic potential of these health evangelism programs. He just wasn't interested in what I was trying to do in our church. After a couple of months, the pastor excused himself from participation in health evangelism and from then on boycotted every program I conducted. He never showed his face again in anything I did in that church.

We had up to 100 non-Adventist participants at every program and the popularity of the Seventh-day Adventist church was growing. The church members were excited and were involved with every program we did. I am sorry to report that attendance at prayer meeting dwindled. The pastor's influence with his members was falling off.

In my youthful inexperience I went and discussed this with the Conference president. He was fully sympathetic with my plight and appreciated the work I was doing in the church. He called the pastor in and read him the riot act. The pastor knew that I was the one who turned him in. He was very resentful. We never spoke to one another again except on Sabbaths when we were in church.

I didn't know how to remedy this situation until I was instructed by God as to what to do. I was reading the Desire of Ages and came to the chapter "He Must Increase" that begins on page 178. This chapter describes the conflict that developed between the disciples of John the Baptist and

Christ's disciples over the form of the words to be used when conducting a baptismal service. Additionally, John's disciples were concerned with John's decreasing popularity and Christ's increasing popularity.

When John's disciples presented their concerns to John the Baptist his reply was "He must increase, but I must decrease" John 3:30. These were certainly the right words, but John did not respond with the correct action and so Jesus did. "Wishing to avoid all occasion for misunderstanding or dissension, He quietly ceased His labors, and withdrew to Galilee." Desire of Ages, 181.

The agenda of the King of the Universe was altered because of a quibble between the disciples of John and Christ. I would think that Christ's response would mirror that of John the Baptist. Christ could well have said. "John must decrease, and I must increase." It didn't happen this way. John said the right thing, but it didn't solve the problem. The problem was only solved when Jesus and His disciples packed up and moved to Galilee.

When the possibility of conflict arises between you and your pastor and it doesn't appear that harmony can be established, you are advised to do as Christ did when controversy threatened His ministry.

> "We also, while loyal to truth, should try to avoid all that may lead to discord and misapprehension. For whenever these arise, they result in the loss of souls. Whenever circumstances occur that threaten to cause division, we should follow the example of Jesus and of John the Baptist." **Desire of Ages, 181.**

At this point I reluctantly terminated what I was doing and rapidly transferred my membership to another church about 20 miles away and began health evangelism activities there. The conference terminated its financial support of my health evangelism activities, and I began a very limited practice of medicine to support myself. My work was arranged so I had every evening and every weekend free to conduct health evangelism activities in my new church location.

My leaving one church for another almost resulted in serious controversy. The head elder, who was a strong supporter of health evangelism, came to me privately and said. "I know why you are leaving. You and the pastor do not get along. Well, that's too bad. We like what you are doing in our church, and we are prepared to fight to keep you here." It was only with considerable effort on my part that we were able to keep the lid on dissension.

Of course, it was natural and vindictive for me to wish the pastor's efforts to languish once I left that church. I was humbled when God richly blessed that small church once I left it. The pastor had record baptisms the next year and the church prospered. Eventually, I came to rejoice in this. Harmony in the local church is more important than any program you conduct within its walls.

In summary, health evangelism needs to be conducted with the blessing, understanding and cooperation of your local pastor. Do not make the pastor's role in health evangelism too big. Respect that pastors are busy people with many burdens. If the pastor is against health evangelism, do not attempt to do it in his church.

## Church Members

Health evangelism activities should largely be conducted by church members. There are many roles for church members in doing medical missionary work. Perhaps the most obvious reason to use church members in conducting health evangelism is their sheer numbers. At this writing the church has about 22 million members. There are less than 10,000 doctors, less than 30,000 nurses, and less than 10,000 dentists.

There is an important role for health professionals in conducting health evangelism programs if they are available in your community. The role of health professionals will be discussed in the next section. If you just look at the numbers, the largest pool of prospective workers is found among ordinary church members who sit in the pew from week to week.

Here is the gold mine of health evangelism personnel. The local church will always have more members than pastors or health professionals. If you want to have an effective program, plan on filling most of your personnel needs with church members.

## Problems with Church Members.

There are certain drawbacks in using church members in conducting health evangelism programs. These shortcomings should be recognized up front. It takes time to adequately develop this resource.

Most church members are not well educated in health lines. This is not a major problem. The church members will learn just what they need to know during the first program you conduct. Church members will be able to handle most questions and situations by their second or third program.

A bigger problem with church members is their lack of interest in health evangelism. Too many members are seemingly indifferent as to what is going on in the church. They may not be living up to the light on healthful living that has been shown them in the past. Some church members need health reform just as badly as the community they are asked to help.

Some of the most sincere and enthusiastic but potentially detrimental volunteers will be church members who have a line of "health products" to promote or sell. They would like to integrate their product line into your health evangelism program. Do not sell, distribute, or give away vitamins, potions, protein powders, nutritional supplements, etc. at a health evangelism program. Do not allow a church member with a private agenda push some product in their small group.

And then there are church members who hold some currently popular but scientifically unsound health information which they will want to share with their small group members. Church members should limit the information they discuss in small groups to that which is part of the program. Only qualified health experts should expand or enhance the prepared lecture materials.

This timely advice from Ellen White is applicable to these wrongly educated church members.

> "It is time that something was done, that **novices** may not be allowed to take the field, and advocate health reform. Their works and words can be spared; for **they do more injury** than the most wise and intelligent men, with the best influence they can exert, can counteract. It is impossible for **the best qualified advocates** of health reform to fully relieve the minds of the public from the **prejudice received** through the **wrong course** of these **extremists**, and to place the great subject of health reform upon the right basis in the community where these men have figured. The **door is also closed** in a great measure, so that unbelievers **cannot be reached** by the present truth upon the Sabbath, and the soon coming of our Saviour. The most precious **truths are cast aside** by the people as unworthy of a hearing. These men are referred to as representatives of health reformers and Sabbath-keepers in general. A great responsibility rests upon those who have thus proved a stumbling block to unbelievers." *Pamphlet 101, 21*

## Preparing Church Members

When you first start to conduct health evangelism programs, your personnel will consist of church members who are largely unskilled recruits. This situation requires a considerable amount of preparation time. Take several weeks to organize and train your church members before you launch into your program.

The time taken in preparation will weed out church members who, after looking at the details of the program, will decide that they cannot commit to the time it is going to take to do the program. It is sad to see helpers pull out of a program even before it starts, but these are the very church members who would likely be pulling out of your program in the middle, leaving you high and dry anyway. It is better to lose helpers before the program begins than to lose them during a great work.

This was a truth that Gideon learned in Old Testament times, and it is just as true today. Going through a process to remove those who are not dedicated, ill prepared, and halfhearted in service will help ensure success once your program begins.

It is best to conduct your training program for church members on the same nights of the week that you intend to conduct your health evangelism program. If members can come out to training meetings, they will be able to come out to the program as well. If you conduct your training over a weekend or two, yet your program will be on Tuesday nights, you will find that several who can attend training on the weekend will find that they do not have time to do the program on Tuesday nights.

The importance of using church members in conducting health evangelism programs is stressed repeatedly in Spirit of Prophecy writings. Some counsel to consider along these lines is found in the following passages.

> "We have come to a time when every member of the church should take hold of medical missionary work. The world is a lazar house filled with victims of both physical and spiritual disease. Everywhere people are perishing for lack of a knowledge of the truths that have been committed to us. The members of the church are in need of an awakening, that they may realize their responsibility to impart these truths. Those who have been enlightened by the truth are to be light bearers to the world. To hide our light at this time is to make a terrible mistake. The message to God's people today

is: "Arise, shine; for thy light is come, and the glory of the Lord is risen upon thee."" *Vol. 7 Testimonies for the Church, p. 62.*

There is a sad situation described in the following passage. Church members have had much education and are knowledgeable regarding healthful living. Unfortunately, many, if not most, have not made any significant effort to reform their lives. In doing this they are deliberately choosing evil instead of righteousness. Church members who are not living health reform become agents of Satan and further his cause.

> "We have come to a time when every member of the church needs to take hold of medical missionary work. On every hand we see those who have had much light and knowledge and all the advantages that could be given them, deliberately choosing evil in the place of righteousness, mercy, and the love of God. Making no attempt to reform, they are becoming agents of Satan, and are continually growing worse and worse." *Vol. 16 Manuscript Releases p. 145.*

To live the life that Christ lived means to do the work he did. This is a work for every member of the church. We are to carry forward the healing and health educational work that He did when he was here.

> "We have come to a time when every member of the church should take hold of medical missionary work." "Christ is no longer in this world in person, to go through our cities and towns and villages, healing the sick. He has commissioned us to carry forward the medical missionary work that He began." *Testimonies and Experiences Connected with the Loma Linda Sanitarium and College of Medical Evangelists, p. 7.*

What fascinates me most about this next passage is that it specifies who the church members are. Businessmen, farmers, mechanics, merchants, lawyers, and others are singled out here. Each is to advance the cause of Christ by personal effort. Oh, yes, money is mentioned but not as a substitute for personal effort and only after personal effort is mentioned.

> "When men of business, farmers, mechanics, merchants, lawyers, etc., become members of the church, they become servants of Christ; and although their talents may be entirely different, their responsibility to advance the cause of God by personal effort, and with their means, is no less than that which rests upon the minister. The woe which will fall upon the minister if he preach not the gospel, will just as surely fall upon the businessman, if he, with his different talents, will not be a co-worker with Christ in accomplishing the same results. When this is brought home to the individual, some will say, "This is an hard saying;" nevertheless it is true, although continually contradicted by the practice of men who profess to be followers of Christ." *Vol. 4 Testimonies for the Church Volume, p. 469.*

Next, we see that the local church is to be organized in such a manner that every member has a work to do. None are to lead an aimless Christian life. All are to be active according to their abilities. This organization is to be accomplished by the church elders and those who have "leading places" in the church.

> "The elders and those who have leading places in the church should give more thought to their plans for conducting the work. They should arrange matters so that every member of the church shall have a part to act, that none may lead an aimless life, but that all may accomplish what they can according to their several ability. . . . It is very essential that such an education should be given to the members of the church that they will become unselfish, devoted, efficient workers for God; and it is only through such a course that the

church can be prevented from becoming fruitless and dead. . . . Let every member of the church become an active worker,--a living stone, emitting light in God's temple." *Christian Service, p. 62.*

Church members are able to provide the one-on-one interface that changes lives. Church members can provide the personal labor for souls that is required for success in God's work.

"The Lord desires that His word of grace shall be brought home to every soul. To a great degree this must be accomplished by personal labor. This was Christ's method. His work was largely made up of personal interviews. He had a faithful regard for the one-soul audience. Through that one soul the message was often extended to thousands." *Christ's Object Lessons, 229.*

Church members are to make personal efforts to help those in need. This is accomplished in a health evangelism program by church members providing this personal effort in small groups. Every church member needs to be involved in some type of work. For many this can be through involvement in health evangelism activities.

"Service to God includes personal ministry. By personal effort we are to co-operate with Him for the saving of the world. Christ's commission, "Go ye into all the world, and preach the gospel to every creature," is spoken to every one of His followers. (Mark 16:15.) All who are ordained unto the life of Christ are ordained to work for the salvation of their fellow men. Their hearts will throb in unison with the heart of Christ. The same longing for souls that He has felt will be manifest in them. Not all can fill the same place in the work, but there is a place and a work for all." *Christ's Object Lessons, 300-301.*

Giving money to the cause of God is not a substitute for personal labor on behalf of those who need our help in overcoming bad habits in their lives.

"Now is our time to labor for the salvation of our fellow men. There are some who think that if they give money to the cause of Christ, this is all they are required to do; the precious time in which they might do personal service for Him passes unimproved. But it is the privilege and duty of all who have health and strength to render to God active service. All are to labor in winning souls to Christ. Donations of money cannot take the place of this. *Christ's Object Lessons, 343*

The work may be small to start with, but it should be designed to create a one-on-one contact between church members and the public. This personal influence is powerful. The Holy Spirit is present to convict and change minds and lives.

"In every new field, patience and perseverance must be exercised. Be not disheartened at small beginnings. It is often the humblest work that yields the greatest results. The more direct our labor for our fellow-men, the greater good will be accomplished. Personal influence is a power. The minds of those with whom we are closely associated, are impressed through unseen influences. One cannot speak to a multitude and move them as he could if he were brought into closer relationship with them. Jesus left heaven, and came to our world to save souls. You must come close to those for whom you labor, that they may not only hear your voice, but shake your hand, learn your principles, feel your sympathy. *Gospel Workers, 340.*

While church members do health evangelism, they should do so with kindness and politeness. They should be empathetic. This will result in a hundred-fold increase in conversions to the church.

"If we would humble ourselves before God, and be kind and courteous and tenderhearted and pitiful, there would be one hundred conversions to the truth where now there is only one." *Vol. 9 Testimonies for the Church, 189*

Finally, an emphatic statement of urgency. Church members need to get to work now!

"The world needs laborers now. From every direction is heard the Macedonian cry, "Come over and help us." Our success consists in reaching common minds. Plain, pointed arguments, standing out as mile-posts, will do more toward convincing people than will a large array of arguments which none but investigating minds will have interest to follow. And if the laborers are pure in heart and life, if they use to the glory of God the talents that he has committed to their keeping, they will have God on their side and heavenly angels to work with their efforts." *The Signs of the Times 10-28-1886*

## Health Professionals

It seems only natural that a health evangelism program would require the services of health professionals. While this is ideal, it is not always possible. Health evangelism programs in your church should not be delayed or postponed if you do not have any health professionals among your members.

It is better to utilize the services of health professionals who are members of your own local church than to bring in some specialist from the community or from some long distance. A guest health professional will divert the ownership and authority of the program away from the local church.

A lecture or even just the presence of a health practitioner of any level of education who is a practicing member of your church will be more effective than some highly educated specialist brought in from the outside. It is not so much the quality or quantity of health information that is needed in a health program so much as a clear identification with the local church and involvement of local church members.

Health professionals supply information and recommendations about your participant's lifestyle. In a smoking cessation program, the information will relate to the health problems associated with smoking and the benefits of quitting. In an exercise program the information will focus on the benefits of exercise. In a nutrition program, foods that are healthful and foods that are unsafe will be reviewed.

If the health professional is well trained and makes a good presentation, not only will the participants be educated, but the church members who are small group leaders will be educated at the same time. The people who meet in small groups will have a chance to discuss the health information that was presented and to personalize it to their own lives.

This work cannot be accomplished by the health professional by saying. "Well, that is about it for tonight. Go home and put this into practice." The health recommendations need to be discussed and digested in small groups. Group leaders will ask for commitments to specific behavior changes from each group member.

I ask the health professional who spoke for the evening to remain during the small group sessions. They should move around from group to group answering questions that come up. This takes the pressure off the small group leaders. If a small group leader does not know the answer to some technical question he or she can say, "I do not know but I will try to get an answer by next week."

The health professionals you work with do not have to be an expert on the topic that is being presented. Any health professional will do. A physical therapist, nurse, dentist, dietician, dental hygienist, health educator or nursing home administrator can present information on the harmful effects of smoking. You do not have to have a board-certified oncologist to talk about smoking and lung cancer. You do not need a pulmonary specialist to talk about emphysema.

It may take a health professional who works on the periphery of an issue a bit more time to study up on a given topic, but they will do just fine. If you do not have any health professionals in your church, let a layperson give the health lecture. You do not have to be a health professional to know that smoking is bad for you and that you ought to eat right and exercise on a regular basis.

If you use a lay person to make the health presentation, it should be acknowledged that he or she is not a trained health professional but keep the apology to a minimum. A layperson that goes to the trouble to learn something about a topic is still more knowledgeable than most of those who are coming for help.

One final word of caution. If you are going to conduct a health evangelism program without the services of a health professional, the layperson presenting the health information should stick with the basic facts included in the materials of your health program.

Do not present any new material you download from the Internet unless it is reviewed and approved by a knowledgeable health professional. Do not present any material you get from lay magazines. This especially applies to lay health magazines. There is a lot of true and useful information available on health topics from these sources, but it is often mixed with so much erroneous material that it is better to stay away from such information unless it can be screened by someone who is skilled in separating truth from error.

# 14

# Behavior Change

---

## Overview

THIS IS THE MOST IMPORTANT CHAPTER OF THIS BOOK. BEHAVIOR change lies at the heart of every self-help program. All health evangelism programs are about behavior change. Modern psychological models have been developed which accurately describe the mental and physical steps people take when they change their behavior for the better. One of these models will be reviewed briefly in this chapter.

Some people are successful in their own strength in giving up a bad habit or overcoming an addiction. The psychological and sociological disciplines have studied these successful people. There is a common process underlying most behavior change. These steps document how people change.

These models describe how some people changed their behavior, but just because someone else was successful doesn't mean that you are going to be successful if you try the same steps. These behavior change models describe what some people have done to change their behavior, but these models fail to help most people who want to change their behavior. Most people who are stuck in a harmful habit or addiction just cannot make these models work. These models may motivate but do not enable people to change.

Here is the problem. Just because some are successful in behavior change doesn't mean that others will be able to follow in their footsteps. Just because you have identified the incremental steps that eventually lead to behavior change in one person doesn't mean that someone else is going to be able to take that same journey. For some it is a matter of motivation. For others it is a matter of ability. Millions want to change but cannot.

Inability to change is fundamentally a spiritual problem that is described in many places in scripture. Among the more famous texts in this regard are the following.

> "Can the Ethiopian change his skin or the leopard its spots? Then may you also do good who are accustomed to do evil" **Jeremiah 13:23 (NKJV)**

> "For we know that the law is spiritual, but I am carnal, sold under sin. For what I am doing, I do not understand. For what I will to do, that I do not practice; but what I hate, that I do. If, then, I do what I will not to do, I agree with the law that it is good. But now, it is no longer I who do it, but sin that dwells in me. For I know that in me (that is, in my flesh) nothing good dwells; for to will is present with me, but how to perform what is good I do not find. For the good that I will to do, I do not do; but the evil I will not to do, that I practice." **Rom 7:14-19 (NKJV)**

These texts refer not only to spiritual aspects of our lives but the mental and physical dimensions as well. We all have behaviors that we need to change. We all can change some behaviors on our own, but every one of us has at least one, and usually multiple behavioral problems, that we just cannot permanently change no matter how much effort we put into it or how many times we try.

The human will, in and of itself, is not capable of producing permanent change in the life. This applies to the physical and mental dimensions of our life as well as the spiritual. Notice this quotation.

"Man cannot transform himself by the exercise of his will. He possesses no power by which this change can be effected. The leaven--something wholly from without-- must be put into the meal before the desired change can be wrought in it. So the grace of God must be received by the sinner before he can be fitted for the kingdom of glory. All the culture and education which the world can give will fail of making a degraded child of sin a child of heaven. The renewing energy must come from God. The change can be made only by the Holy Spirit. All who would be saved, high or low, rich or poor, must submit to the working of this power. *Christ's Object Lessons 96-97*

Here is the solution for everyone. God has the power to change us. The more times we have failed on our own, the more wonderful is the deliverance we gain through a relationship with Jesus Christ. This deliverance is what the world needs. Health evangelism programs bring addictions and bad habits face to face with Christ. Health evangelism programs should do this simply and in a straightforward manner without bringing up more advanced doctrinal issues.

In your health evangelism program do not be hesitant about this. Promise permanent deliverance to everyone who attends your program. This type of deliverance is a miracle. It is your privilege to be the messenger of this good news. The realization of miraculous behavior change will thrill many in your audience. As they come to experience previously elusive success, they will confirm these miraculous changes have occurred as a result of God's power.

This is a faith-healing service but not in the tradition of the modern faith-healing services we see around us today. The miracles I see are not a cure for lung cancer but a miraculous deliverance from the tobacco addiction. I do not see cures for cirrhosis of the liver, but deliverance from alcoholism through the power of God. I do not see a cure of arthritic knees in the overweight glutton, but I do see successful weight loss with

God's help. I do not see very many miracles that cure diseases so much as I see miracles resulting in changed behaviors that cause disease.

Despite these miraculous deliverances from harmful habits and addictions, the church hasn't been very supportive of health evangelism. The church is certain about eternal salvation through Jesus Christ but has been decidedly less certain about how Jesus delivers a person from harmful behaviors, habits, and addictions.

Some might deny this, but I ask you to articulate the doctrine of behavior change as it relates to harmful health practices. Sermons are not preached on this topic. Church members are generally not encouraged to change unhealthy behaviors except for cigarette smoking and public alcohol drinking. Overweight and obesity resulting from gluttony is entirely overlooked by pastors and church members alike.

There is a considerable difference of opinion among pastors and teachers as to how behavior change is accomplished through a relationship with Jesus. There is broad agreement that behavior change can occur through a relationship with Jesus, but the steps haven't been formalized very well. The details are fuzzy.

Most churches and denominations focus on their own unique and distinctive doctrines as these are important for denominational affiliation. Behavior change issues are often postponed until after you accept the doctrines of the church and often, they are overlooked entirely.

Habits and addictions are problems that equally afflict members of all churches and denominations. I think the fear among many pastors and churches is that focusing on problems such as obesity, poor nutritional habits, and a sedentary lifestyle will result in a label of "legalism"–a kind of salvation by works. Pastors have told me that church members are already guilt-ridden to begin with. If the church harps on common behavior problems, the guilt would only increase. This could result in members transferring to another church where they will be left alone. Giving is also likely to be affected.

In the following section I develop the doctrine of how God helps people change behavior. This material is a synthesis of principles from the Holy Bible and the Spirit of Prophecy. I will also use some concepts on behavior change from a book, ***Changing for Good*** by J. O. Prochaska, et al. I will also utilize some concepts on addiction from the book, ***Addiction and Obesity*** by G. May, M.D. In addition, I will relate principles from my own experience conducting health evangelism programs over the last 50 years.

## Awareness of a Problem

There are many people who are simply unaware that they have a behavior that will lead to a loss of health. These people are not necessarily stuck in a bad behavior; they just do not perceive their problem. They have never tried to change their behavior because they do not think they have any bad behaviors.

These persons feel safe. They are not afraid of failure. They have no guilt. They do not feel any family or social pressure to change. Some would say that if people are not aware of something then it really isn't a problem, but this isn't true. This is a difficult group to reach. Waiting for these people to develop a few symptoms that will wake them up to the reality of their situation is painful for us to watch and risky for them. Too often the first sign of heart disease is sudden death.

The longer people wait to change, the more difficult change becomes. Behavior change programs are more effective in reducing the risk of disease and death when the interventions occur early in a person's life before permanent damage has been done.

> *The longer people wait to change, the more difficult change becomes.*

How do you motivate people to change who do not know that they are at risk for anything? These people will not attend a health evangelism program because they do not recognize their problem. What to do? There is something you can do and there is something God can do.

Wake up the unaware by education. A direct appeal might be helpful, but you cannot push someone into action if they are not ready to act. Nagging is repetitive and often backfires. At the same time, you shouldn't give up your efforts. Apathy on your part may communicate a lack of caring about the problem. Do not be an enabler who helps a problem persist. Do not buy beer, wine, cigarettes, ice-cream, cake, or cookies for anyone if these are part of their problem.

God is the One who finally wakes us up to our problems and motivates us to change. God works in the life long before we are aware of who He is or our need for His help in our lives. God will bring an awareness of problems to our attention. The mind may wake up slowly or suddenly, but it will be the drawing, wooing of God that wakes us up to the dangers we face if we persist in health destroying behaviors

This unconscious drawing of persons to God is described in the following passages:

> "It is true that men sometimes become ashamed of their sinful ways and give up some of their evil habits before they are conscious that they are being drawn to Christ. But whenever they make an effort to reform, from a sincere desire to do right, it is the power of Christ that is drawing them. An influence of which they are unconscious works upon the soul, and the conscience is quickened and the outward life is amended." *Vol 2 Mind, Character, and Personality 600.*

> "Christ is the source of every right impulse. He is the only one that can implant in the heart enmity against sin. Every desire for truth and purity, every conviction of our own sinfulness, is an evidence that His Spirit is moving upon our hearts. *Steps to Christ 26.*

So where does the motivation for change come from? It comes from God. You should pray that God will wake up those who would benefit from your health evangelism program. You can educate, but unless God wakens the desire for change it will not occur. Be content to leave the unmotivated in the hands of God. God will continue to try to wake them up.

## Thinking About Change

Once a person becomes aware of a health problem, they begin to think about changing. Thinking about changing represents some progress toward the goal of healthful living. Those who contemplate change, really do want to change. They intend to change someday--but not today.

Those who want to change worry a lot but do not get around to working on their health problems. They are worried about heart attacks, cancer, obesity, addiction, cirrhosis and on and on, but they do not get around to doing something about it. This is because they are also worried about cravings, mental anguish, grieving, sadness, and loss, associated with efforts to change. Change requires a mental and physical struggle. It takes a high level of motivation to finally get around to doing something about destructive behaviors that lead to disease.

Many who want to change are looking for an easy, foolproof plan that will work for them. A plan is helpful because it organizes the process of change. A plan outlines the steps you must take and warns you to lookout for pitfalls of various types. Many will want a plan they can work on in the privacy of their own homes, just by themselves. Do not worry about these people. Others will do better in a structured program, in a group setting. A health evangelism program, conducted in your church will be just what they need.

## Preparation for Behavior Change

Many who change will make preparation for behavior change. Preparation readies you to take action and prepares you to handle unexpected challenges. Commitment is the most important element in preparation for change. Commitment is a high level of motivation that fully devotes the will to the process of change. At the point of commitment all ambivalence is lost, and courage is high. Certainty of success is in view.

As part of the commitment process, developing and signing a formal contract is often useful. Setting a definite date to change puts the process of quitting clearly in motion. These concepts can all be incorporated into your health evangelism program.

Going public with your commitment to change is also helpful. It is more shameful to fail in front of friends and colleagues. Going public provides you with a high level of motivation not to fail because you know that others are watching your progress. Of course, your health evangelism program is a public program and helps provide motivation for your audience as well.

## Action

This is actively working on your problem. Your health evangelism program is all about action. Your program should focus on the process of giving up old behaviors and working on new behaviors. There are some specific things you can do to help yourself. Many of these things have a general application to all behavior changes. These activities are reviewed here.

**Diversions** are helpful in getting people to drop old behaviors. Diversions keep you from focusing on the pain and difficulty in breaking old habits and addictions. Keep the mind and body busy. Do things that occupy the mind with other things that have nothing to do with your old behaviors. Focus your energy on new behaviors, projects, and activities. The possibilities are endless.

**Exercise** is important in helping you change behavior. Exercise results in an improved body image. A person experiences increased energy, metabolism, and cardiovascular function. Those who exercise have less anxiety and depression and they sleep well. Exercise decreases physical and emotional pain. There are also benefits to body fat and cholesterol levels. Design regular exercise into your health evangelism programs.

**Relaxation** is an important ingredient in achieving success. Changing behavior is hard emotional and physical work. The battle will often leave you exhausted. There is a need for frequent periods of rest during the struggle. Your prescription should include early to bed, a quiet work and home environment, body positioning that is comfortable, comfortable clothes, and a letting go of other concerns that might be a trigger for relapse.

**Counter thinking** is a mind game. Your mind will suggest dozens of reasons as to why you should return to your old ways. Rehearse positive responses in your mind. Use the logic and authority of your mind to keep yourself in your new behaviors. Irrational thoughts should be countered by the reality of what you are accomplishing.

**Prayer** is the most important key to success. Prayer will be a new experience for many in your audience. Many who are agnostics, atheists, or nonreligious people in your audience will actually try prayer at your suggestion. This is not because they know and believe in God, but they are in a desperate situation and are willing to try almost anything to experience deliverance from their behavioral problem. Of course, this is just what God wants. God delights to answer the prayers of all who are struggling. God is willing to surprise someone with success who has never known Him before. What a great way to be introduced to a helping God.

Here are two famous texts which have a bearing on behavior change and prayer. A section that follows will deal in greater detail with specifics on the help that God gives to those who ask for help in changing behavior.

> "Ask, and it will be given to you; seek, and you will find; knock, and it will be opened to you" **Matthew 7:7 (NKJV).**

"If any of you lacks wisdom, let him ask of God, who gives to all liberally and without reproach, and it will be given to him" **James 1:5 (NKJV).**

Mrs. White indicates that it is when prayer is neglected that temptations come upon us. Prayer opens heaven's resources to help us overcome.

"The darkness of the evil one encloses those who neglect to pray. The whispered temptations of the enemy entice them to sin; and it is all because they do not make use of the privileges that God has given them in the divine appointment of prayer. Why should the sons and daughters of God be reluctant to pray, when prayer is the key in the hand of faith to unlock heaven's storehouse, where are treasured the boundless resources of Omnipotence?" *Steps to Christ, 94-95.*

When you have prayed to God for help, you need to act. You must act as if you have received the help for which you asked. God's help in overcoming will now be blended with the effort you make. Success will be certain.

"While you pray that you may not be led into temptation, remember that your work does not end with the prayer. You must then answer your own prayer as far as possible, by resisting temptation, and leave that which you cannot do for yourselves for Jesus to do for you. *Signs of the Times 11-18-1886.*

**Assertiveness** is helpful. Communicate your thoughts, feelings, wishes and intentions clearly. Positive talk influences your ability to respond. Hearing yourself speak positively helps you to act positively.

**Your Environment.** It is helpful, as far as possible, to control the **environment** in which you live and work. Avoid people, places or things that might trip you up. This is not a sign of weakness or poor self-control. Do not invite temptation but rather avoid it as much as possible.

You may not be able to avoid all tempting situations but remaining steadfast in the face of temptation is easier the more distance and time there is between you and your old habits and addictions.

**Cues that Trigger Cravings.** Avoid these kinds of cues. Destructive behaviors are usually triggered by certain cues in the environment. Smokers light up with a cup of coffee or after a meal. For every habit there are dozens of cues that need to be dealt with. Identify and then avoid as many cues as you can. Doing this will be easier if you can identify them in your mind beforehand and if you can practice what you will say or tell yourself if you encounter one of these triggers for your addiction.

**Reminders.** It is helpful to leave reminders to yourself in various places. These are positive messages confirming the wisdom of the new behaviors you are modeling. Write messages of encouragement to yourself. Reminders strategically placed at home and at work will go a long way to keep your new behaviors in view and help you forget the old behaviors you are trying to change. Video reminders from supportive family members can be reviewed when temptation strikes.

**Rewards** are useful. When you give up bad habits, you usually save some money. Reward yourself on a regular basis for the progress you are making. This is important on anniversaries at one week, one month, and one year.

**Support** from others. Utilize the sympathy and support of family, friends, and colleagues as you change. They will be supportive and will lend a listening ear to the struggles you are facing. They will rejoice when you rejoice. These close ones will confirm you in your new behavior and celebrate each victory with you.

## God's Special Help with Bad Habits and Addictions

I have already mentioned prayer; but there is much more to learn about God's special help for those who want to overcome. God will help you overcome every bad habit and addiction. God is the answer to life's failures and unfulfilled desires. God wants you to know Him as a helper.

God does not usually save us from the consequences of the diseases we get from years of indulgence, but God will always help us change our destructive behaviors. You may not know God personally. You may not even believe in God. You may not want to know God, but God wants you to experience Him as a Helper in your life. God will prove to you that he is real. If after asking God for help, you find that you experience success in overcoming bad habits where you had only experienced failure before, you will have first-hand, personal experience that there is a God who helps you in your time of need.

Preachers and evangelists want unbelievers to come to know Jesus Christ as a redeemer of the "soul" and acknowledge the life, death, and resurrection of Christ as realities before moving on to other issues in the Christian life. This is a rather narrow and limited approach to God. In many ways it restricts God's influence and activity in human life.

When Jesus was here on earth working miracles, he opened blind eyes and then the person saw their Savior. Jesus opened the ears of the deaf who then heard the good news of salvation. The healing of disease in Christ's day, in many cases, preceded belief in Christ as Savior. And so today, many who are struggling with destructive habits and addictions can be healed of these deadly behaviors by God as a first step in convincing a person that He is real.

God's help is available to all, but God's help will not be dispensed to all. The conditions to be met for receiving help from God are very specific, yet not unreasonable. It is necessary to become familiar with God's formula for behavior change.

It is important to be positive regarding the outcome of the struggle. Help is at hand. Jesus will be there throughout the struggle. Do not dwell on the negative aspects of behavior change. Fear of consequences discourages, but God encourages.

"In working for the victims of evil habits, instead of pointing them to the despair and ruin toward which they are hastening, turn their eyes away to Jesus. Fix them upon the glories of the heavenly. This will do more for the saving of body and soul than will all the terrors of the grave when kept before the helpless and apparently hopeless." *The Ministry of Healing, 62-63.*

We should inform people of the certainty of behavior change and point the discouraged to God as the One who helps us accomplish what would otherwise be impossible for us to do by ourselves. God wants us to enjoy the benefits of healthful living. The behavior change God wants us to implement in our lives is not impossible to achieve.

"Our heavenly Father presents before his finite creatures no impossibilities; he requires not at their hands that which they cannot perform. He has not set before his church a standard to which they cannot attain; yet he designs that they shall labor earnestly to reach the high standard set before them in the text. He would have them pray that they may be "filled with the fruits of righteousness," and then expect this blessing and receive it, and in all things grow up into Christ their living Head." *The Signs of the Times, 12-09-86*

## Admit You Cannot Change on Your Own

God wants to demonstrate a person's inability to succeed without Him. It is always necessary for those who do not have a relationship with God to realize their inability to change on their own. If a person is self-confident and believes that he or she can bring about a permanent change for the better in their lives, God doesn't step in to help. Self-confident people must try again and again until they experience enough repeated failures that they become convinced of their own inability to change.

This may seem discouraging, but it is a setup for eventual success. If you have failed miserably to change yourself, if you have repeatedly failed to change yourself, but you suddenly become successful after calling on God for help, you will know that divine help came from outside yourself.

This is the true point of conversion. It doesn't really matter if you start your walk with God by trusting your lost "soul" to God or your lost physical or mental self to God.

God saves us when we trust Him to save us. Being saved from the sin of smoking is a good a place to start your walk with God. Being saved from your perverted appetite for food is a good way to be saved. Being saved from some addiction is just as valid as being saved from some "spiritual" sin.

A person who has just been saved is now a "babe" in Christ. Growth and maturity are necessary to round out the Christian experience. This is known in theological circles as the process of "sanctification." I do not believe any church would be willing to baptize a person whose only experience with God was salvation from smoking or obesity, but God saved that person just the same. As long as a person is willing to grow from that point, God will continue to work with them.

I want people to know our wonderful God. He loves, he cares, he saves, he changes behavior. I want people to get to know God. Everyone who comes to know God must start somewhere. Where and under what circumstances are people most likely to know God? At the point of failure and futility, God will be there to save and change the life.

Yes, baptism and church membership are important in the Christian life, in their own good time. Baptism and church membership are steps in the Christian life that come later. They do not mark the beginning of the Christian life. Baptism indicates that a person has grown to the point that he or she is ready to join a body of Christian believers.

For unbelievers it is a long walk to the baptismal tank. That walk must begin at some point. Everyone has a behavior problem that is keeping them back from personal fulfillment. They have destructive habits, addictions, and strained relationships. Let's introduce these hurting and defeated people to God as the agent of change in human life. God will help all defeated people who are willing to call on his name.

In the wilderness of Moses time, the poisonous snake bite that resulted in a painful and rapid death was neutralized by a look at the uplifted serpent. So today, the bite of death that comes from drugs, smoking, a sedentary life, alcohol, and bad eating habits can all be changed by a look at the uplifted Savior. Jesus changes our behavior. Jesus saves us from our bad behaviors. Jesus saves us. For many, this will begin in a health evangelism program right in your church.

## Be Honest with God

God is honest with you and expects you to be honest with Him in return. This is difficult to do. To receive God's help with any behavior you want to change, it is necessary for you to be honest with God. Think about this implication of honesty.

If God delivers you from cigarette smoking, someone is going to notice your new smoke-free status and ask how you did it? What is your answer going to be? You may not be a religious person. Up to this point in your life you may have been an atheist or a blasphemer, but now you have experienced supernatural help. You are now off cigarettes, and someone wants to know how you did it. What is your answer going to be? You must be honest in your answer.

Your answer should be, "I smoked for years and years and tried to quit dozens of times, but without success. I asked God to help me quit and He did it. I am free of this habit due to the specific intervention of God in my life. I am so thankful to God for the deliverance He provided me in this case."

In scripture there is the story of a woman who suffered for 12 years with an illness. She was healed when she stretched out her hand and anonymously touched the hem of Jesus garment. This is recorded in Mark 5:25-34. This woman was instantly healed. She would have been satisfied to slip away unnoticed from the crowd and quietly enjoy God's blessing of healing in the privacy of her own home. But Jesus wanted her to acknowledge that He was the one who healed her. She really didn't want to publicly acknowledge this but when she couldn't hide her healing she spoke up.

> "But the woman, fearing and trembling, knowing what had happened to her, came and fell down before Him and told Him the whole truth" **Mark 5:33 (NKJV)**

Is telling the truth an unfair requirement? Not really. There is a world out there filled with people who need to change and are discouraged due to their many failures. You are to share the fact that God changes lives. You are to tell your own story of repeated trials and failures until you achieved success when you finally asked God for help.

A second reason Jesus wanted the woman with the issue of blood to come forward was to let her know, that by that simple touch of his garment, she was connected with the God of the universe. God is not hard to contact. God is very near. God wants to help you. If you simply reach out to him, he will be right there to bring healing to your life.

> *"The humblest soul that looks up to Christ in Faith is connected with the God of the universe."*

> "We should reach out the hand of faith, and grasp the arm of infinite power. The simplest prayer that is put up in faith is acceptable to heaven. The humblest soul that looks up to Christ in faith is connected with the God of the universe." **Signs of the Times, March 10, 1890.**

God will meet you in any place, at any time, when you bring a problem to Him that needs to be changed. It doesn't have to be in church, although it is especially meaningful if the health evangelism program is conducted in the church. You may have come to a church just to stop smoking, but you met God in a health evangelism program. He is the helper for all who need behavior change.

## Asking for Help.

The next step in receiving God's help is to simply ask. Words need to be spoken. You may have thought about and wished that God would help you. This is not enough. God doesn't respond to random thoughts and wishes. Relationships are formed by an exchange of words. Often, thoughts and wishes remain vague and nebulous until they are put into words. Putting our desires and requests into words has a way of sharpening and strengthening them. Put your longing for behavior change into words. Speak them aloud. It is often helpful to write them down.

Christians know this process as prayer. This is a word that may scare away those who do not yet have a relationship with God. It is not necessary to even call this process of talking with God as prayer. It is enough to call it talking with God.

God has been leading you for months, years, even your whole life, but now is the time to open a return channel. This is done by talking with God. There are no special words that need to be spoken. The conversation should be short and to the point. Here is an example.

"God, I am overweight. I have tried many diets. Some of them worked for a while but never for very long. I look horrible. Obesity is going to ruin my relationship with others. Obesity is going to ruin my health. I want to change. I need to change. I am not able to change permanently by myself. I need help. Please help me lose weight. Oh yes God, I will be honest about this. If You help me lose weight, I will tell others that my help came from You. Thank you in advance. Let's get to work."

This is the first of many conversations you will have with God. You will find it necessary to talk with God many times a day. But if you do not feel anything when you ask God for help, how do you know that God has helped you? When will you know that God is helping you? What will God's help be like? How long will God's help last? Will God help for one meal, one hour, one day, one week? The answers to these questions are exactly what everyone needs to know.

Here is what I have learned from my experience and the experience of others. Frequent conversations with God are needed because it is so easy to forget that you have requested God's help. If you carelessly consider and then yield to your old habits, it is not a failure on God's part but a simple negligence on your part. Additionally, God is seeking a "real time" relationship with you. If you drop the ball and leave God's presence, He is not obligated to rescue you from your own carelessness.

You may in some way I can't define for you feel or sense the presence of God or some assurance from God when you ask for help, but many feel nothing after praying. God will still help you. You will know that God is helping when you successfully resist a temptation that used to be an unbearable urge.

The duration of God's help depends on the duration of your practicing the presence of God. God will help for one meal, one day, or one week, but it requires a continuing commitment to the process of depending on God for the success you know you can't provide yourself.

Prayer is vital to success. Review these promises God makes.

> "Ask, and it will be given to you; seek, and you will find; knock, and it will be opened to you. For everyone who asks receives, and he who seeks finds, and to him who knocks it will be opened" **Matthew 7:7-8 (NKJV).**

> "And whatever you ask in My name, that I will do, that the Father may be glorified in the Son. If you

> ask anything in My name, I will do it" **John 14:13-14
> (NKJV)**

> "Now this is the confidence that we have in Him, that
> if we ask anything according to His will, He hears us"
> **1 John 5:14 (NKJV)**

Prayer is powerful. If prayer can subdue kingdoms, quiet roaring lions, and stop fire from consuming, then prayer can help you with your problems and bring about new behaviors.

> "The children of God are not left alone and defenseless.
> Prayer moves the arm of Omnipotence. Prayer has
> 'subdued kingdoms, wrought righteousness, obtained
> promises, stopped the mouth of lions, quenched the
> violence of fire.'" *Christ's Object Lessons, p. 172.*

God is pictured as eagerly leaning forward to catch the plea of one who is struggling to overcome. God has a blessing for us just waiting for us to make our needs known.

> "God is bending from his throne to hear the cry of the
> oppressed. To every sincere prayer he answers, "Here am
> I." The prayer that ascends from a broken and contrite
> heart is never disregarded; it is as sweet music in the ears
> of our heavenly Father: for he waits to bestow upon us
> the fullness of his blessing." *The Oriental Watchman,
> 12-01-1909.*

God doesn't respond to ceremonious prayers. He wants to hear the frank, desperate, disorganized cry of one facing temptation.

> "There are two kinds of prayer--the prayer of form and
> the prayer of faith . . . But the prayer that comes from
> an earnest heart, when the simple wants of the soul are
> expressed just as we would ask an earthly friend for a

favor, expecting that it would be granted--this is the prayer of faith." *My Life Today 19.*

Though God is the Lord of the Universe, He wants us to approach him as a friend.

> "Prayer is the opening of the heart to God as to a friend. Not that it is necessary in order to make known to God what we are, but in order to enable us to receive Him. Prayer does not bring God down to us, but brings us up to Him." *Steps to Christ 93.*

> "Those who decide to do nothing in any line that will displease God, will know, after presenting their case before Him, just what course to pursue. And they will receive not only wisdom, but strength. Power for obedience, for service, will be imparted to them, as Christ has promised. *The Desire of Ages 668.*

In this struggle to live better, you can eventually overcome all the harmful habits you have acquired through life's experiences and even congenitally acquired tendencies toward bad habits as well. The child of an alcoholic has an addictive personality. This may be overcome through the power of Christ. There are other inherited tendencies that predispose us to harmful behaviors. Many suppose that their natural tendencies are excused or unchangeable because of the laws of nature. This is not true. God has clearly indicated what constitutes healthful behavior. You may have inherited many harmful tendencies, but all this can be overcome through the grace of God.

> "It is by the Spirit that the heart is made pure. Through the Spirit the believer becomes a partaker of the divine nature. Christ has given His Spirit as a divine power to overcome all hereditary and cultivated tendencies to evil, and to impress His own character upon His church." *The Desire of Ages 671*

# Action

After asking God for help there is another step you need to take to receive the requested assistance. There is something you need to do. Here is an unfortunate experience of a lady who failed to understand this.

She was a lady who attended a 5-Day Plan to Stop Smoking I conducted in Towson, Maryland. I had talked about how God helps smokers quit. After the program she lit up a cigarette in the parking lot of the church. She told me, "I have been asking God to help me stop smoking for the past 20 years and He hasn't done it yet."

I asked what she expected God to do to help her to quit. I asked whether she expected God to make her lighter so it wouldn't light. Was she expecting matches to fizzle and go out before she could light up? Did she expect God to work on the mind of the checkout clerk at the local store when she tried to buy cigarettes, so the checkout person would refuse to sell her any cigarettes because God was trying to get her to quit?

She was repeatedly asking God to help her quit smoking but without her doing anything. She was expecting God to force her to stop smoking in response to her prayer. Prayer doesn't work that way. God doesn't work that way. This lady needed to act on her request. She needed to act like she was a nonsmoker.

Immediately after asking God for help is the time for action. You should have a plan to put to work. For the obese person, that plan will include a diet and eating behavior changes. For the smoker it is time to throw away the cigarettes, lighters, and ash trays. For the sedentary person it is initiating a regular program of exercise. For the alcoholic it may be attending Alcoholics Anonymous meetings. For those with a bad temper it may be an anger management program. For those attending your health evangelism program, you will be providing the plan of action a person needs to follow.

Working at behavior change may seem too familiar. You have done this before. You know what a tremendous effort and strain it is. For you, diet, or exercise programs, and in fact all programs you have ever tried have been frustrating and did not produce lasting success.

The difference in this program is that you have asked God to help you. God does not dispense with your effort or cooperation when He provides help for you to overcome. God works with your efforts. God helps you work the plan you intend to follow.

So, if you have a plan and are working it, do you now have a brighter vision of success? Are you brimming with confidence? Do you know that this plan is going to work for you this time? Possibly not. So, when will you know that God has been helping you? When and how will you experience God's help?

The simple answer is, "Just when you need it, God's help will be there." God's acting in the human life is often not felt at the time the plea for help is made, but God's help will show up when you need it.

Here are examples of where God exercised miraculous power on behalf of a person, but a cooperative effort was required on the part of the person or persons nearby at the time the miracle was performed.

## The Raising of Lazarus

The raising of Lazarus recorded in John 11 is an important example. Raising Lazarus to life, four days after he died, was Christ's greatest miracle. As Jesus stood at the tomb, He instructed that the stone be rolled away. This command to remove the stone seems strange.

It takes less divine power to move a stone than it does to raise a person from the dead. It would have added significant drama to the scene if the stone had mysteriously moved all by itself or been shattered with a bolt of lightning.

The point is this, in every miracle God performs for you, there is a part for you to play. God will not do for you what you can do for yourself. Jesus required someone to roll away the stone from the opening of the tomb. Martha objected to removing the stone. If there had been a lot of sympathy for Martha's point of view in the crowd that was standing there, if there had been a general outcry for the stone to stay in place, Lazarus would not have been raised from the dead.

I do not think the men who rolled away the stone went home that evening and boasted to their family how they and Jesus had raised Lazarus from the dead. Yet, if the stone didn't get rolled away Lazarus wouldn't have been raised.

The part you play in any miracle is necessary for the miracle to happen, but it has absolutely nothing to do with the power it takes to perform the miracle. All the power comes from God, but your cooperation is necessary. Your efforts are acts of faith moving or even just leaning in the direction you want to go, but God supplies all the ability.

## The Water to Wine Miracle

Another example of divine and human cooperation in performing a miracle is when Jesus turned water into wine at the wedding feast in Cana as recorded in John 2. Jesus required the household servants to fill the stone jars with water and then dip it out and serve it. The water was suddenly turned into wine.

If the servants had objected and refused to fill the jars with water, there wouldn't have been any wine. When those servants went home that night, they certainly recounted to their families what a great miracle Jesus had performed, but I doubt they took any credit for the miracle because you can fill jars with water all day long and the water will never turn to wine unless there is a miracle from God.

I am repeatedly making the point that it is necessary for people to participate in the performance of a miracle. If we do not do our part,

God doesn't do His part. Our part is essential but ineffectual. God does it all but waits for us to cooperate with him.

## Crossing the Jordon River

Here is a third example. When the children of Israel crossed the Jordan River, they all marched forward even though the river was at flood stage. This is recorded in Joshua 3. There was no bridge and no boats, but they lined up and marched forward.

The children of Israel headed in the direction they were instructed to go. When the feet of the priests touched the flood waters, the Jordan was held back, and they all crossed over on dry ground. A miracle happened. The people marched forward indicating a willingness to do what God requested. God provided the miracle. Again, we see the cooperation between the human and the Divine. Man acted as though God was going to do something, and He did. God requires you to act and then He provides ALL the power to accomplish the act.

Cooperation between the human and the Divine is necessary to form a correct character. We must make serious efforts, but our efforts are not sufficient to accomplish anything. We are still wholly dependent on God for Success.

> "The work of gaining salvation is one of co-partnership, a joint operation. There is to be co-operation between God and the repentant sinner. This is necessary for the formation of right principles in the character. Man is to make earnest efforts to overcome that which hinders him from attaining to perfection. But he is wholly dependent upon God for success. Human effort of itself is not sufficient. Without the aid of divine power it avails nothing. God works and man works. Resistance of temptation must come from man, who must draw his power from God. On the one side there is infinite wisdom, compassion, and power; on the other,

weakness, sinfulness, absolute helplessness." *The Acts of the Apostles 482*

Human effort is worthless unless energized by divine power. Divine help is unavailable unless there is human endeavor.

"Human effort avails nothing without divine power; and without human endeavor, divine effort is with many of no avail. To make God's grace our own, we must act our part. His grace is given to work in us to will and to do, but never as a substitute for our effort. . . . Those who walk in the path of obedience will encounter many hindrances. Strong, subtle influences may bind them to the world; but the Lord is able to render futile every agency that works for the defeat of His chosen ones; in His strength they may overcome every temptation, conquer every difficulty." *God's Amazing Grace 253*

Actions essential for success are themselves gifts which we have already received from God. The use of these talents and skills helps us move in the direction we want to go. God will not duplicate that which He has already enabled us to do.

"The Lord does not propose to perform for us either the willing or the doing. This is our proper work. As soon as we earnestly enter upon the work, God's grace is given to work in us to will and to do, but never as a substitute for our effort. Our souls are to be aroused to cooperate. The Holy Spirit works the human agent, to work out our own salvation. This is the practical lesson the Holy Spirit is striving to teach us. "For it is God which worketh in you both to will and to do of His good pleasure." *Testimonies to Ministers and Gospel Workers 240*

In all your efforts to overcome bad habits you must constantly be aware that you are weak. Success at this moment does not guarantee your success in the next hour or tomorrow. You need God's constant help, but you must never let down your guard or relax your own efforts to succeed.

"In order to receive God's help, man must realize his weakness and deficiency; he must apply his own mind to the great change to be wrought in himself; he must be aroused to earnest and persevering prayer and effort. Wrong habits and customs must be shaken off; and it is only by determined endeavor to correct these errors and to conform to right principles that the victory can be gained. *Patriarchs and Prophets 248*

As you make constant, earnest struggles, you should be looking to and contemplating the goodness of God and how it is His strength that enables you to be successful.

"Let every one who desires to be a partaker of the divine nature appreciate the fact that he must escape the corruption that is in the world through lust. There must be a constant, earnest struggling of the soul against the evil imaginings of the mind. There must be a steadfast resistance of temptation to sin in thought or act. The soul must be kept from every stain, through faith in Him who is able to keep you from falling. We should meditate upon the Scriptures, thinking soberly and candidly upon the things that pertain to our eternal salvation. The infinite mercy and love of Jesus, the sacrifice made in our behalf, call for most serious and solemn reflection. We should dwell upon the character of our dear Redeemer and Intercessor. We should seek to comprehend the meaning of the plan of salvation. We should meditate upon the mission of Him who came to save His people from their sins. By constantly contemplating heavenly themes, our faith and love will grow stronger. Our prayers will be more and more acceptable to God, because they will be more and more mixed with faith and love. They will be more intelligent and fervent." *Sons and Daughters of God 109*

There are stern battles with self that need to be fought. You need to examine your progress regularly. God gives you the talents and the powers of mind that you can use in developing your habit free character.

"A noble character is earned by individual effort through the merits and grace of Christ. God gives the talents, the powers of the mind; we form the character. It is formed by hard, stern battles with self. Conflict after conflict must be waged against hereditary tendencies. We shall have to criticize ourselves closely, and allow not one unfavorable trait to remain uncorrected." *Christ's Object Lessons 331*

It is amazing to me that with God's help even hereditary traits can be corrected. Think of the health problems and harmful practices for which a congenital component has been identified. All this can be changed.

"Through the Spirit the believer becomes a partaker of the divine nature. Christ has given His Spirit as a divine power to overcome all hereditary and cultivated tendencies to evil, and to impress His own character upon His church." *The Desire of Ages 671*

When you have done all that you can God will do all that you cannot.

---

*Once you have done all that you can God will do all that you cannot.*

---

"Some reason that the Lord will by his Spirit qualify a man to speak as he would have him; but the Lord does not propose to do the work which he has given man to do. He has given us reasoning powers, and opportunities to educate the mind and manners. And after we have done all we can for ourselves, making the best use of the advantages within our reach, then we may look to God with earnest prayer to do by his Spirit that which we cannot do for ourselves, and we shall ever find in our Saviour power and efficiency." *Gospel Workers 148*

Constant watchfulness, persevering effort, severe discipline, and tough conflict will be your lot but as you depend on God you can right the deformity of your character. There is a lifetime of struggle, but with God's help the outcome is certain.

"It will cost us an effort to secure eternal life. It is only by long and persevering effort, sore discipline, and stern conflict, that we shall be overcomers. But if we patiently and determinedly, in the name of the Conqueror who overcame in our behalf in the wilderness of temptation, overcome as he overcame, we shall have the eternal reward. Our efforts, our self-denial, our perseverance, must be proportionate to the infinitive value of the object of which we are in pursuit. . . . Wrongs cannot be righted, nor reformations in character made, by a few feeble, intermittent efforts. Sanctification is not a work of a day or a year, but of a lifetime. Without continual efforts and constant activity, there can be no advancement in the divine life, no attainment of the victor's crown. . . . You have need of constant watchfulness, lest Satan beguile you through his subtlety, corrupt your minds, and lead you into inconsistencies and gross darkness. Your watchfulness should be characterized by a spirit of humble dependence upon God. It should not be carried on with a proud, self-reliant spirit, but with a deep sense of your personal weakness, and a childlike trust in the promises of God." *Gospel Workers 205*

Living a healthful life is not an option. Once we know what should be done, we need to act.

> "The time of ignorance God winked at, but as fast as light shines upon us, He requires us to change our health-destroying habits, and place ourselves in a right relation to physical laws." ***Counsels on Diet and Foods 19***

There is a need for struggle and perseverance.

> "Those who, after seeing their mistakes, have courage to change their habits will find that the reformatory process requires a struggle and much perseverance; ***Counsels on Diet and Foods 24***

# Temptation

Temptation shows up in many ways. For the smoker trying to quit there is a craving for cigarettes. For the alcoholic it is a craving for the numbing nothingness that alcohol brings to the battered brain. For the sedentary it is the urge to stay in bed and not hit the jogging trail. For the obese it is the urge to snack or take second helpings. For those with anger issues it is an urge to yell at a stupid employee, family member, or a careless driver on the road. For the sex addict it is the drawing of the eyes to pornography on the internet or in magazines. To the lazy it is a lineup of entertaining TV programs for the evening. For the spiritually indolent it may be missing church or Sabbath school, prayer meeting or the omission of daily devotions.

These are all temptations, barriers between you and success. Temptations are often resisted for a few hours, days, weeks or even years but then at some point of weakness you give in and experience failure once again. Here you also need God's help.

What does God do about temptations? Well, if you didn't ask God for help, God isn't going to do anything about your temptations. If you did ask God for help, you are about to succeed where you only experienced failure before.

Temptations come in varying intensities. There are small brief temptations that come when you are busy. Something crosses your mind, but because you are so busy, you barely give the temptation a passing thought. I believe some temptations will be with you all your life. God does not prevent you from being tempted. In fact, God allows you to be tempted. Satan tempts you to bring out the worst in you, but God allows temptation to bring out the best in you.

Being a child of God does not exempt you from temptation but being a child of God puts resources at your disposal you can use to resist temptation. When you ask God for help in overcoming some destructive behavior, you can expect frequent and intense temptations that you can successfully meet and overcome with God's help.

Fortunately, over time, temptations about a specific problem tend to become less intense and less frequent, but even after several months or years of successful living, temptations can return in strength. This is not a sign that God has abandoned you. It is a sign that Satan hasn't given up on you and is determined to break you down if he can. When Satan finds he is unable to overcome you in one area he shifts his efforts to some other area of weakness in your life in the hopes of breaking you down one way or another.

For example, when a person stops smoking, in addition to temptations to return to smoking, there is a tendency on the part of many to want to eat more. Food tastes better when you are not smoking. The hand-to-mouth motions of eating are like the actions of smoking. I have seen people put on 30 or 40 pounds after quitting smoking. It is good to stop smoking but it is bad to become a glutton as a consequence. Here, one bad habit replaced another. This is how Satan works. Temptations in one area may decrease, only to be replaced by a whole new set of temptations in some other area of life.

So, where and when does God help you when you are fighting temptation? God doesn't very often remove a temptation altogether. But God does keep you from yielding to temptation and falling back into your old ways. In some rare cases God will eliminate all temptation about a certain problem.

In one of my stop smoking clinics I had a man who quit smoking with God's help. I saw him several months later. He said that God had eliminated the desire for tobacco. He didn't have a single craving at any time since he committed the problem to God. It was a wonderful deliverance. God can do this for anyone, and God may do this for you, but this type of deliverance is unusual.

God often lets people be tempted and get pretty close to failure before stepping in. There is a certain intensity of temptation where you have always failed before. You know where this point is and you know when you are getting close to it.

If God doesn't seem to be doing much about your temptation, do not despair. God will not let you fail. There is a point where God always steps in and gives you success. If relief doesn't come early in the temptation, at least will come before you reach the point of failure.

*God will not let you fail! Just at the point where you have always failed before God will now give you success!*

God will not let you fail. Just when you feel you have reached the point of failure, God will enable you to say "No" to your temptation. At just the point where you have always failed before you will now have success. This is where God's help shows up every time. Instead of experiencing repeated failures as you did in the past you will now experience repeated victories.

Why does God sometimes wait until you reach the point of failure before stepping in? There are several reasons why God may allow this to be your experience. All these reasons for temptation need to be understood.

First, God wants to demonstrate your honesty and sincerity before the universe before He steps in to help you. For this reason, your temptations may be strong on occasion. You may become very uncomfortable. It is good to keep in mind that every effort you make in your own behalf is a measure of your honesty and sincerity.

To be sure, every effort you make in your own behalf is totally inadequate to keep you from falling back into bad behaviors. You remember that your best effort has never been able to deliver you in the past, but your best effort is a measure of the intensity of your desire to receive God's help. God honors that and will not let you fail.

> "No temptation has overtaken you except such as is common to man; but God is faithful, who will not allow you to be tempted beyond what you are able, but with the temptation will also make the way of escape, that you may be able to bear it" **1 Corinthians 10:13. (NKJV)**

> In the Lord's Prayer we are admonished to pray about temptations and to ask for deliverance from them.

> "And do not lead us into temptation, but deliver us from the evil one. For Yours is the kingdom and the power and the glory forever. Amen" **Matthew 6:13 (NKJV)**

Jesus reminded his disciples that by prayer they would be able to avoid or overcome temptation.

> "Watch and pray, lest you enter into temptation." **Matthew 26:41 (NKJV)**

Another safeguard against temptation is contained in the parable of the sower in Luke 8. This describes those who have heard the good news but who are overcome by temptation. These start out well, but because they remain superficial in their experience and do not advance in their relationship with God, they are unprepared for severe temptations.

> "But the ones on the rock are those who, when they hear,
> receive the word with joy; and these have no root, who
> believe for a while and in time of temptation fall away"
> **Luke 8:13 (NKJV)**

Temptations have a purpose. If we maintain our hold on God and with His help endure temptations, we will be approved by God and will receive the crown of life. This may be the experience of those who learn to trust God at a health evangelism program.

> "Blessed is the man who endures temptation; for when
> he has been approved, he will receive the crown of life
> which the Lord has promised to those who love Him"
> **James 1:12 (NKJV)**

It is my reasoning that the next text applies to all those who are trying to overcome temptation. Some would argue that a secular people do not have the opportunity or right to apply this text to their lives because they have not been born of God. My point is that being born of God occurs at the point where you avail yourself of God's help. Being born of God is associated with altar calls at evangelistic meetings, but it must be applied as well to the person who, for the first time, claims God's special help for a problem area in the life no matter where they are.

> "For whatever is born of God overcomes the world. And
> this is the victory that has overcome the world—our
> faith" **1 John 5:4 (NKJV)**

In referring to the temptation of Peter, Mrs. White indicates that in the Christian life the Lord does not save us from trial but does save us from defeat.

> "It was necessary for Peter to learn his own defects of
> character, and his need of the power and grace of Christ.
> The Lord could not save him from trial but He could
> have saved him from defeat . . . he would have received

divine help so that Satan could not have gained the victory." *Christ's Object Lessons 155*

Once you have entered the struggle to overcome a bad habit, there will be many situations that will come up to divert you from the problem you are trying to overcome. You will be successful as you keep our mind on Christ.

"You have Satan to contend with, and he will seek by every possible device to attract your mind from Christ. But we must meet all obstacles placed in our way, and overcome them one at a time. If we overcome the first difficulty, we shall be stronger to meet the next, and at every effort will become better able to make advancement. By looking to Jesus, we may be over comers. *The Youth's Instructor, 01-05-1893.*

Many who avail themselves of God's help will eventually fail to overcome their bad habits. This is not God's fault or the fault of your health evangelism program.

"Those who work for the fallen will be disappointed in many who give promise of reform. Many will make but a superficial change in their habits and practices. They are moved by impulse, and for a time may seem to have reformed; but there is no real change of heart. They cherish the same self-love, have the same hungering for foolish pleasures, the same desire for self-indulgence. They have not a knowledge of the work of character building, and they cannot be relied upon as men of principle. They have debased their mental and spiritual powers by the gratification of appetite and passion, and this makes them weak. They are fickle and changeable. Their impulses tend toward sensuality. These persons are often a source of danger to others. Being looked upon as reformed men and women, they are trusted with responsibilities and are placed where their influence corrupts the innocent." *The Ministry of Healing 177*

You can overcome some temptations by yourself on certain occasions, but you cannot have long term success without Gods help. God expects you to recognize your weakness yet make determined efforts to correct your faults and errors.

> "In order to receive God's help, man must realize his weakness and deficiency; he must apply his own mind to the great change to be wrought in himself; he must be aroused to earnest and persevering prayer and effort. Wrong habits and customs must be shaken off; and it is only by determined endeavor to correct these errors and to conform to right principles that the victory can be gained. Many never attain to the position that they might occupy, because they wait for God to do for them that which He has given them power to do for themselves. All who are fitted for usefulness must be trained by the severest mental and moral discipline, and God will assist them by uniting divine power with human effort." *Patriarchs and Prophets 248*

Satan may tempt you, but Satan cannot make you give in to temptation. Christ repulsed all temptation and will give you strength of meet all temptations as well.

> "Satan assailed Christ with his fiercest and most subtle temptations, but he was repulsed in every conflict. Those battles were fought in our behalf; those victories make it possible for us to conquer. Christ will give strength to all who seek it. No man without his own consent can be overcome by Satan. The tempter has no power to control the will or to force the soul to sin. He may distress, but he cannot contaminate. He can cause agony, but not defilement. The fact that Christ has conquered should inspire His followers with courage to fight manfully the battle against sin and Satan." *The Great Controversy 510*

## Keeping it up

Success comes a day at a time. Success today may be followed by failure tomorrow, but this need not be. Success today is proof that we can be successful tomorrow. The formula that worked today will also work tomorrow. At times you fail because you fail to maintain your connection with God. You start out well but do not keep it up.

---

*Success comes a day at a time!*

---

I had a lady in my office practice who had successfully lost 40 pounds with God's help. She was so happy. She had previously never lost more than 5 pounds on any diet. She was praying to God every day and God was giving her success.

One day, she came into my office and was a bit concerned. She said, "If I do not pray to God at breakfast, I overeat at breakfast. If I do not pray at noon, I overeat at lunch time. If I do not pray at dinner time, I overeat in the evening. If I do not pray to God all the time this just doesn't work!" She was upset and brought her fist down forcefully on my desk.

We discussed the nature of God's help. God is willing to help us as long as we maintain a relationship with Him. If we lose our contact with God, we will rather immediately revert back to our old behaviors. God desires to maintain a long-term relationship with us. As long as we maintain our connection with Him, He is actively working on our behalf. I explained that God admonishes us to "pray without ceasing."

> "Rejoice always, pray without ceasing, in everything give thanks; for this is the will of God in Christ Jesus for you" **1 Thessalonians 5:16-18 (NKJV)**

This lady immediately saw the significance of what I was saying. She realized that she was complaining about having to maintain a continuous connection with God. She brightened and said she would never again complain about having to keep in touch with God. I am pleased to report that she kept her weight off until the time of her death sometime later.

It is wearisome at times to keep focused on your problem and to constantly be in prayer to God. It is easy to be diverted from your important goals. With time however, you become accustomed to being in God's presence and learn to always depend on Him for all things. Jesus admonishes you to take His yolk upon you.

> "Take My yoke upon you and learn from Me, for I am gentle and lowly in heart, and you will find rest for your souls" **Matthew 11:29 (NKJV)**

In order for you to always succeed you must continue to keep the Lord always before you.

> "The reason why so many are left to themselves in places of temptation is that they do not set the Lord always before them. When we permit our communion with God to be broken, our defense is departed from us. Not all your good purposes and good intentions will enable you to withstand evil. You must be men and women of prayer. Your petitions must not be faint, occasional, and fitful, but earnest, persevering, and constant. It is not always necessary to bow upon your knees in order to pray. Cultivate the habit of talking with the Saviour when you are alone, when you are walking, and when you are busy with your daily labor. Let the heart be continually uplifted in silent petition for help. *The Ministry of Healing 510-511*

We should plan on obtaining a new victory every day.

> "God is our strength. We must look to Him for wisdom and guidance, and keeping in view His glory, the good of the church, and the salvation of our own souls, we must

overcome our besetting sins. We should individually seek to obtain new victory every day. We must learn to stand alone and depend wholly upon God. The sooner we learn this the better. Let each one find out where he fails, and then faithfully watch that his sins do not overcome him, but that he gets the victory over them. Then can we have confidence toward God, and great trouble will be saved the church." *Early Writings of Ellen G. White 105*

Keeping up with successful living results from abiding in Christ and thorough continual communication with Him.

"This union with Christ, once formed, must be maintained. Christ said, "Abide in Me, and I in you. As the branch cannot bear fruit of itself, except it abide in the vine; no more can ye, except ye abide in Me." This is no casual touch, no off-and-on connection. The branch becomes a part of the living vine. The communication of life, strength, and fruitfulness from the root to the branches is unobstructed and constant. Separated from the vine, the branch cannot live. No more, said Jesus, can you live apart from Me. The life you have received from Me can be preserved only by continual communion. Without Me you cannot overcome one sin, or resist one temptation. *The Desire of Ages 676*

If you have learned to abide in Christ, you will identify new problems in your life that need to be corrected. You can overcome each one through the strength that Christ provides. This will result in a string of uninterrupted victories.

"Christ rejoiced that He could do more for His followers than they could ask or think. He spoke with assurance, knowing that an almighty decree had been given before the world was made. He knew that truth, armed with the omnipotence of the Holy Spirit, would conquer in the contest with evil; and that the bloodstained banner would wave triumphantly over His followers. He knew that the life of His trusting disciples would be like His, a series of uninterrupted victories, not seen to be such here, but recognized as such in the great hereafter. *The Desire of Ages 679*

Those situations which seem sure to trip you up will disappear as you make a consistent effort to do the will of God.

"Those who would walk in the path of obedience to God's commandments will encounter many hindrances. There are strong and subtle influences that bind them to the ways of the world; but the power of the Lord can break these chains. He will remove these obstacles from before the feet of his faithful, humble children, or give them strength and courage to conquer every difficulty, if they earnestly beseech his help. All hindrances will vanish before an earnest desire and persistent effort to do the will of God. Light from Heaven will illuminate the pathway of those who, no matter what trials and perplexities they may encounter, go forward in the way of obedience, looking to Jesus for help and guidance. *The Signs of the Times, 07-22-1886*

There was another lady who was visiting with me after a Smoking Cessation Clinic. She was smoking in the parking lot just before she left for the evening. She had heard what I had said about how God helped smokers quit. She remarked to me, "I quit smoking with God's help."

I was surprised because she was smoking as she told me this. I asked her, "What happened?" She said that after about six months she decided she could stay off cigarettes by herself. She felt she didn't need God's help with smoking anymore. Well, obviously she had failed, because she was smoking as she was talking with me.

I next asked her, "What do you plan to do about your smoking?" Her response was, "I will just keep trying." Notice the "I." She was determined to quit on her own and was not meeting with any success. It is my belief that she will never be able to quit smoking on her own. She needs to find God again. She needs to start working with God once again. She knows just where she left Him, and she knows exactly what help is available.

## Thankfulness

Another key to long-lasting success is being thankful for the success you have experienced up to this point. If you go an hour without smoking, that represents success, and you should thank God. If you go a whole day without smoking, it is time to thank God again.

If you have asked God to help you overcome an addiction or habit and you now have had the problem under control for a few days, how do you know that God is in fact helping you? You may not feel very different from what you did before you changed. The proof that God is helping you is that you are not doing what you used to do. You are living a successful life.

> *The proof that God is helping you is that you are not doing what you used to do.*

At this point some people want to think that they are the ones that are responsible for their own success. This is a mistake that leads to failure. The best way to avoid this mistake is to always be thankful to God for all the success you have.

After an hour without a cigarette, thank God for success. After a day without snacking or overeating, thank God for success. After a day without drugs, pornography, or alcohol; thank God for success. The more you thank God for what He is doing for you the more convinced you will be that it is He who is helping you and not you by yourself.

Scripture advises us to be thankful for what God has accomplished for us.

> "But thanks be to God, who gives us the victory through our Lord Jesus Christ. Therefore, my beloved brethren, be steadfast, immovable, always abounding in the work of the Lord, knowing that your labor is not in vain in the Lord" **1 Corinthians 15:57-58 (NKJV)**

> "Now thanks be to God who always leads us in triumph in Christ, and through us diffuses the fragrance of His knowledge in every place. For we are to God the fragrance of Christ among those who are being saved and among those who are perishing" **2 Corinthians 2:14-15. (NKJV)**

> "Be anxious for nothing, but in everything by prayer and supplication, with thanksgiving, let your requests be made known to God; and the peace of God, which surpasses all understanding, will guard your hearts and minds through Christ Jesus" **Philippians 4:6-7 (NKJV)**

> "And whatever you do in word or deed, do all in the name of the Lord Jesus, giving thanks to God the Father through Him" **Colossians 3:17 (NKJV)**

> "Rejoice always, pray without ceasing, in everything give thanks; for this is the will of God in Christ Jesus for you" **1 Thessalonians 5:16-18 (NKJV)**

You should thank God that you are not left alone in the struggle to change your behavior.

> "To every Christian comes the word that was addressed to Peter, "Satan hath desired to have you, that he may sift you as wheat: but I have prayed for thee, that thy faith fail not." Luke 22:31. Thank God we are not left

alone. This is our safety. Satan can never touch with eternal disaster one whom Christ has prepared for temptation by His previous intercession; for grace is provided in Christ for every soul, and a way of escape has been made, so that no one need fall under the power of the enemy. *Our High Calling 311*

In summary, with our cooperation God's power provides everything we need to successfully overcome all cultivated and inherited habits and addictions This needs to be the key message in all health evangelism programs.

# 15

# A Biblical Model of Health Evangelism

EARLY IN MY EXPERIENCE WITH HEALTH EVANGELISM I WAS TRYING to figure the best way to do things. I was struggling with ways to involve the pastor and church members more in the programs I was conducting. I was trying to determine how much spiritual content to include in programs and what types.

As I was driving in Baltimore, Maryland I had my radio tuned to a local religious station. I happened to catch the last few minutes of a sermon by Theodore H. Epp who was the founding director and speaker of the Back to the Bible broadcasts that were on the air between 1939 and 1985.

His text was 2 Kings 4:1-7. He was spiritualizing this Old Testament story about the widow's oil. In just a few minutes his application answered several questions I had about health evangelism. He didn't provide all the details just the application to the last few verses. In his closing remarks he indicated that there was much more to the story and that it should be studied carefully.

This story was my study for several days. It is the most comprehensive picture of health evangelism to be found in scripture. The use of Old Testament stories to learn how to work today is justified by Paul in the following texts.

"Now all these things happened to them as examples, and they were written for our admonition, upon whom the ends of the ages have come" **1 Corinthians 10:11 (NKJV)**

"For whatever things were written before were written for our learning, that we through the patience and comfort of the Scriptures might have hope" **Romans 15:4 (NKJV)**

The following story tells us how to do health evangelism. I have spiritualized the various elements in this story. You will see how God wants us to work for others in our community from the home base of the local church. I am going to analyze this passage verse by verse and word by word.

## 2 Kings 4:1

"A certain woman of the wives of the sons of the prophets cried out to Elisha, saying, "Your servant my husband is dead, and you know that your servant feared the LORD. And the creditor is coming to take my two sons to be his slaves" **2 Kings 4:1 (NLJV)**

*A Woman:* This story is about a woman. In scripture a woman symbolizes the church. This story is about the church. Support for this is found in Jeremiah and Isaiah.

"I have likened the daughter of Zion to a lovely and delicate woman" **Jeremiah 6:2. (NKJV)**

"For your Maker is your husband, The LORD of hosts is His name; He is called the God of the whole earth" **Isaiah 54:5 (NKJV)**

Christ is the Bridegroom and Husband, and the church is His bride. Parables in the New Testament support this concept as well. See: **Matthew 9:15; Mark 2:19,20; Luke 5:34,35; and Matthew 25:1-11 (NKJV)**

*Certain Woman:.* This story is about a certain woman which would be a certain local church.

*Cried Out:* This is an indication of distress. This local church is in trouble. Churches today have numerous problems. Many churches are experiencing falling membership, diminished attendance at services, plummeting offerings, and a general lack of vitality. What is the problem in the local church?

*Husband Is Dead:* Christ is the husband of the church. This passage indicates that Christ who is the husband of the church has died. Christ did die. Christ's death has created a problem which is actually a challenge and opportunity for the church.

This passage might also indicate the attitude of some churches today. Christ may no longer be the living, energizing force in the church. Some churches languish in formalism and meaningless rounds of religious activities. To such a church, Christ is still dead.

*Creditor:* A creditor is someone to whom you owe something. In this case, the death of the husband created a debt for this woman. This means that the death of Christ has created a debt for the church. What debt could this mean?

Paul understood that the death of Christ made him a debtor.

> "I am a debtor both to Greeks and to barbarians, both to wise and to unwise. So, as much as is in me, I am ready to preach the gospel to you who are in Rome also" **Romans 1:14, 15 (NKJV)**

The debt the church owes is to both the Greeks and barbarians, both to the wise and unwise. In other words, the whole world. But in a local sense, your local church owes a debt to your community, your neighbors and friends.

Your community has a right to ask, "What role do you have in the life of the community? Justify yourself. Show us that you are worthy. What are you doing for us? How are you helping us? How are you an asset rather than a liability?"

These are the questions every local church must answer. Your community has a right to know who you are, why you exist and what your business is. You and your local church owe a debt to your community.

*Two Sons:* The two sons represent church members. The number two indicates that there are two classes of people in the church. The following texts are about two sons and refer to the different experiences of church members.

> "But what do you think? A man had two sons, and he came to the first and said, 'Son, go, work today in my vineyard.' He answered and said, 'I will not,' but afterward he regretted it and went. Then he came to the second and said likewise. And he answered and said, 'I go, sir,' but he did not go. Which of the two did the will of his father?" They said to Him, "The first." Jesus said to them, "Assuredly, I say to you that tax collectors and harlots enter the kingdom of God before you" **Matthew 21:28-31 (NKJV)**

In this passage the contrast is between talkers and doers. Some in the church talk a good story but do not do much. There are others who quietly go about doing good. Church members are represented by the two sons in the story of the prodigal son. Each son represents a class of church members.

> "Then He said: 'A certain man had two sons. And the younger of them said to his father,

'Father, give me the portion of goods that falls to me.' So he divided to them his livelihood. And not many days after, the younger son gathered all together, journeyed to a far country, and there wasted his possessions with prodigal living. But when he had spent all, there arose a severe famine in that land, and he began to be in want. Then he went and joined himself to a citizen of that country, and he sent him into his fields to feed swine. And he would gladly have filled his stomach with the pods that the swine ate, and no one gave him anything.

'But when he came to himself, he said, 'How many of my father's hired servants have bread enough and to spare, and I perish with hunger! I will arise and go to my father, and will say to him, "Father, I have sinned against heaven and before you, and I am no longer worthy to be called your son. Make me like one of your hired servants."'

"And he arose and came to his father. But when he was still a great way off, his father saw him and had compassion, and ran and fell on his neck and kissed him. And the son said to him, 'Father, I have sinned against heaven and in your sight, and am no longer worthy to be called your son.'

"But the father said to his servants, 'Bring out the best robe and put it on him, and put a ring on his hand and sandals on his feet. And bring the fatted calf here and kill it, and let us eat and be merry; for this my son was dead and is alive again; he was lost and is found.' And they began to be merry.

"Now his older son was in the field. And as he came and drew near to the house, he heard music and dancing. So he called one of the servants and asked what these things meant. And he said to him, 'Your brother has come, and because he has received him safe and sound, your father has killed the fatted calf.'

"But he was angry and would not go in. Therefore his father came out and pleaded with him. So he answered and said to his father, 'Lo, these many years I have been serving you; I never transgressed your commandment at any time; and yet you never gave me a young goat that I might make merry with my friends. But as soon as this son of yours came, who has devoured your livelihood with harlots, you killed the fatted calf for him.'

"And he said to him, 'Son, you are always with me, and all that I have is yours. It was right that we should make merry and be glad, for your brother was dead and is alive again, and was lost and is found'" **Luke 15:11-32 (NKJV)**

In this story, both boys were lost. One in the church and the other in a far country.

Church members are also symbolized as being the children of Abraham.

"For it is written that Abraham had two sons: the one by a bondwoman, the other by a freewoman" **Galatians 4:22 (NKJV)**

Here again two sons represent different types of church members. Some are still in bondage as represented by Ishmael and the others are free because they have been born again. These church members are represented by Isaac.

*Slaves:* The creditor is coming to make slaves of this woman's sons. The world is coming to make slaves of church members. The church is daily being converted to the world. We see members drifting into sin. Compromise within the church is rampant. Church members are becoming slaves to fashion. Church members are becoming slaves to appetite. Church members are becoming slaves to alcohol. Church members are becoming slaves to entertainment and ease.

The church might well cry out in distress for her cold experience and loss of her members. The world has come and has stolen the hearts and minds of many church members. This is the condition of the Laodicean church which exactly describes the condition of the church today.

## 2 Kings 4:2

Look at 2 Kings 4:2 to see the problem develop further.

> "So Elisha said to her, "What shall I do for you? Tell me, what do you have in the house?" And she said, "Your maidservant has nothing in the house but a jar of oil" 2 **Kings 4:2 (NKJV)**

*Elisha:* Elisha was the spiritual leader of his day and symbolically represents the authority and leadership of the church. Elisha represents church administration at its various levels. It is natural for a local church to turn to the conference administration for help in times of distress.

*What Shall I Do for You?* This indicates some limitation on the part of church administration. Just as the Christian experience of one person cannot substitute for another; just so, church administration cannot compensate for any deficits to be found in your congregation. The role of church administrators is primarily advisory. Church leaders may counsel with us, pray with us and study the problem with us but in the end, the local church still has the problem. In the end, the local church must be the institution to take care of the problem.

*What do You Have in The House?* This is a logical question. It calls for an inventory of resources. It asks, "What assets exist at the local level that can be utilized to help solve the problem?"

*Your Maidservant Has Nothing:* Now here is a dishonest assessment of the situation. This lady had two sons but didn't value them as highly as she should. She didn't mention them. Her sons should have been counted among her assets. So it is today in local churches. The pastor is shouldered with too many of the responsibilities that should be carried by church members. The church members are less and less involved in the life of the church.

*A Jar of Oil:* I suspect this is a complaint rather than a boast. The lady only had a jar of oil. Oil in scripture represents the Holy Spirit. Anointing with oil was used to symbolize the anointing by the Holy Spirit. It is to be applied in the name of the Lord.

> 'I have found My servant David; With My holy oil I have anointed him" **Psalm 89:20 (NKJV)**

> 'Is anyone among you sick? Let him call for the elders of the church, and let them pray over him, anointing him with oil in the name of the Lord" **James 5:14 (NKJV)**

This connection between oil and the Holy Spirit is mentioned in Testimonies to Ministers in the following passage.

> "Read and study the fourth chapter of Zechariah. The two olive trees empty the golden oil out of themselves through the golden pipes into the golden bowl from which the lamps of the sanctuary are fed. The golden oil represents the Holy Spirit. With this oil God's ministers are to be constantly supplied, that they, in turn, may impart it to church. "Not by might, nor by power, but by My Spirit, saith the Lord of hosts." ***Testimonies to Ministers and Gospel Workers 188***

*Oil Creates Light:* Look at the role of oil a bit more. It was used in lamps to create light. What does light represent? Light represents good works.

> "Let your light so shine before men, that they may see your good works and glorify your Father in heaven." **Matthew 5:16 (NKJV)**

In this next passage light describes the work of health evangelism.

> "Is this not the fast that I have chosen:
> To loose the bonds of wickedness,
> To undo the heavy burdens,
> To let the oppressed go free,
> And that you break every yoke?
> Is it not to share your bread with the hungry,
> And that you bring to your house the poor who are cast out;
> When you see the naked, that you cover him,
> And not hide yourself from your own flesh?
> Then your light shall break forth like the morning,
> Your healing shall spring forth speedily,
> And your righteousness shall go before you;
> The glory of the LORD shall be your rear guard.
> If you extend your soul to the hungry
> And satisfy the afflicted soul,
> Then your light shall dawn in the darkness,
> And your darkness shall be as the noonday" **Isaiah 58:6-8, 10 (NKJV)**

Helping people stop smoking, eat right, lose weight and exercise are all comprehended in loosening the bonds of wickedness, undoing heavy burdens, and letting the oppressed go free. Isaiah 58 describes health evangelism. Health evangelism is good works, and it results in light.

The lady in this story was low on oil. This means that this local church was low on the presence and influence of the Holy Spirit. It was a cold and lifeless church with members disappearing out the back door. This church was deficient in good works. The members were not involved in any outreach activities. They didn't have a health evangelism program. Look at the advice Elisha gave in this crisis situation.

## 2 Kings 4:3

"Then he said, "Go, borrow vessels from everywhere, from all your neighbors—empty vessels; do not gather just a few." **2 Kings 4:3 (NKJV)**

*Go:* Here is beginning of the solution to the problem. The word is "GO." This means get busy. Do something. It represents action. The problem in the local church is a lack of action. The answer to the problem is increased activity. Start to do something. The instruction doesn't stop here. Very specific instruction is given.

*Borrow Vessels:* Vessels in scripture represent people.

"But in a great house there are not only vessels of gold and silver, but also of wood and clay, some for honor and some for dishonor. Therefore if anyone cleanses himself from the latter, he will be a vessel for honor, sanctified and useful for the Master, prepared for every good work" **2 Timothy 2:20, 21 (NKJV)**

"And the vessel that he made of clay was marred in the hand of the potter; so he made it again into another vessel, as it seemed good to the potter to make.

"O house of Israel, can I not do with you as this potter?" says the LORD. "Look, as the clay is in the potter's hand, so are you in My hand, O house of Israel! **Jeremiah 18:4, 6 (NKJV)**

"I am forgotten like a dead man, out of mind; I am like a broken vessel." **Psalm 31:12 (NKJV).**

The vessels are to be borrowed. They are not to be bought but borrowed. Borrowing is an act of asking. In our work with those whose lives need to be changed by health evangelism we are to invite and ask. We want to borrow them for a few days to introduce them to

God who has the power to change their lives. No force is to be used in the work of God.

The word "Go" indicates that action was necessary. The action was to involve people in the community around the church. Next, we learn the scope of the work.

*Everywhere, from all your neighbors:* The activities of the local church are to involve neighbors. This indicates that the local church is supposed to do a work in its own community. Oh, yes, you need to support global missions and radio and TV ministries, but your most important work and first responsibility is to your neighbors.

All neighbors are included in the instruction. All neighbors are to be the field of labor. But there is a certain restriction which is placed on the selection of a neighbor to be served. There is a form of discrimination and exclusiveness which is to be practiced. The labor is to be confined to *empty* vessels.

*Empty vessels:* Empty vessels represent people who feel empty. These are not the proud, egotistical people who are brimming with self-esteem. Proud people think they have a power within themselves that will propel them to success. Empty vessels are those who realize their own weakness. They have tried to succeed on their own but have found their own efforts to be inadequate. These are the ones who are hungering and thirsting after righteousness. Our health evangelism activities should be confined to those who need and want help.

*Do not borrow just a few:* Here is another reminder of the scope of activity. The local church is not to be content with feeble, intermittent, or spasmodic efforts. The church is to reach every interested and eligible person in the community.

The admonition to do a thorough work is emphasized three times in this one verse with the words, "everywhere," "all your neighbors" and "do not gather a few."

## 2 Kings 4:4

"And when you have come in, you shall shut the door behind you and your sons; then pour it into all those vessels, and set aside the full ones" **2 Kings 4:4 (NKJV)**

*When you have come in, you shall shut the door behind you.* Come in where? In the house of this woman. The house is the church building itself. Here is a strong indication that the major emphasis in any Holy Spirit related activity is to be in the local church itself. This is why I do not like to conduct health evangelism in any other setting than the local church. The church is the Christian's home. The sooner a person gets there the better off he or she will be.

To the extent that you conduct health evangelism in high school auditoriums or other public places, the church doesn't get the recognition, church members do not help, and people do not get into the church. It is harder to get people to come to your local church for traditional doctrinal presentations. It is easier to get people to come to your local church for health evangelism activities. The church is designated by this scripture as the place for evangelistic activity.

I think this is also indicated by the shutting the door behind you. In this story a very special miracle is about to take place and it only occurs in connection with the church. The church is God's appointed agency for the salvation of the world. This activity is to take place in the church.

*Then pour into all those vessels:* Here is where the advice seems illogical. This woman only had a jar of oil. How is she going to pour out into all those vessels? If she put a teaspoon of oil in each vessel, she wouldn't have enough to go around. If she poured her entire jar of oil into one big vessel, she would only be able to recover a small amount if she tried to get it all back.

In God's instruction as to how we should work and what we should do, there is always room for doubt, questioning and speculation. The instruction given here seems unrealistic and unreasonable, but it is very specific, and it is clear. Here is where faith is to be exercised.

The pouring out is especially significant and needs some further exploration. The goal here is to fill the vessels with oil which is synonymous with filling people with the Holy Spirit. The miracle is only going to occur when the pouring begins. This lady didn't want to lose the little bit of oil she did have. She could have placed the jar of oil on a board that stretched across the opening of a 50-gallon drum. She could have prayed for God to cause the jar to overflow with oil so that the little bit she had wouldn't be risked, wasted, or lost.

In other words, the lady could have asked or prayed for an abundance of the oil to spill over the sides of the jar. She could have asked for oil above and beyond the small amount she had, without risking her own pitifully small supply.

This is a critical principle in spreading the Gospel. The Holy Spirit is dispensed by God in proportion to our efforts to work in God's cause in spreading the Good News. If we do not give away what we have, we will never get any more. If you have too little of the Holy Spirit in your local church, the key to getting an abundant outpouring from God is not found in praying for more of the Holy Spirit but by doing something with the pitifully small amount you have.

This principle is made perfectly clear in these selected passages.

> "The capacity for receiving the holy oil from the two olive trees which empty themselves, is by the receiver emptying that holy oil out of himself in word and in action to supply the necessities of other souls. Work, precious, satisfying work--to be constantly receiving and constantly imparting! The capacity for receiving is only kept up by imparting." **S.D.A. Bible Commentary Vol. 4, 1180.**

"Our mission to the world is not to serve or please ourselves; we are to glorify God by co-operating with Him to save sinners. We are to ask blessings from God that we may communicate to others. The capacity for receiving is preserved only by imparting. We cannot continue to receive heavenly treasure without communicating to those around us." *Christ's Object Lessons 142-143*

Church members are like pipes through which the Holy Spirit flows to others. If the faucet is shut off nothing will flow through the pipe. If the spigot is open, there is flow. You may be just a small section of pipe in the plumbing of the church but there is an unlimited amount of the Holy Spirit that can flow through you to bless others.

*Set aside the full ones:* Is there ever a sense that we set aside those for whom we are working? Certainly! As soon as people become filled with the Holy Spirit it is time to set them beside us so they too can help us work for others. This is not setting aside people to discard them. We set them aside because we no longer need to work over them. They themselves are filled with the Holy Spirit and are enabled to impart the Holy Spirit to others.

As soon as a person has been converted it is time to put them to work. There is something they can do. They should become part of a team so they will not work independently or unwisely.

"Just as soon as a church is organized, the members should be set to work, taught to go forth in God-given power to find others and tell them of the story of redeeming love. The power of the gospel is to come upon the companies raised up, fitting them for service. Some of the new converts will be so filled with the power of the Lord that they will at once enter the work, imparting that which they have received." *Vol. 5 Manuscript Releases 331*

"I saw that the servants of God should not go over and over the same field of labor, but should be searching out souls in new places. Those who are already established in the truth should not demand so much of their labor; for they ought to be able to stand alone, and strengthen others about them, while the messengers of God visit the dark and lonely places, setting the truth before those who are not now enlightened as to the present truth." *Early Writings 104*

Now for the results of this story.

## 2 Kings 4:5

"So she went from him and shut the door behind her and her sons, who brought the vessels to her; and she poured it out" **2 Kings 4:5 (NKJV)**

*So she went:* This is the correct response. The first advice was, "Go." So she went. We know from the previous verses that this corrective activity occurred behind closed doors in the church. Notice the next phrase.

*Her sons, who brought the vessels to her:* Here is a surprise. The work of bringing people into the church is not the work of the pastor. It is the work of church members. This is why health evangelism activities are not designed correctly unless they are designed to create an interface between church members and the public. This one-on-one interaction between the sons of the woman, (church members) and the empty vessels occurs in the setting of the local church.

*And she poured out*: This represents activity for the lost. For those who have spiritual needs, those who have physical needs, and those who have bad habits and addictions. They can change their behavior once they have a relationship with God and are filled with the Holy Spirit. This occurs in the local church.

## 2 Kings 4:6

> "Now it came to pass, when the vessels were full, that she said to her son, "Bring me another vessel." And he said to her, "There is not another vessel." So the oil ceased 2 **Kings 4:6 (NKJV)**

*Now it came to pass:* There is a lot to understand in these few words. The work of God in the earth takes time. Time, effort, and means are required. We should not become weary in doing good.

*"she said to her son:"* Perhaps this is a sad part of the story. There were two sons to begin with, but now she appears to be working with just one son. Some like to work in the church. Some like to shirk in the church. Not all are wise virgins. There are foolish virgins. Not all will actually go and work in the vineyard. Perhaps this is a sad reminder that not all who begin the work will finish the work.

*"Bring me another vessel"*: What a change has taken place in the attitude and experience of this woman! At the beginning of this story, she was crying and worried about the state of her home, and family. Now this woman is excited. She likes the work she is doing. The work is satisfying and effective. It is enjoyable. When the work appears to be done and there are no more vessels to be filled, she urges her remaining son to "Bring me another vessel".

Working for souls is very exciting and satisfying. The more you do the more you want to do. It is exciting to see lives changed through the wonder-working power of the Holy Spirit. Start doing health evangelism and you will create an excited, vibrant church that loves to reach out to the community.

*"There is not another vessel"*: This indicates that the sons of this woman did a thorough work. They were busy. They scoured the neighborhood to find empty vessels. The work didn't cease until everyone who was empty was filled. And so it will be in the last days. The gospel must go to every kindred, tongue, and nation. It will largely be done one

community at a time. But there is an end to the work. Once everyone who is going to respond to the call decides to follow God, the work will be finished.

*So the oil ceased:* How comforting to know that there will be enough oil until every empty vessel is filled. There will be enough converting power of the Holy Spirit until all have decided one way or another. The oil will cease someday. That day is spoken of in Matthew and Revelation.

> "And this gospel of the kingdom will be preached in all the world as a witness to all the nations, and then the end will come" **Matthew 24:14 (NKJV)**

> "He who is unjust, let him be unjust still; he who is filthy, let him be filthy still; he who is righteous, let him be righteous still; he who is holy, let him be holy still." **Revelation 22:11 (NKJV)**

## 2 Kings 4:7

> "Then she came and told the man of God. And he said, "Go, sell the oil and pay your debt; and you and your sons live on the rest." **2 Kings 4:7 (NKJV)**

*Pay your debt:* How can anything we do pay our debt? Our debt was paid once and for all on Calvary. The abundance of oil that was produced through this miracle was in no way the property of the widow. It was God's oil and how could that in any way pay her debt?

The debt mentioned here is not the "eternal debt" we owe our Saviour but the debt we owe our friends and neighbors. In our working for them we do gain reward. Stars in our crowns and a hearty "Well done" from Jesus at his second coming.

"His lord said to him, 'Well done, good and faithful servant; you were faithful over a few things, I will make you ruler over many things. Enter into the joy of your lord.'" **Matthew 25:21 (NKJV)**

*And live:* The gift of God is eternal life, but we cooperate with Him in working for the betterment and salvation of our neighbors and friends. This is the Biblical model of health evangelism. Church members working out of the local church in the surrounding neighborhood finding people in need and providing whatever services they can and pointing to God as the agent of behavior change in human life.

"These are words which Christ addresses to his redeemed people. He invites them to become patient toilers in a field which calls for self-denying labor; but it is a glorious work, and one that Heaven smiles upon. Faithful work is more acceptable to God than the most zealous formal worship. True worship consists in working together with Christ. Prayers, exhortations, and talk are cheap fruits, which are frequently tied on; but fruits that are manifested in good works, in caring for the needy, the fatherless, and widows, are genuine, and grow naturally upon a good tree." *The Signs of the Times 02-17-1887*

# 16

# Best Weigh: Nutrition and Weigh Loss Program

BEST WEIGH IS A WEIGHT MANAGEMENT AND NUTRITION PROGRAM designed by the author of this book that incorporates the evangelistic elements presented here. Best Weigh incorporates sound nutrition and exercise elements but also incorporates spiritual components. Data collection and analysis validate the principles advocated here. Best Weigh is now owned and distributed by Eric Nelson, MD. See Appendix D for additional details.

A detailed look at Best Weigh is presented here to illustrate the practical ways in which evangelistic principles can be incorporated into a health program.

The Best Weigh weight management component focuses on limiting caloric intake and promoting moderate exercise. Nutrition education focuses on limiting fats, sugars, and flesh foods while at the same time promoting fruits, grains, nuts, and vegetables. Nutritional supplements are discouraged. The Best Weigh program meets once a week for 10 weeks.

A typical program consists of a weigh-in followed by a 30-minute PowerPoint illustrated nutritional lecture. This is followed by a 10-15-minute spiritual presentation by the pastor of the church. This talk is focused on spiritual dynamics behavior change.

The last half of each session takes place in small groups of not more than six participants hosted by two Seventh-day Adventist helpers. These helpers facilitate discussion and decision-making. Specific dietary changes for each participant are discussed and determined. Helpers follow instructions contained in the Best Weigh Helpers Guide. Participants are dismissed to go home from the small groups.

The nutritional information provided in Best Weigh is general in nature and is consistent with the recommendations of the American Dietetic Association and the dietary principles espoused by the Seventh-day Adventist church.

It is preferable for the nutritional lectures to be presented by a health professional who understands the basics of nutrition. Informed laypersons can give the nutritional lectures in the absence of a health professional. The nutritional information is contained in 10 PowerPoint presentations.

Participants are encouraged to avoid snacks between meals including diet soda, and gum. Participants are also asked to eliminate one or two food items from the diet that are high in calories and nutritionally questionable. These foods are allowed once a week without penalty.

The exercise recommended in Best Weigh is walking for a minimum 30 minutes, 5 days a week. Bicycling and swimming are acceptable alternatives to walking. Duration is emphasized over pace. A target safety-number for maximum recommended heart rate is calculated by subtracting a participant's age from 180. This simple calculation is in line with other more complicated methods of calculating an ideal target heart rate. The Best Weigh "safety number" is a bit more restrictive for older individuals and a bit more liberal for younger persons.

Best Weigh is overtly evangelistic because it encourages each participant to develop a new or deeper relationship with God. Best Weigh is designed with the confidence that Jesus provides the power to achieve permanent weight loss and to eat in a healthful manner. The evangelistic components of Best Weigh include, daily Bible study, prayer at mealtimes, coming repeatedly to a Seventh-day Adventist church, daily contact with Seventh-day Adventist helpers, and repeated exposure to the pastor of the local church who makes the brief spiritual presentation each week.

## Materials and Methods:

The materials used in the Best Weigh program consist of a Director's Manual containing specific instruction on how to organize and conduct the Best Weigh program.

Each participant receives a Best Weigh Workbook. By the end of the program the Workbook contains ten handouts totaling about 100 pages. Each handout summarizes the nutritional lecture material, contains quizzes, exercises, and a New Direction section where participants formalize their commitment to specific, self-determined, dietary changes. Recipes and tips on exercise are included in each handout. The last page is a list of seven Bible verse assignments for each day of the coming week.

The small group leaders are guided by the Best Weigh Helpers Guide. This document contains a copy of the entire Workbook as well as directions on how to conduct small groups. The Helpers Guide also contains all the answers to all the questions, quizzes, and exercises in the Workbook.

The materials include all the forms, The Registration Form, Group Weight Loss Record, Final Session Questionnaire and Follow-up Questionnaires. There are nametags and the Progress Card, and advertising aids including containing a sample brochure, letters to doctors, letters to alumni, newspaper advertisements, bulletin announcements and other handouts that promote Best Weigh.

Data concerning a person's compliance are collected on the participant's Progress Card. Best Weigh data are entered at the bestweigh.us website.

Participants and church members designated for data entry enter Best Weigh data into the database.

# Sample Score Card

| Name | | | | | | Week | Start Wt | | Wt End | |
|---|---|---|---|---|---|---|---|---|---|---|
| Number | Group | Dates | 12 | 13 | 14 | 15 | 16 | 17 | 18 | |
| Breakfast Score | | | | | | | | | | |
| Lunch Score | | | | | | | | | | |
| Dinner Score | | | | | | | | | | |
| Snack Score | | | | | | | | | | |
| Food Item to Avoid Score | | | | | | | | | | |
| Walking Score | | | | | | | | | | |
| Prayer Score | | | | | | | | | | |
| Inspirational Study Score | | | | | | | | | | |
| Contact Group Leader Score | | | | | | | | | | |
| Total Daily Score | | | | | | | | | | |

| Meal Score | | Walking Score | |
|---|---|---|---|
| Skipped a meal | 6 | 1 Hour and more | 6 |
| 75% Less | 5 | 45 Minutes | 5 |
| 50% Less | 4 | 30 Minutes | 4 |
| 25% Less | 3 | 15 Minutes | 1 |
| Same as Usual | 2 | Didn't Walk | 0 |
| 10% More | 1 | **Prayer at Meals** | |
| 25% More | 0 | 3 Times or More | 3 |
| **Snack Score** | | 2 Times | 2 |
| No Snacks | 4 | 1 Time | 1 |
| 1 Snack | 3 | No Prayer | 0 |
| 2 Snacks | 2 | **Inspirational Reading** | |
| 3 Snacks or more | 0 | You Read | 2 |
| **Food to Avoid** (FTA) | | You Didn't Read | 0 |
| Ate No FTA | 4 | **Called Best Weigh Helper** | |
| Ate 1 FTA | 2 | Yes You Called | 3 |
| Ate 2 FTA | 1 | No Call | 0 |
| Ate 3 FTA | 0 | | |

Each Progress Card contains data collected during one week of the program. Participants keep score of the amount eaten at each meal, the amount of exercise, between meals snacks, and the food item to avoid.

The progress card also provides a place to record various spiritual parameters. These include scores for prayer, Bible study, and contact with Seventh-day Adventist helpers by phone, in-person, or by texting.

The scores are self-reported estimates of each participant's compliance with the principles of Best Weigh. The Progress Card also contains an objectively determined Start Weight and End Weight obtained at the weekly, confidential weigh-ins throughout the program.

Data collected on each progress card is entered in a cloud based database accessed through www.bestweigh.us. Individual participants have access to their own data and can enter or modify their own data day by day during the program.

At each local Best Weigh program location, one or more church members are designated as data entry individuals. These church members enter data for people who are not computer literate or who choose not to record their own data into the database. These church members can review the progress of all the participants from that one church location. At the national level the Best Weigh webmaster and the author review all data from all programs.

## Study Population:

Participation in the national Best Weigh database is optional. Many Best Weigh results are never entered into the national database. The analysis presented here is based on 28 separate Best Weigh programs conducted at various times and places. These 28 Best Weigh programs were conducted in 20 different locations. (Some locations have conducted more than one Best Weigh event.)

Data sets were analyzed for 13 separate sites across Texas, four sites in Florida, and sites in Washington, and Ohio. Other places where Best Weigh programs have also been conducted but data NOT entered into the database include New York, Alabama, Oregon, Florida, Illinois, Michigan, Texas, and international sites in the UK and Australia.

For the present analysis, there were 524 individual participants. Some participants, over time attended more than one Best Weigh program. A few participants attended three or four Best Weigh programs. A total of 89 attendees were repeat participants.

In this analysis these repeat participants were included as if they were first time participants. By including repeat participants in this data analysis, we have a total of 613 participants in this study population. There were 113 men (18.4%) and 500 women (81.6%).

An important variable we measured was the Non-Adventist Person Visit (NAPV). A non-Adventist is counted every time he or she comes through the door of the Seventh-day Adventist church. The 28 Best Weigh programs generated a total of 4723 NAPV. This represents 4723 separate visits to the church by people who are not members of the church.

The NAPV is an important evangelistic measure. People do not become members of the church unless they become familiar with and are comfortable coming to church. If this important step can be achieved in a health evangelism program a big step toward baptism has taken place.

The NAPV is a useful denominator in determining economic value of a given program. In a recent Best Weigh conducted at the Crowley Seventh-day Adventist church the cost of the program was divided by the NAPV and it was discovered that the cost per NAPV was $2.36. A Health Evangelism program is a highly cost-effective method of bringing non-Adventists into the Seventh-day Adventist Church.

Attendance at many weight management programs drops off after the first few weeks. Best Weigh is no exception. The attrition rate is 11-15% for each of the first three sessions. At the beginning of the 4th session 60%-80% of the original audience remains. While occasional subsequent sessions are missed by a few individuals after the 4th session, the group largely remains stable throughout the remainder of the program. It has been noted that the attrition rate is higher for larger programs. The retention rate is greater in smaller programs.

An intake questionnaire administered the first session obtained baseline demographic data and determined some of the spiritual practices of the participants. Not all questions were answered by all participants and therefore some of the totals do not equal the total population who attended Best Weigh

The distribution of ages of men and women who attended the Best Weigh programs in this analysis is presented in Table 1. Best Weigh draws the most men and women in the 51-60 age groups but a number of the very young and very old are also represented.

| Table 1. Distribution of Best Weigh Participants by Age | | | | |
|---|---|---|---|---|
| Age Range | Women | Men | Total | Percent |
| 10-20 | 3 | 2 | 5 | 1.4 |
| 21-30 | 15 | 3 | 18 | 4.6 |
| 31-40 | 39 | 14 | 53 | 13.7 |
| 41-50 | 57 | 10 | 67 | 17.3 |
| 51-60 | 96 | 27 | 123 | 31.8 |
| 61-70 | 52 | 17 | 69 | 17.8 |
| 71-80 | 36 | 16 | 52 | 13.4 |
| Total | 298 | 89 | 387 | 100.0 |

The marital status was reported by 455 participants. This is displayed in Table 2.

| Table 2. Distribution of Best Weigh Participants by Marital Status | | |
|---|---|---|
| **Marital Status** | **Number** | **Percent** |
| Single | 70 | 15.4 |
| Married | 300 | 65.9 |
| Separated or divorced | 65 | 14.3 |
| Widowed | 20 | 4.4 |
| **Total** | **455** | **100.0** |

Church attendance prior to attending Best Weigh is one marker of religious conviction. Since Best Weigh has a strong spiritual component, it was hypothesized that Best Weigh might only be an attractive weight loss program for those who attend church regularly.

The spiritual emphasis found in Best Weigh does not appear to be a barrier to attendance for the unchurched population. Over 40% of Best Weigh participants do not regularly attend church. This would indicate that those with weight problems are comfortable attending a weight loss program that has a spiritual component. This is especially true if the spiritual emphasis is focused on overweight and obesity. The custom of church attendance of participants prior to taking Best Weigh is outlined in Table 3.

| Table 3. Distribution of Best Weigh Participants by Church Attendance | | |
|---|---|---|
| **Church Attendance** | **Number** | **Percent** |
| Rarely or Never attend Church | 256 | 41.8 |
| Quite often or Regularly attend Church | 357 | 58.2 |
| **Total** | **613** | **100.0** |

Best Weigh also determined the Bible study habits of participants before attending Best Weigh. The hypothesis was that Best Weigh might not be well attended by individuals who did not have regular Bible study habits. This turned out to not be a significant barrier. Over half the people who attend Best Weigh do not regularly read the Bible. These results are in Table 4

| Table 4. Distribution of Best Weigh Participants by Bible Study | | |
|---|---|---|
| **Bible Study** | **Number** | **Percent** |
| Rarely or Never read the Bible | 310 | 50.6 |
| Often or daily Bible study | 303 | 49.4 |
| **Total** | **613** | **100.0** |

The prayer practices of those who attend Best Weigh were determined at the beginning of the program. It was thought that Best Weigh might only attract people who had a religious bias and who already had strong spiritual practices. More than 40% of those who choose to attend Best Weigh do not regularly pray. These results are in Table 5.

| Table 5. Distribution of Best Weigh Participants by Prayer Practices | | |
|---|---|---|
| **Prayer Practices** | **Number** | **Percent** |
| Pray sometimes or less than once a day | 254 | 41.4 |
| Pray often or daily | 359 | 58.6 |
| **Total** | **613** | **100.0** |

It was desirable to determine how experienced the Best Weigh participants were with previous attempts to lose weight. Obese individuals are open to trying multiple different approaches to weight loss. Nearly two thirds of Best Weigh participants have previously tried to lose weight. These characteristics are presented in Table 6.

| Table 6. Best Weigh Participants by Previous Attempts to Lose Weight | | |
|---|---|---|
| **Previous Attempts to Lose Weight** | **Number** | **Percent** |
| None. This is the first attempt to lose weight | 227 | 37.0 |
| One or more previous attempts to lose weight | 386 | 63.0 |
| **Total** | **613** | **100.0** |

An attempt was made to determine the degree of confidence or optimism Best Weigh participants had, that the current attempt to lose weight was going to be successful. How confident were the participants that they would weigh less than they currently do two years from this current Best Weigh program? Nearly 84% of participants were confident that they would not weigh the same as they do now in two years' time.

The 16% who felt they would probably weigh the same in two years may have failed multiple times to be successful in keeping weight off. This may be a pessimistic yet realistic view of the difficulty of controlling appetite by human ability alone. This presents an opportunity to especially encourage the discouraged that God provides help to those who are weak. Best Weigh may be particularly effective for this group of discouraged people. The results are in Table 7.

| Table 7. What is the likelihood that you will weigh the same two years from now? | | |
|---|---|---|
| Will Weigh the Same Two Years from Now | Number | Percent |
| Probably or definitely not | 512 | 83.5 |
| Probably or most likely will weigh the same | 101 | 16.5 |
| Total | 613 | 100.0 |

# Results:

The data analyzed in this paper are limited to those who attended at least 7 sessions of Best Weigh. Attending 7 sessions indicates a high level of commitment to the program and a serious attempt to utilize Best Weigh principles in losing weight. The figures in the tables below are standardized so the comparisons are of 133 individuals in each column. The numbers are of the number of days on which individuals reported that particular score during the 10 weeks of the program

Each component of the Best Weigh program was found to enhance weight loss. In the analysis that follows, the adherence to Best Weigh recommendations are examined in 133 persons who lost 1-9 pounds during the program and in "133" of those who lost 10 or more pounds during the program. The analysis examines each program component in the order it appears on the Progress Card.

Meal scores are based on an eyeball assessment of the amount of food on the plate at mealtime. Second helpings are discouraged. There was no weighing or measuring of foods. There was no counting of calories. The less food eaten at a meal the higher the score.

Here is a comparison of those who lost 0-9 pounds and those who lost 10 pounds or more. Those who lost less weight were 44% more likely to eat the "Same as usual" at breakfast compared to those who lost 10 or more pounds. Best Weigh encourages eating a hearty breakfast. It was interesting to find that those who ate less than usual for breakfast lost the most weight.

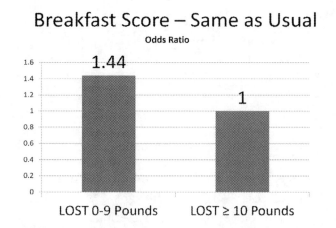

Here are those who those who ate "75% less" for breakfast. Those who lost more weight were more than twice as likely to eat "75% less" for breakfast.

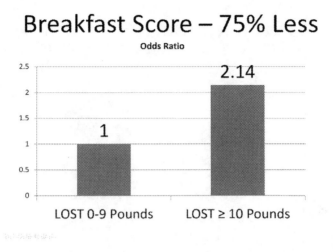

Those who lost the most weight were three time more likely to eat "75% less" for the evening meal compared with those who lost less than 10 pounds. Clearly, weight loss is related to the amount of food eaten at mealtime.

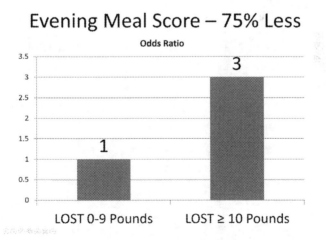

The Best Weigh program encourages participants to avoid all snacking between meals. We include diet drinks, chewing gum, and even "healthy" snacks in this recommendation. This figure shows that those who lost more weight were 50% more likely to avoid all snacks. Snacks represent extra calories and work against losing weight.

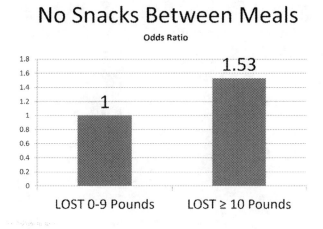

## No Snacks Between Meals

### Odds Ratio

There is a time to eat and a time not to eat. Overweight and obese individuals need to learn to deny the clamor for flavor in the mouth that occurs at various times during the day. Water is the best between meal snack. Best Weigh recommends 6-8 glasses of water between meals each day.

Many Best Weigh participants continue to eat snacks. It is clear from the next figure that snacking between meals keeps you from losing weight. This shows that those who lost less weight were 42% more likely to eat "Two Snacks" per day. This is another way show that calories count whenever you eat them.

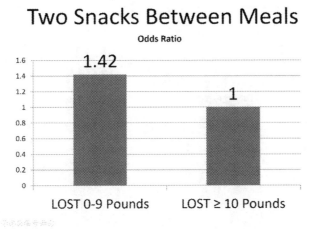

Best Weigh advocates "giving up" one or more foods that contribute to obesity. It is recommended that people give up things that are high in fat or sugar that are consumed excessively on most of the days of the week. Participants are allowed to have these "foods to avoid" once a week without penalty.

Many people chose to give up desserts while others chose to give up butter, margarine, or salad dressings. These choices are formalized in writing on the first session of Best Weigh. Those who lost more weight were 32% more likely to stay away from the "Food Items to Avoid" than those who lost less weight.

The next figure shows that those who give into temptation are much less likely to lose weight. Here we compare those who had two of the "Food Items to Avoid" during the week in addition to the one allowed. Those who lost less weight were nearly 50% more likely to have the "Food Item to Avoid" compared with those who lost more weight.

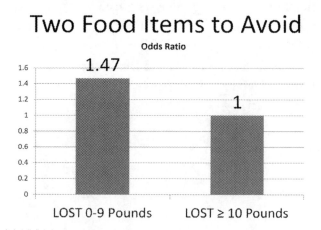

Exercise is an important component of any weight loss program. The extra exercise burns off a few more calories. Exercise also maintains a normal if not slightly enhanced metabolic rate that keeps those pounds coming off even though calories have been restricted in the diet.

Best Weigh recommends walking a minimum of 30 minutes, 5 days a week. Extra points are gained for walking 45 minutes or an hour a day. Best Weigh demonstrates that the more you walk the more weight you lose. Those who lost more weight were 23% more likely to walk the recommended 30 minutes per day.

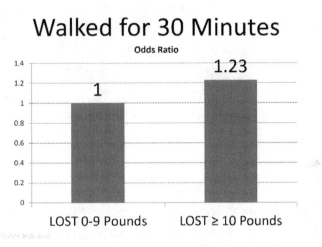

Those who lost more weight were 64% more likely to walk for the bonus 45 minutes than those who lost less weight.

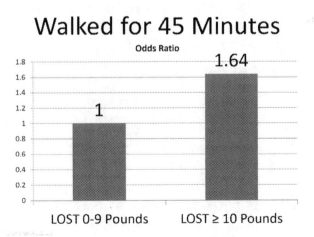

Not surprisingly, those who lost more weight were nearly twice as likely to walk for one full hour compared to those who lost less weight.

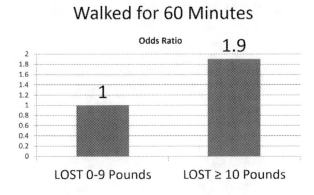

## Walked for 60 Minutes

Up to this point, the results of Best Weigh are exactly what you would expect from a weight management program. If you eat less and exercise more, you will lose weight. The less you eat and the more you exercise the more weight you will lose.

Best Weigh is a health evangelism program. What has never been examined before in a Seventh-day Adventist program are variables that pertain to the evangelistic components of the program including prayer, Bible study, and frequent contact with Seventh-day Adventist helpers. These data will be examined next.

Prayer is an important component of Best Weigh. Participants are encouraged to pray at mealtimes. The prayers are in part, expressions of gratitude for God's provision of food, but the prayers are also requests for deliverance from an unhealthy appetite.

In the 28 Best Weigh programs reported here, a total of 13,197 prayers were offered. The 87 SDA participants offered 1953 prayers (average 22 prayers/SDA participant). The 526 Non-SDA participants offered

11,244 prayers (average 21 prayers/ Non-SDA participant). Best Weigh is a program that results in much prayer.

Prayer results in more weight loss. Those who lost more weight were 25% more likely to pray three times a day compared to those who lost less weight.

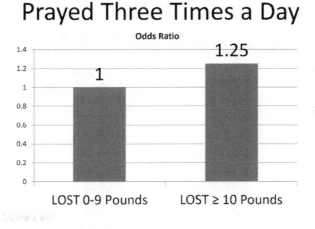

Those who lost less weight were 22% more likely to pray only once a day.

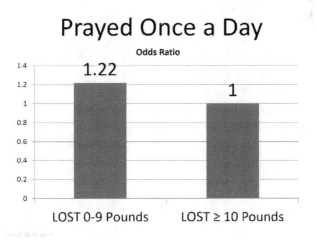

Best Weigh encourages daily Bible study. Specific scripture assignments are made for each day of the program. These Bible verses have a spiritual application to weight management. Each participant is encouraged to analyze the Bible verses assigned to discover this specific application of the Bible to the issue of weight loss.

In the 28 Best Weigh programs, the Bible was studied 11,224 times by all participants. The 87 SDA participants were responsible for 1724 (average 20 times/SDA participant) of these studies and the Non-SDA participants studied the Bible 9500 times (average 18 times/participant).

Daily Bible study is an important contributor to successful weight loss. Those who lost more weight were 21% more likely to study their Bible study assignment for the day compared with those who lost less weight.

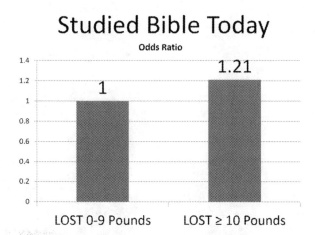

Best Weight participants are encouraged to call Seventh-day Adventist helpers on a daily basis to report progress, whether good or bad, and to receive encouragement.

These helpers are not professional counselors, but they are given some instruction on phone etiquette and have been prepared by reading the chapters, "In Contact with Others," and "Helping the Tempted," from the Ministry of Healing by Ellen G. White.

In the 28 Best Weigh programs a total of 6511 phone calls occurred between participants and the Seventh-day Adventist helpers. The 526 Non-SDA participants made 5403 calls to SDA helpers for encouragement (average of 10 calls per participant). The 87 SDA participants made 1108 calls to SDA helpers for encouragement (average 12.7 calls per participant).

Calling helpers not only creates friendships with those who come to the church for help but this frequent contact also results in increased weight loss. Those who lost more weight were 50% more likely to contact their SDA helper than those who lost less weight.

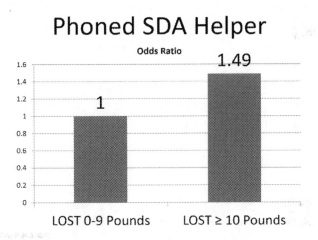

Measuring the impact of prayer, Bible study, and contact with church members on weight loss expands our understanding of behavior change. To the extent that health programs conducted by Seventh-day Adventists omit evangelistic components, just to that extent they are limiting the successful outcome of the programs. To the extent that health programs conducted by Seventh-day Adventists omit evangelistic components, just to that extent they are secular programs that merely duplicate secular programs that are widely available.

# Discussion

A health program is designed to modify the lifestyle of individuals so that improved health and longer life are the result. An evangelistic program is designed to bring eternal life to those who are dead in trespasses and sin. Those who initially benefit from a secular health program will still die. Those who are saved through a relationship with Christ will live forever.

A health evangelism program is designed to successfully and permanently improve the lifestyle through the power that a relationship with Christ brings into the life. Health evangelism is an intensely practical application of Christian principles to the harmful habits and addictions that shorten life. Health evangelism programs are usually focused on a single problem and should be seen as examples of problem-specific evangelism.

The Best Weigh program has several components that qualify it as a unique example of health evangelism. These are:

1.  Best Weigh is conducted in Seventh-day Adventist Churches
2.  Best Weigh utilizes daily Bible study as an adjunct to diet and exercise
3.  Best Weigh recommends prayer three times a day to seek God's help in controlling the appetite.
4.  Best Weigh brings the public in contact with a Seventh-day Adventist pastor who has a short homily at each session.
5.  Best Weigh creates an interface between the public and Seventh-day Adventist church members who bring encouragement and support to those seeking help with weight management.
6.  Best Weigh encourages follow-up visits in participant's homes at three monthly intervals for a period of at least one year. Many people inquire regarding the beliefs of the Seventh-day Adventist church in the privacy of their own homes.
7.  Best Weigh introduces people to 11 of the 28 fundamental beliefs of the Seventh-day Adventist church.

8. Best Weigh is scientifically sound. A health evangelism program that is based on sound scientific principles strengthens the credibility of our spiritual message. Sound science contributes to confidence in the soundness of our spirituality.

9. Best Weigh is economical. The low cost of Best Weigh is quickly perceived by the non-Seventh-day Adventists as being a great return on their investment. They are refreshed to see that the program is not driven by a profit motive. The Best Weigh participants sense a spirit of sacrifice and volunteerism (servanthood) on the part of the health professionals, church members and pastor. This contributes to the evangelistic potential of the program.

The attrition rate of any health program is of concern. Several factors affect drop-out rates. One factor is the cost of the program. Another factor in Best Weigh may be the offence of the gospel.

An expensive program always has a lower attrition rate than an inexpensive program. A high-cost program selects from the public those who are highly motivated enough to invest a large sum of money to achieve success. An expensive program serves a much smaller portion of the problematic population than an inexpensive program. An inexpensive program such as Best Weigh attracts larger numbers of participants, but because a person has so little invested in the program drop-outs are more likely to occur.

Best Weigh is also an overtly spiritual program. Some are offended with the mention of God and the help that Jesus brings to the person struggling with appetite issues. Fortunately, there are dozens of Godless weight management programs a person can chose to attend if they do not want to be connected with the God of the universe as presented in the Best Weigh program.

There are several unanswered questions regarding Best Weigh and all health evangelism programs that are conducted using the principles of health evangelism outlined in this book. These questions can only be answered if more complete and extensive data collection becomes a component of both health evangelism programs and traditional evangelistic series.

One unanswered question is that of baptisms. Will a person who attends Best Weigh eventually be baptized? One step indicating an increased potential for baptism would be an individual's susceptibility to attend traditional evangelistic meetings.

There is some preliminary evidence that Best Weigh participants are much more likely to attend traditional evangelistic meetings than the general public. When presented with advertising and personal invitations to attend a series of traditional evangelistic meetings at the same church where Best Weigh was conducted, Best Weigh alumni have responded in higher numbers than those who simply receive advertisements at home in the mail.

This is because the Best Weigh alumni have already been to the church several times and have become friends with several Seventh-day Adventist helpers. Best Weigh alumni know that the church puts on quality programming. Many have found a new or deeper relationship with God because of the spiritual elements in the Best Weigh program.

Will Best Weigh alumni be more likely to be baptized after attending evangelistic meetings? Will Best Weigh alumni be more likely to become active members of the church? Will Best Weigh alumni have a higher retention rate a year after baptism than newly baptized members who didn't have a multi-week exposure to SDAs in a health evangelism program such as Best Weigh?

These questions can be answered with further research. Efforts should be made to discover the most efficient (not necessarily the quickest) methods of evangelism in our health conscious but increasingly gluttonous society. Health evangelism will receive a broader endorsement from the church when it is shown to be an effective activity initiating new believers into the family of God.

# 17

# Evaluating Health Evangelism

## The Importance of Data

WE LIVE IN A SOCIETY WHERE EVERYTHING IS DRIVEN BY DATA. THE more you know about anything, the better decisions you will make. Products have lengthy specification sheets that describe the product in great detail. Your doctor makes a diagnosis and recommendations based on your history, physical examination, lab tests, and X-rays. The effectiveness of any program is demonstrated by some type of evaluation.

The church measures the effectiveness of evangelistic efforts by the number of baptisms that follow a series of meetings. The church is also highly efficient in counting money. As previously discussed, there are several intermediate steps that usually take place before a person is baptized. These intermediate steps are not measured by the church at any level or in any detail.

Health evangelism is more involved with the several phases of candidate development prior to baptism. For this reason, baptism is not the best measure of the effectiveness of health evangelism.

Many measures of health status have been developed by the scientific community. There are literally thousands of tests which can confirm any one of hundreds of diseases. It is valuable to measure some of these variables on people who attend health evangelism programs.

Improvements in blood chemistries, blood sugars, weight, and blood pressure are important markers that indicate improvement in physical health for your program participants.

Measures of progress on the evangelistic/spiritual side of health evangelism are different, poorly defined, and are not routinely collected. Until these important evangelistic variables are developed and measured, the full effectiveness of health evangelism will not be known or appreciated.

It is necessary to identify and measure the unique spiritual variables of health evangelism. One reason health evangelism has not advanced in the Seventh-day Adventist church is because no one has proven the effectiveness of health evangelism. What needs to be measured? What are health evangelism variables?

The most basic variable that needs to be measured is the number of non-Adventists who attend a program or "non-Adventist person visit" or NAPV. (Guest visit or GV would be a more euphemistic if somewhat less specific designation for this variable.)

Non-Adventists may be identified on your registration form. You might include a question that asks for a person's preferred religious affiliation. Have a short list that might include Baptist, Methodist, Catholic, Muslim, Jewish, Seventh-day Adventist, Assembly of God, Protestant, and "other."

You count the non-Adventists every time they come through the church door to attend your program. If a non-Adventist comes to all 10 sessions of a program, that counts as 10 NAPV. If two people come five times, that totals 10 NAPV as well. If ten people come only once, that also counts as 10 NAPV.

The NAPV is a more valuable number than the total number of people who attend a program. You are trying to document the impact of a program on the non-Adventist community. You will never be able to isolate the impact on non-Adventists until you count them.

The NAPV should be determined for traditional evangelistic series as well as health evangelism programs. In order to compare the effectiveness of any two programs it is necessary to generate the NAPV from each type of meeting.

The NAPV may not seem as important as counting baptisms, but baptisms never occur unless there have been dozens of NAPV that preceded the baptism. Health evangelism generates NAPV, but the church counts baptisms. The effectiveness of health evangelism cannot be known unless the NAPV totals for a program are measured and recorded.

## Calculations using the NAPV

The NAPV is a number that has many other useful purposes—particularly as related to cost or expense of a program. An important figure to generate is the cost required to produce a single NAPV. For example, if you had 50 people register for a program. After 10 sessions there were 400 NAPV (perfect attendance for 10 weeks would have generated 500 NAPV) and the cost of advertising was $300 and the cost of materials was $200. Expenses total $500 and you had 400 NAPV.

By simply dividing the dollars by the NAPV you generate the cost of each NAPV. In this example you would calculate the cost of a single NAPV by dividing the total cost of the program by the number of NAPV: $500/400 NAPV = $1.25/NAPV. If you charged more than $1.25 as a registration fee you would generate a profit for the program. Each NAPV actually created income for the program and your church.

It has been my experience that health evangelism programs generate actual income per NAPV. Traditional evangelism activities often cost hundreds of dollars per NAPV. Church administration will take notice of NAPV if we start generating them. NAPVs are a prerequisite to baptism. By knowing the NAPV values of a health evangelism program, you are beginning to show that health evangelism creates steps that lead to baptism.

# Measure Bible Reading

Another important pre-baptism health evangelism variable to measure is personal Bible study. All health reform principles are found in the Bible. True health evangelism programs will integrate Bible study into the curriculum of the program. I like to assign a Bible text for participants to look up and study each day. These Bible texts should be relevant to the problem with which the participant is struggling.

Bible study is documented by creating a progress card on which Bible study is documented day after day. If the Bible is studied, a participant gets a score for this. The progress cards are collected each week and new cards are distributed for the coming week. Measuring Bible study is an important marker that a person is on the path leading to baptism.

Future church members should be familiar with their Bibles and study them on a daily basis. If this habit is developed during a health evangelism program, the participant is moving along the path that leads to baptism. The church should also incorporate this level of documentation from traditional evangelistic meetings. Current evangelistic meetings do not document the amount of Bible Study that is taking place during the program.

It is also important to correlate an improvement in health behaviors with Bible study. In the programs I have conducted, I have found that those who have positive behavior change are about three times more likely to study their Bible daily compared with those who are less successful in changing their behavior.

# Measure Prayer

Another important variable to measure in health evangelism programs is the frequency with which a person prays. Prayer is as essential to success in changing health behaviors just as prayer is necessary in maintaining a close walk with Jesus in the spiritual life.

It is not easy to measure the duration or intensity of prayer, but it is quite easy to measure the frequency of prayer—the number of prayers offered each day. The progress card is useful to record these prayers. In the Best Weigh program, we recommend prayer at mealtimes and give one point for each prayer. Points are awarded for up to three prayers a day.

It is not uncommon for several thousand prayers to be offered to God during a 10-week program. Demonstrating that your health evangelism program is leading people to take prayer seriously and to pray regularly is an important sign of spiritual growth.

Spiritual growth in prayer should occur because of a well-designed health evangelism program. Prayer numbers should also be of interest to church officials and help foster administrative support for health evangelism. If a person is developing a consistent prayer life in a health evangelism program this marks progress along the path leading to baptism.

It is important in health evangelism programs to correlate the prayer life of participants with their success or failure in changing health behaviors. The most successful participants in my programs are about three times more likely to pray in contrast to less successful participants. Prayer changes things in terms of physical health as well as spiritual health.

## Measure Each Contact Point with Church Members

Another important health evangelism variable is contact with Seventh-day Adventist helpers. Health evangelism programs should be designed to create an interface between church members and non-Adventist guests from the community. Too often, we are satisfied to have church members attend meetings to help swell the audience. Too often, members just sit there with nothing to do but "support" the program. This is an extremely limited use of talent and does little to create a spiritual or social interface with the public.

One evangelistic goal of the church is to create a fellowship among believers and to create fellowship with people from the public at large. Those who have come to the church for help with health problems need to become integrated with the body of believers. This can be accomplished during health evangelism programs. A good way to do this is to create something useful for church members to do with participants during your program.

Deliberately design activities for your church members. Ask church members to lead small group discussions during a program. Church members should be available to help participants 24/7. I like church members to be "on call" at all times during a program. I like to require participants from the public to contact church members in some fashion at least once a day between the weekly sessions of my program.

These frequent contacts between church members and participants can be documented on a progress card. Contacts do not just happen; they need to be designed into health evangelism programs. This type of contact should also be designed into traditional evangelistic meetings—not just health evangelism activities.

In my experience, participants with the most success in overcoming bad habits are about four times as likely to have daily contact with church members compared with those who are having less success in behavior modification. Regular contact with church members is a strong determinant of success.

Church members will need some training for them to provide meaningful help to program participants. I find the best preparation is achieved by assigning church members reading assignments from scripture and Spirit of Prophecy. I like to start by assigning the chapter titled "In Contact with Others" in the Ministry of Healing. At training sessions, church members are encouraged to share with one another the instruction they receive from this chapter. When you add a season of prayer to the devotions, the result is a body of church members with soft hearts and loving attitudes. They are better prepared to interact with their non-Adventist friends from the community.

## Lack of Evaluation Tools

Standardized questionnaires and software databases for evaluating health evangelism are not available in off-the-shelf computer programs at the present time. As you conduct health evangelism programs in your church, you will need to design questionnaires, create databases, collect, and keep track of data yourself. No one has done this for health evangelism.

The great benefits and cost-effectiveness of health evangelism have never been demonstrated.

The Health Ministries departments of the church, at various levels, do not collect these data. Tools for evaluation have not been forthcoming from our colleges or universities. Sadly, the church at large has no process of measuring the effectiveness of health evangelism. For the present, this task is going to be up to you.

## Useless Numbers

Let me further illustrate the nature of this data collection problem. When I was the Medical Staff Director of the United States Office on Smoking and Health, the Five-day Plan to Stop Smoking was near its peak of popularity in the United States and around the world. The U.S. government was interested in preventing people from starting smoking and getting current smokers off cigarettes. We were very interested in the effectiveness of the 5-Day Plan to Stop Smoking.

I traveled the few miles from my federal government office to the Temperance Department of the General Conference, then located in Washington, D.C., (in 1980 the Temperance department was joined with the Health Department and is now known as the Health

Ministries Department) and conferred with the leaders in charge of the Five-day Plan. I received only two pieces of information. One was that the program had been instrumental in helping 20 million people stop smoking. This statistic was derived from the number of Five-day Plan Control Booklets which had been sold over time.

This statistic is impressive because it is a big number. We would like to think that we have helped millions of people stop smoking. Of course, 20 million it isn't an accurate number. Many organizations stockpiled these control booklets to use in future programs. Many of these booklets were eventually used but many were not. The total number of booklets shipped is a very soft number that doesn't reflect an actual count of people served. Hard numbers are needed to establish convincing statistics.

The second number I received from the Temperance Department of the General Conference was that the effectiveness of the program was very close to 100%. This statistic was derived by counting those who were present on the last session of the program and who had not had a cigarette during the previous 24-hours.

This is an overly optimistic number. To be more accurate it would have been better to compare those who were successful on the last night of the program against the number who registered. If 50% of those who registered for the Five-day plan dropped out during the program, you didn't really help those people. They most likely dropped out because they went back to smoking. That would be a 50% success rate even if 100% of those who remained in the program didn't smoke on the last night of the program.

The number of people who quit smoking on the last night of a program is not as important as the number of people who are still off cigarettes at three months, six months, or a year. Studies have shown that there are very few who relapse if they successfully stay off cigarettes for a whole year. For this reason, the true, long term, effectiveness of a stop smoking program should be measured at the end of a year. The denominator used in calculations should include all who initially registered for the program.

The United States Office on Smoking and Health was willing to financially support a scientifically accurate analysis of the long-term effectiveness of the 5-Day Plan. Dr. Daniel Horn, Ph.D. the Director of the Office on Smoking and Health considered church officials as being either incredibly naive at best, or at worst basely dishonest people. The Temperance Department had no understanding of, or respect for, scientifically accurate smoking cessation data from the 5-Day Plan.

The Five-day plan, in a very limited way, has been studied in a scientific manner. Sadly, this research was not done by the church and was not funded by the church. The church has not used these more accurate numbers in their advertisement of the Five-day Plan and do not usually discuss these numbers in public.

The success rate of the Five-day Plan at one year varies from 10% at the low end up to 35% at the high end at one year. It should be observed that of the "20,000,000" who supposedly have taken the Five-day Plan that less than 1000 of these smokers have ever been studied in a systematic way.

I have given you these details to make an earnest plea for you to design a strong and evaluation component into your health evangelism program. You need truthful, reliable data to prove to yourself, the church, and others the effectiveness of your program. Programs that are shown to produce long term success will eventually receive the blessing of the God, the church and community.

## Basic Data Collection for Health Evangelism

Do not be discouraged by the prospect of having to collect and maintain data. Start with a simple computer spreadsheet or database.

# Data Points

You need to collect data at several points during every program.

| | |
|---|---|
| 1. Registration. | These document initial behaviors, knowledge, and attitudes. |
| 2. Intervals during the program. | These document progress during the program. |
| 3. The last session. | These summarize changes during the program. |
| 4. One-month follow-up. | These document short term adherence to the program. |
| 5. Three-month follow-up. | These create an opportunity to contact new friends. |
| 6. Six-month follow-up. | These measure intermediate success. |
| 7. One-year follow-up. | These measure of long-term success. |

Most of the data you collect the first night you will want to re-collect the last night. This will document the kinds of changes that have occurred during the program. So, most of the questions asked at registration need to be asked again at the last session.

Each of the follow-up questionnaires should be the same as well. The 1, 3, 6, and 12 month questionnaires are all the same.

# Demographic Data

This is basic information about a person. For every kind of program, you will need these data. I suggest you collect the following.

1.  Last name
2.  First name
3.  Middle name or initial
4.  Date of birth (calculate age from this)
5.  Address (You prefer the home address)

6. Phone numbers (get daytime, evening, work and cell phone numbers)
7. Other contact avenues. (E-mail address, Facebook or twitter account information.)
8. Gender (Male or Female)
9. Religious preference (Used to identify non-church members who attend)
10. Marital Status (May affect outcomes. Divorced people do not do as well.)
11. Occupation (Blue collar workers may not do as well as white collar workers.)
12. Educational Level (Highly education people often do better)
13. Number of Children (May indicate a need for childcare)

## First and Last Session Behavioral Data

The behavior data you should collect depend on the nature of your program. If you are going to conduct a stop smoking clinic you should ask questions about smoking. If you are planning a weight management program, you need to ask questions about eating habits. If you are going to conduct an exercise program, you need to ask questions about health and fitness.

The questions you ask should probe a person's knowledge and attitudes about the behavior that needs to be changed. You should ask about a person's health practices. What has a person tried in the past? What do he or she plan to do at the present? As an example, the following questions are questions I would ask those who registered for a weight control program.

Questions for a weight management program questionnaire.

1. How much do you weigh today? (Compare with actual weight)
2. What is the most you have ever weighed?
3. How many times have you made a serious attempt to lose weight?

4. How much weight would you like to lose in this 10-week program?

5. What are foods you snack on the most? List three.

6. What is the most weight you have lost following a diet?

7. How many others in your immediate family would you say are overweight?

8. Do you believe that God helps a person lose weight?

9. At what age would you say that you were first overweight?

10. Do you have high cholesterol?

11. Do you have diabetes?

12. Do you have high blood pressure?

13. Has your doctor advised you to lose weight for health reasons?

14. Do you have a regular exercise program?

You can add or subtract questions from this list. Do not make the questionnaire too long. It shouldn't take more than 5-10 minutes to complete. You do not want excessive delays in the registration area on the first night.

You should ask most of the same questions on the last session. By comparing answers given on the last session with the answers given to the identical questions at registration, you can measure the changes in attitude, beliefs, and practices that resulted from your program. If smokers said they didn't believe that God helped smokers quit on the first night, but on the last night had changed their mind, you can see that these people are closer to the kingdom.

## Data Collection During the Program

To document behavior change from week-to-week I like to use a "Progress Card." This card is given out at every session of the program and is collected for data entry when a participant returns the following week. New cards are distributed when last week's cards are picked up. Designate one or more persons to collect and hold the data you generate.

## Data Entry

Data should be entered onto a spreadsheet or into a database from week to week throughout the program. Your registration questionnaire, the progress cards, your last session questionnaire, and all follow-up questionnaires are entered. Before your program begins identify the individuals who have the computer equipment, knowledge of spreadsheets or databases, and who will do the data entry for you.

The Best Weigh program has this software online and your data is kept in the cloud. If your program is registered well before it begins potential participants can register online. Some basic reports are generated continuously as your data is entered throughout the program.

## Data Analysis

The purpose of data analysis is to answer questions about the impact of your program on individuals and the group that attended. The simplest information you should extract has to do with attendance and attrition.

Next analyze the changes that occurred in the health variables you were tracking. What kind of changes to weight, cholesterol levels, blood sugars, blood pressure, or indicators of depression resulted from your program? What were the elements of your program that contributed the most to these changes?

Most important to document are the changes in the spiritual variables you were tracking. How did belief in God change? Measure how people applied prayer, Bible study, and interaction with church members. How many non-Seventh-day Adventist visits resulted from this effort?

# 18

# Susceptibility

SUSCEPTIBILITY IS THE TENDENCY TO BE AFFECTED BY SOMETHING external to yourself. It is the capacity to be influenced by receiving mental impressions. Susceptibility to evangelism is the tendency to respond positively to invitations to believe in salvation through Jesus Christ. These responses can be measured by a willingness to study the Bible in a systematic was and eventually by a willingness to be baptized and join the church.

Susceptibility to evangelism is a positive trait that is developed by the Holy Spirit working on the mind of people who are consciously or unconsciously searching for the truth. There are various degrees of susceptibility. These can be measured. Studies need to be done to measure how the susceptibility of people is influenced by various measures of intervention. This is a way to measure the return on investment.

## Susceptibility to Advertising

Evangelistic efforts are widely advertised for a couple of weeks before the meetings begin. Which methods of advertising attract the largest number of people? Which methods of advertising are most cost effective?

A few years ago, the Crowley Seventh-day Adventist church in Texas held four weeks of traditional evangelistic meetings. These were advertised through a variety of means. There was the traditional mail out of "Prophecy for America" cards to every household in the surrounding postal zip codes at a cost of $8,000.00. A letter from the pastor was mailed to those who had stopped along the highway to go through a model of the ancient sanctuary tent of the children of Israel billed as Messiah's Mansion at a cost of $225.00.

There was a letter mailed to the 100 plus previous attendees of the Best Weigh nutrition and weight loss program conducted in the church at a cost of $125.00. There was $200 invested in Facebook advertisements. The church had a large video sign on the road in front of the church and it was estimated that $50.00 of electricity was used to promote the meetings. Church members were encouraged to invite their neighbors and friends. A few brochures were made available at the checkout counter of a local thrift shop cosponsored by the church.

As non-Seventh-day Adventists arrived at the evangelistic meetings they were asked which modality of advertising influenced them the most to attend the meetings. The number of attendees that came because of each method of advertising were tallied and the cost per attendee calculated. The numbers are small but revealing.

| Response and Cost per Attendee to Advertising an Evangelistic Meeting | | | |
|---|---|---|---|
| Advertisement Modality | Number attended | Cost invested | Cost/ Attendee |
| Letter to Messiah's Mansion | 8 | $225.00 | $28.13 |
| Letter to Best Weigh | 3 | $125.00 | $41.67 |
| Mass Mail Out | 5 | $8,000.00 | $1,600.00 |
| Church Video Sign | 0 | $50.00 | NA |
| Facebook Advertisement | 1 | $200.00 | $200.00 |
| Personal invitations | 15 | $0.00 | $0.00 |
| Good News TV Stations | 3 | $1,200 | $400.00 |
| Fliers in Thrift Shop | 2 | $12.50 | $6.25 |
| Total Investment* | 37 | $23,805.00 | $580.61 |

* Included a $15,000 investment from the Texas Conference.

The most cost-effective invitations were those personally made by friends to friends. These are the kinds of friendships developed at health evangelism programs when conducted with small groups.

Other highly effective methods of advertising were letters sent to alumni of previous health evangelism activities held at the church. Prior exposure to Seventh-day Adventists through health programming greatly increased the susceptibility of persons to attend evangelistic meetings.

If this was generally understood and appreciated by the denomination's community of evangelists, they would require local churches to conduct health evangelism programs for a year or two before traditional evangelistic "reaping" meetings were held.

Mass mailing of invitations was the least effective modality of advertising. This method of finding an audience is expensive, unfruitful, is now obsolete and should no longer be used in evangelism.

## Susceptibility to Stay

It has been estimated that about 50% of those who join the church leave within one year. The susceptibility to stay in the church following evangelistic meetings need to be measured. I do not have any figures on this, but I predict that new church members who were first cultivated in health evangelism programs will be much more susceptible to staying with us. The success rate might at the end of a year might be as high as 80%-90%. This is a number that needs to be measured by those who conduct health evangelism.

## Susceptibility to be Active

There are members who support the church by becoming involved in church culture. They attend Sabbath School, prayer meeting, and regularly attend services on Sabbath. It is my prediction that new church members whose first exposure to Seventh-day Adventists was in health evangelism programs will be more susceptible to become active participants in the activities of the church. It couldn't be otherwise because they had friends in the church well before they were baptized.

## Susceptibility to Give

Lastly, there are members who support the mission of the church by regularly depositing their tithes and offerings in the church coffers. About half the members in my local church don't pay tithe. There are several others who only pay tithe and don't support the local church in any other financial way. The church is very good at counting money. It is my prediction that new church members whose first exposure to us was through health evangelism will be faithful in returning their tithes and offerings.

This needs to be measured. Once it is known that giving is enhanced by health evangelism, church administrators will insist that all traditional evangelistic meetings be preceded by one or two years of health evangelism activity. It will be a financial boon to the denomination.

## Tracking Susceptibilities

The various practices of individuals who join the church need to be measured. The tool has two parts to it. One is data collected from a new member at the point of baptism. This needs to include basic demographic information but most importantly information about the steps that led to baptism. How long were they actively connected with Seventh-day Adventists before baptism? How many members in this local church do they know and interact with? What meetings or programs did they participate in before baptism?

These data will identify those who attended an evangelistic meeting in response to a flyer mailed to their residence and those who have attended one or more health evangelism programs prior to more formal Bible studies or participation in traditional evangelistic meetings.

The second tool needed is a bit more complicated. It is a report card on progress in the Christian life. To be most accurate it should not be completed by the person being tracked. It could be completed weekly, monthly, or quarterly. Attendance at Sabbath School, church services, prayer meeting and other activities needs to be monitored by someone who takes a census of the church members who attend every meeting.

This is not just a count of how many attended a given meeting but identifying every individual who shows up to every service of the church. This census could be performed by a church member who is personally acquainted with every member of the church. Another way is to issue a bar code identification to every church member to be scanned every time they come to church. Another way is to place a kiosk in the entryway of the church for people to sign in on each time they arrive for services.

Beyond simple attendance other measures of involvement in activities of the church can be documented on a quarterly basis. Does the new member help in Sabbath School departments? Does the new member support Pathfinders or be a helper in one of the frequent health evangelism programs?

The giving habits of new members can be obtained from the church treasurer. This is confidential information and should be deidentified before being attached to a members file. A simple scoring system would be sufficient. A=tithes and offerings, B=tithe only, C=offerings only, D=rarely gives, E=never gives.

# 19

# The Program is Not the End!

---

FOLLOW-UP HAS BEEN THE WEAKEST COMPONENT IN ALL THE HEALTH evangelism programs. Follow-up is as important as the program itself. Follow-up is often more time consuming than conducting the program. It takes effort and planning.

In planning to include follow-up activities in a health evangelism program it is important to inform the small group helpers that you require their help for follow-up activities as well as their help during the program. Follow-up should occur at least quarterly for a period of one year.

Follow-up means you do not let go of people once you get to know them. Participants have been coming to your church week after week. You know them by their first names. They have become educated. They have new health practices. Many of them will slip back into their old ways of living if you do not keep in touch with them to encourage them.

The easiest but least effective way to conduct follow-up activities is to hold them at the church. At the last session of any program there is a spirit of fellowship and gratitude. People want the effect to last. There is always a sincere desire to continue meeting on a regular basis for follow-up.

But follow-up meetings at the church do not work well. They are always poorly attended. There are two reasons for this. One reason is that your participants are successful in maintaining their new behavior. They do not need follow-up meetings. They are doing just fine so they do not come to follow-up.

The second reason people do not return to follow-up meetings is because they have relapsed into their old habits and are too ashamed to return. So, whether your participants experience success or failure, few of them will ever return to follow-up meetings at the church. They are more likely to return to your next regular program for more encouragement or a second try if they have failed.

The most effective type of follow-up is in each participant's homes. Though some church members dread house-to-house work, in-home follow-up is pleasant and not difficult. These are not "cold calls." You know the people you are reaching out to. You saw these people from day to day and from week to week during your program. You are friends.

The same two small group leaders should be the ones to call on the members of their own small group. This means that they will only have to make six or seven calls to complete each round of follow-up.

This in-home follow-up activity should not be a surprise to your program participants. During the program you told them there was going to be this kind of follow-up. Your program participants will be expecting you to call on them. Most participants will be glad to see you.

There are important reasons for doing your follow-up in the home. One reason is to help reinforce the participant's new behaviors. Smokers will be less likely to relapse if they know you will be calling on them soon.

Another reason to do follow-up is to document the long-term effectiveness of your health evangelism program. You need to document what they are doing. This information will go into your database and fulfills one of the scientific purposes of your program.

This scientific evaluation is the perfect "official" reason for a follow-up visit. You are dropping by for data collection. That is non-threatening and will not be a barrier to your home visit. You need a clipboard, pencil, and follow-up forms with you; they should be in your hand when you knock on the door.

The most important reason for an in-home follow-up visit is that this is probably the very first time you will be one-on-one with an individual member of your small group. This creates a type of contact in which spiritual issues can be explored.

The polite thing to do is to call ahead and make a definite appointment for a follow-up visit. In this way participants can have their houses in order and will not be embarrassed as they would be if you make an unannounced call.

If you call for an appointment and the participant says that he or she would like to skip the follow-up visit you can ask if they would be willing to complete the follow-up questionnaire over the phone. The participant will almost always say, "Yes" and you can obtain your follow-up data. It should be noted in your database that the follow-up was a phone visit and not a face-to-face interview.

While you are on the phone, after the participant has answered the questions for the questionnaire, you can then assume a more casual voice and make inquiry as to how the person is doing spiritually. I like to use the same approach whether I am in the home or conducting the interview over the phone.

How is the in-home visit structured? After initial casual comments, you announce the desire to obtain follow-up information you need for the study. Ask the few questions on your follow-up questionnaire. Then you put your clipboard down, sit back, relax, and casually ask three more "unofficial" questions which should not appear to be related to the purpose of data collection.

The first question I like to as ask is, "How are you doing physically since you . . ." (quit smoking or lost weight or finished the program)? The usual answer is, "Your program has helped me so much, etc."

The second question has to do with mental issues. I ask, "How are you doing mentally/psychologically? Is it still a struggle? How are you keeping it up?"

The third question is the most important, "How are you doing spiritually with regard to your habit?" This is the key moment of your entire health evangelism program. You are one-on-one in the privacy of a person's home. There are no other group members watching or listening. If a participant is thinking about spiritual things, if they want to talk about what God is doing in their lives, they will talk to you about it right now.

Health evangelism programs should be evangelistic. They are made evangelistic during the program when you explain the ways in which God helps with behavior change. Health evangelism programs are most evangelistic when you get to ask a person about his or her personal relationship with God in the quietness of their own home.

What kind of responses will you get to this question? A common response is, "Oh, fine, just fine. What did you think about the football game last weekend?" This indicates a reluctance to speak to you directly about spiritual things. Do not press the point. These people think a lot of you and your health evangelism program. They are not offended that you brought up the subject. There was a spiritual emphasis in the program, and it was conducted by religious people in a church.

Without a connection with God, participants are not likely to maintain their new behavior very long. Perhaps the Holy Spirit will impress them to come to another program. Do not push the people into a discussion of spiritual things if they do not want to go there.

Many people will respond positively to your question about spiritual things. They will gladly confess that they are maintaining their new behaviors through a relationship with God. They will rejoice that they have a new and more practical understanding about what the Christian life is all about. They will praise your church for having such a practical religion that helps people with real problems.

Others will be anxious to know more about your church and what you believe. They will want to know about such things as the Sabbath and other distinctive doctrines. You should be prepared for anything and everything. I like to keep a variety of pamphlets, Bible study lessons and several books and Bibles in the car to use under these circumstances. If a person expresses an interest in spiritual things, and wants to begin a discussion with you, be prepared.

It will not appear to the participant that spiritual concerns were the real reason you came calling. Spiritual issues came up after you obtained your scientific data. The religious materials you are going to leave weren't under your arm when you came to the door. You go back out to your car to get the extra materials.

If you have a positive spiritual interaction with a former program participant, it is important to offer a prayer before you leave the home. It is important for you to pray again once you return to your car. Thank God for the developing spiritual relationship and ask for continued guidance.

Follow-up activities should be initiated soon after the end of a program. I suggest intervals of one month, three months, six months, and a year. Most people who relapse do so fairly quickly. An early follow-up visit will be helpful in preventing relapse. There is room for flexibility here. You may want to conduct follow-up activities even more frequently than I have suggested. Negotiate this with your small group leaders who will be doing most of the follow-up.

If two small group leaders cannot go together for some reason, it may be necessary for the pastor, health professional or some other helper to go with one of the helpers. Remember, two-by-two is a Biblical principle and is the appropriate way to make follow-up calls.

A follow-up newsletter and additional "alumni" meetings at the church are good ideas but not a substitute for in-home visits. In a newsletter the success of various individuals can be reviewed, spiritual messages about overcoming can be included, and the dates for the next programs at the church can be announced.

## Spirit of Prophecy Quotations on Follow-up Activities

Follow-up will result in baptisms.

> "For years light has been given upon this point, showing the necessity of following up an interest that has been raised, and in no case leaving it until all have decided that lean toward the truth, and have experienced the conversion necessary for baptism, and united with some church, or formed one themselves." *Evangelism 324*

If we do not do follow-up, the gains may unravel. This advice applies to health evangelism activities as well as to other ministerial activity.

> "I hope you will look at things candidly and not move impulsively or from feeling. Our ministers must be educated and trained to do their work more thoroughly. They should bind off the work and not leave it to ravel out. And they should look especially after the interests they have created, and not go away and never have any special interest after leaving a church. A great deal of this has been done." *Evangelism 324*

Follow-up activity is mandatory and not optional. This would apply to health evangelists as well as pastors.

> "There are no circumstances of sufficient importance to call a minister from an interest created by the presentation of truth. Even sickness and death are of less consequence than the salvation of souls for whom Christ made so immense a sacrifice. Those who feel the importance of the truth, and the value of souls for whom Christ died, will not leave an interest among

the people for any consideration. They will say, Let the dead bury their dead. Home interests, lands and houses, should not have the least power to attract from the field of labor." *Evangelism 324*

A follow-up letter can be mailed. Tracts and Bible study guides can be distributed at follow-up visits.

"When at our large gatherings, make all the discourses highly reformative. Arouse the intellect. Bring up the talents possible into the efforts made, and then follow up the effort with tracts and pamphlets, with articles written in simple form, to make the subjects brought before them distinctly stated, that the word spoken may be repeated by the silent agent. Short, interesting articles should be arranged in cheap style, and scattered everywhere. They should be at hand upon every occasion where the truth is brought before the minds of those to whom it is new and strange." *Counsels to Writers and Editors 126*

Follow-up activities should be aggressive. It will be appropriate to chase people down under some circumstances. Do not give up.

"We must not think of such a thing as discouragement, but hold fast to souls by the grasp of faith. Do not give up those for whom you are working. Go out in the mountains and seek the lost sheep. They may run from you, but you must follow them up, take them in your arms and bring them to Jesus. Pulpit effort should always be followed by personal labor. The worker must converse and pray with those who are concerned about their souls salvation. Those who listen to discourses should see in those who believe, an example in life and character that will make a deep impression upon them." *The Home Missionary, February 1, 1890.*

Medical missionaries are true evangelists. They should always go out two-by-two. This is especially important in urban areas.

> "It is medical missionaries that are needed all through the field. Canvassers should improve every opportunity granted them to learn how to treat disease. Physicians should remember that they will often be required to perform the duties of a minister. Medical missionaries come under the head of evangelists. The workers should go forth two by two, that they may pray and consult together. Never should they be sent out alone. The Lord Jesus Christ sent forth His disciples two and two into all the cities of Israel. He gave them the commission, "Heal the sick that are therein, and say unto them, The kingdom of God is come nigh unto you." ***Medical Ministry 249***

Follow-up activities create the opportunities to cultivate spiritual interests. Do not forget to take with your pamphlets, Bible Study guides, and books which can be handed out when the chance comes up.

> "Now, when we go into the house we should not begin to talk of frivolous things, but come right to the point and say, I want you to love Jesus, for He has first loved you. . . . Take along the publications and ask them to read. When they see that you are sincere they will not despise any of your efforts. There is a way to reach the hardest hearts. Approach in the simplicity, and sincerity, and humility that will help us to reach the souls of them for whom Christ died." ***Welfare Ministry 91***

We are to follow Christ's example and find our ways to the fireside, with families in their own homes. This is so personal and creates opportunities for witness that will not come up in the health evangelism activity at the church.

> "To all who are working with Christ I would say, wherever you can gain access to the people by the

fireside, improve your opportunity. Take your Bible, and open before them its great truths. Your success will not depend so much upon your knowledge and accomplishments, as upon your ability to find your way to the heart. By being social and coming close to the people, you may turn the current of their thoughts more readily than by the most able discourse. The presentation of Christ in the family, by the fireside, and in small gatherings in private houses, is often more successful in winning souls to Jesus than are sermons delivered in the open air, to the moving throng, or even in halls or churches." *Gospel Workers 193*

Follow-up in the home should not be for the purpose of doctrinal presentations but from time-to-time doctrinal issues will come up and can be addressed. Doctrinal presentations should not be the primary purpose of in-home visits, but doctrines can be discussed if they are brought up by those with whom you are visiting.

"There are many souls yearning unutterably for light, for assurance and strength beyond what they have been able to grasp. They need to be sought out and labored for patiently, perseveringly. Beseech the Lord in fervent prayer for help. Present Jesus because you know Him as your personal Saviour. Let His melting love, His rich grace, flow forth from human lips. You need not present doctrinal points unless questioned. But take the Word, and with tender, yearning love for souls, show them the precious righteousness of Christ, to whom you and they must come to be saved." *Welfare Ministry 92*

The in-home visits allow personal appeals to behavior change and personal appeals to accept Christ as the agent of behavior change in human live.

"Personal, individual effort and interest for your friends and neighbors will accomplish more than can be estimated. It is for the want of this kind of labor that souls for whom Christ died are perishing. . . . Your work may accomplish more real good than the more extensive meetings, if they lack in personal effort. When both are combined, with the blessing of God, a more perfect and thorough work may be wrought; but if we can have but one part done, let it be the individual labor of opening the Scriptures in households, making personal appeals, and talking familiarly with the members of the family, not about things of little importance, but of the great themes of redemption. Let them see that your heart is burdened for the salvation of souls". *Welfare Ministry 93-94*

# 20

# As Solid as Science

---

IN THE MINDS OF SOME PEOPLE, SCIENCE AND RELIGION ARE MUTUALLY exclusive disciplines. Science increasingly recognizes that an intelligent designer is required to explain the complexity found in the natural world. As one author said, "science drives us conclusively and compellingly toward the existence of God. The Scriptures and science proclaim the same truth. They support each other because God's revelation of himself in nature is just as true as his revelation of himself in Scripture. The Scriptures and science are united—not without their distinctions, of course—but united. To separate them is to do exactly what the world does."[1]

The role of science in health evangelism is an important one. Science has done much to advance our standard of living and has provided us with wonderful technological advances. The scientific method is an invaluable tool that can validate or discredit the effectiveness of a drug, nutritional supplement, or health practice.

Traditional religious evangelism deals primarily with a person's spiritual condition. Health evangelism deals with both spiritual and physical restoration. The tools of science are essential to measure the effectiveness of health evangelism.

---

[1] Sproul, R.C. Defending Your Faith: An Introduction (p. 86). Good News Publishers. Kindle Edition.

In the area of healthful living, science and religion are both important. Science provides the proof that certain health practices preserve health and promote long life. Health evangelism introduces us to God who provides us with the power to change. God gives us the strength to continue good health practices once they are established.

## The Scientific Method

The scientific method is the tool that science uses to prove or discredit a theory. Science proved that cigarette smoking causes lung cancer and science put robots on Mars. As you conduct health evangelism activities, it is important to use health concepts based on data that are scientifically sound. Selecting accurate information will be easy for someone with a scientific background but will be a challenge for those not trained in understanding the scientific literature.

I have been distressed to find church members who have little scientific background, proclaiming as truth, popular but erroneous health advice that has no basis in fact. These church members often pose as health experts and teach what is contradictory to what has already been established by careful study.

Every recommendation for healthful living you make needs have been tested and proved effective in a human population. You need to be able to look for published studies that support what you are telling people. You should be able to analyze a study to see if it was designed and conducted in such a way as to be able to really prove a point.

## Anecdotal Reports and Endorsements

The most useless and unscientific recommendation for a product, diet, nutritional supplement or proposed lifestyle change is the anecdotal recommendation. Anecdotal endorsements are provided by individuals who are famous or who have respected degrees. When there is no credible science to back up a claim of effectiveness for a product, the most a company can do is to get some recognizable person to recommend it. Scientific articles sharing anecdotal findings are called case reports and are simply for forming hypotheses to test, they do not constitute evidence of effectiveness of whatever is reported.

## Population Studies

The effectiveness of medications can be studied in fairly small populations. Much larger studies are needed to document the benefits or harm from specific lifestyle behaviors. If someone promotes a certain behavior as important to health, it is important for you to learn what you can about the population in which that behavior was studied. Often, studies are just surveys of opinions. Perhaps a few dozen people were polled. Such studies do not establish the benefit of any treatment.

## Retrospective Studies

The simplest type of a population study is the retrospective study. A retrospective study starts with a population that has a certain disease. The researcher then collects data from a second population of people (the control group) who do not have that disease. The more alike the two populations are in every respect, except for the presence of disease, the more valid the conclusions that can be drawn.

In a retrospective study the two populations should be matched for age, sex, geographic area, and many comorbid conditions. Establishing the similarity of the two populations is very important to suggest reliable conclusions. Yet retrospective studies cannot establish cause and effect relationships.

Careful matching of case and control populations is the most important part of a retrospective study. In the 1950's several retrospective studies of men with lung cancer that showed that cigarette smoking was much more common in men with lung cancer than in a matched control group of men who did not have lung cancer. Retrospective studies are most useful in studying rare diseases. Retrospective studies are relatively inexpensive to conduct. Many retrospective studies are conducted with as few as a hundred cases and a hundred controls.

## Prospective/Cohort Studies

A study of an entire cohort of a population is an even better scientific tool. Prospective population studies are conducted on large populations of people and are continued for several years. Prospective studies may enroll thousands to even millions of people.

A cohort study is begun by enrolling people by administering a questionnaire that determines a wide variety of data points such as age, sex, race, and occupation, daily or weekly use of various food items alcohol, tobacco and drug use, levels of exercise at work and at home.

Certain physical measurements such as height, weight, blood pressure, cholesterol levels or other physical parameters may be included. Usually, people with known diseases that might affect the validity of the results are excluded so that you can measure the effect of certain behaviors in healthy people.

Cohort studies take a long time to conduct. They must run for enough years for diseases to develop and deaths to occur. You periodically monitor the health of the population and document the development of disease over time.

The American Cancer Society has conducted large prospective studies that have enrolled over one million people and has followed the subjects for several years. A large Japanese study followed 250,000 people for some 17 years. A single large prospective study can be used to study the development of many different diseases that may be associated with many different behaviors. The Framingham heart study enrolled only 4000 people but followed them for more than 30 years.

Two of the highly valuable cohort studies are the NIH-AARP study of a half million people and the Health Professionals study of physicians and nurses which also has hundreds of thousands of participants.

The most valid data regarding the relationship of various behaviors to health come from prospective studies. Many claims are made for many different health behaviors, but if there are no data from prospective studies to back up the claims, do not put a lot of stock in what is being claimed.

Retrospective studies showed a link between cigarette smoking and lung cancer, but it took large prospective studies to show that cigarette smoking was not only a cause of lung cancer but was also a major cause of cancers at other sites as well. Smoking causes cancer of the oral cavity, larynx, esophagus, pancreas, kidney, bladder, and cervix. Smoking causes emphysema and chronic bronchitis. Smoking is a major cause of heart attacks, strokes, and hardening of the arteries in general. All these facts were discovered in large prospective studies. One large prospective study can prove several things.

*One large cohort study can prove many things.*

Other cohort studies have shown that you can prevent heart attacks by eating nuts frequently, drinking four or more glasses of water a day and by decreasing the amount of meat and dairy products in the diet. Do not believe a health claim unless there is some objective data from a large prospective study or a well conducted retrospective study to back them up.

## The Adventist Health Study

The unusually good health of Seventh-day Adventists is of particular interest to the scientific community and the world at large. As a people, we have more good health behaviors and better health than any population, in any country of the world.

The first study of Seventh-day Adventists began back in the 1950s. The current Adventist Health Study II is a large prospective epidemiological study. There are close to 100,000 participants from across the United States. The Adventist Health Study data collection and analysis is done by Loma Linda University.

The AHS-II study is confirming the validity of the health principles found in the Bible and the writings of Ellen G. White. Hundreds of new and surprising benefits of vegetarian and vegan diets have been discovered for the first time. Diet, exercise, water, avoidance of tobacco, alcohol, and coffee, and dozens of other variables are being examined.

Over the past 60 plus years over 450 articles, based on data from Adventist Health Studies, have been published in peer-reviewed scientific journals. Many more articles will appear every year from this important study.

The Adventist Health Study has discovered significant new health information. Several of these new health facts have been confirmed by other, often much larger studies of secular populations conducted by secular universities.

## Statistical Significance

Some discussion of what constitutes proof is necessary. I do not want to go into a detailed discussion of the mathematics of probability. It is sufficient to say that rigorous mathematical tools exist to exactly measure the significance or validity of data collected.

There is always a possibility that a positive association discovered in a study is due to chance and is not real. The scientific community has agreed that no claim of proof for an association will be made unless there is less than a 5% chance that the outcome was a random occurrence.

Probability is expressed as $p$. Therefore, a finding must have a $p$ value of 0.05 or smaller to be statistically significant.

The proof that an association is real is based on the magnitude of the association, the consistency of an association in multiple studies, and the validity of the association in various populations and demonstrating dose-response relationships. It is also helpful if there is experimental evidence in animal models that support the theory.

## Peer Review and Publication

Research regarding the health of populations has a time-honored mechanism to keep things honest. It is the peer review process. Research at every center of scientific study is monitored by an Institutional Review Board (IRB). Any bias in study design or population selection is pretty much eliminated through the peer review process.

Peer review continues when it comes time to publish research data. Research is introduced to the world through presentation to a skeptical scientific audience at regularly held meetings where research results are first presented.

Scientists also seek to have their findings published in respected science journals. The editors of these journals distribute the articles they receive for publication to several independent (often competing) scientists who are often themselves doing research in the same area.

If the study was sound and the results accurate, the article is recommended for publication. If defects or inaccuracies are found, the article is returned to the author for clarification, revision or perhaps more research is needed to adequately prove the point.

The medical literature of the entire world is catalogued in the United States National Library of Medicine in Bethesda, Maryland. Authors, article title, journal, and a brief abstract are published online at pubmed.gov. The articles from over 5000 different medical journals are catalogued each month and are available for anyone to review. Currently there are over 33 million articles on file in the library.

Do not promote any new health concept, idea, or practice in your health evangelism program unless you can find support for it in multiple places in peer-reviewed scientific articles, preferably large prospective studies. Every health activity promoted in your health evangelism program should be supported by sound scientific evidence.

The Bible supports this type of rigorous accuracy in all we do. "Let all things be done decently and in order, 1 Corinthians 14:40." The Old and New Testaments contain dozens of recommendations to be orderly in all that we do.

## Spirit of Prophecy Comments on Science

Modern science has become powerful because it is discovering truth that God has authored.

> "God is the author of science. Scientific research opens to the mind vast fields of thought and information."
> *Counsels to Teachers, Parents and Students, 426*

Health evangelism should be brimming with high quality scientific medical knowledge. We know science and we know the God of science. Those who come to us for help will recognize we have accurate scientific knowledge and can introduce them to the God of behavior change who designed the science.

> "The light that God has given in medical missionary lines will not cause His people to be regarded as inferior in scientific medical knowledge, but will fit them to stand upon the highest eminence." *Medical Ministry, 65*

In this quotation, Mrs. White correctly recognizes that science properly conducted possesses all kinds of power. Science is useful. Accurate science should be a part of any health evangelism program.

> "The schools established among us are matters of grave responsibility; for important interests are involved. In a special manner our schools are a spectacle unto angels and to men. A knowledge of science of all kinds is power, and it is in the purpose of God that advanced science shall be taught in our schools as a preparation for the work that is to precede the closing scenes of earth's history." *Fundamentals of Christian Education, 186*

In this next quotation, a practical knowledge of the science of human life is advocated. This knowledge has been produced through many millions of scientific research studies conducted over the past 100 years.

> A practical knowledge of the science of human life, is necessary in order to glorify God in our bodies. It is therefore of the highest importance that among the studies selected for childhood, Physiology should occupy the first place. How few know anything about the structure and functions of their own bodies, and of Nature's laws. Many are drifting about without knowledge, like a ship at sea without compass or anchor; and what is more, they are not interested to learn how to keep their bodies in a healthy condition, and prevent disease." *The Health Reformer 08-01-1866*

Understanding God and understanding true science are complementary not mutually exclusive.

> "The closer our connection with God, the more fully can we comprehend the value of true science; for the attributes of God, as seen in His created works, can be best appreciated by him who has a knowledge of the Creator of all things, the Author of all truth. Such can

make the highest use of knowledge; for when brought under the full control of the Spirit of God, their talents are rendered useful to the fullest extent." *Counsels to Teachers, Parents and Students, 38*

Here is nice summary of how health evangelism is to be practiced.

"Whenever possible, let a room be provided where the patrons can be invited to lectures on the science of health and Christian temperance, where they can receive instruction on the preparation of wholesome food and on other important subjects." *Testimonies of the Church, Vol 7, 115*

Rational science was in its infancy in the late 1800's and early in the 20th century. The last 100 years have brought breathtaking advances in all branches of science which continue to this day. Ellen White embraced true rational science while condemning the many harmful practices of health practitioners of her day.

# 21

# The Use of Health Supplements

HEALTH EVANGELISM IS INTENDED TO PROMOTE AND PRESERVE GOOD health in humans whose lifestyle has resulted in risk factors likely to result in disease. A common question has to do with the role of dietary supplements in preserving health.

Supplements are often recommended because they claim to contain elements that are said to be missing in the diet. However, the claim that the natural fresh, frozen, and canned foods generally available no longer possess all the life preserving properties they once contained is actually false.[2]

Supplements are forbidden by law to claim the ability to cure specific diseases. On the other hand, supplements are allowed to make a variety of vague claims. For example, some claim to support digestion, assist the immune system, or help promote brain health.

A false contrast is drawn between supplements and prescription medication. Claims are made that supplements are for "health" and drugs are for "disease." It is true that prescriptions medications are designed to treat specific diseases, but it is not established that supplements

---

[2] D.R. Davis, et.al, "Changes in USDA Food Composition Data for 43 Garden Crops, 1950 to 1999," *Journal of the American College of Nutrition*, Vol. 23, No. 6, 669–682 (2004)

contribute anything to a person's health. The successful promotion of supplements has created a 36 billion dollar a year industry.[3]

Many conscientious church members, who believe the health message of the church, mistakenly feel it necessary to add one or more vitamin or herb supplements to their daily routine. Because most supplements claim to be "simple remedies," "natural," and promote "health" they mistakenly presume supplements are consistent with counsel the church received more than a century ago.

## What is in a Supplement?

A dietary supplement is a tablet, capsule, powder, gel, or liquid product that contains one or more of the following: a vitamin, a mineral, an herb or plant, amino acids, plant or animal enzymes, organ tissue from animal sources, illegally obtained prescription medication, unregulated chemical compounds, or a concentrate, metabolite, constituent, or extract of any of the above singly or in combination.

## How are Supplements Regulated?

The U.S. Federal law that regulates supplements is the Dietary Supplement Health and Education Act (DSHEA) passed by congress in 1994. Products that are labeled and intended for sale as food supplements have great freedom. They are considered the same as food.

Food supplements are not regulated by anyone. No testing of any kind is required. The manufacturer does not have to prove that they work. No evidence of any kind is required to establish that they perform the way they are claimed in advertisements.

---

[3] Supplements are a $36.6 Billion industry in 2021 Source: (https://www.ibisworld.com/industry-statistics/market-size/vitamin-supplement-manufacturing-united-states/ Billion / year industry) Viewed August 2021

Supplements manufacturers are not required to prove that they are safe to take. Many supplements are in fact not safe to take. I have seen dozens of people experiencing liver damage from taking supplements. Fortunately, the liver damage was reversed in the patients once they stopped taking the offending supplement.

Supplement manufacturers are not required to recommend any specific dosage of their products. The supplement bottle may recommend one capsule a day, or one with each meal, or two or three with each meal. The optimum dosage for supplements has not been determined. Dosage recommendations are not required by the government. Take what you want. Take as much or as little as you want.

Legal prescription medications have very exact dosing guidelines. Sometimes drug levels are monitored to make sure that you are taking just the right dose to be effective and to minimize possible side effects.

Supplements are not required to have any purity standards. They often contain contaminants.[4],[5] Many supplement makers claim to have high purity standards. This would be good if in fact the product was useful for health. Purity of something that has no health benefit is of no value and little comfort.

Supplements are sold without supervision by the Food and Drug Administration (FDA). For this reason, there are no studies required to be conducted to establish or disprove the effectiveness of the product being sold. No publishing of data in peer reviewed journals is required.

## Supplements Provide False Security

Claims are made that supplements contain beneficial nutrients no longer found in food, which as noted above is false. So, a pill may contain

---

[4]  P.A. Cohen, et.al, "Nine prohibited stimulants found in sports and weight loss supplements:" Clinical Toxicology, published online March 23, 2021, 7 pages

[5]  P.A. Cohen et.al, "Five Unapproved Drugs Found in Cognitive Enhancement Supplements," *Neurology Clinical Practice*, September 23, 2020

beta-carotene, but there are over 1000 carotene compounds in food. Why limit your carotene intake to just one in a pill when carrots and other orange vegetable contain the full symphony of carotene compounds?

Not all the beneficial nutrients or biologically active factors in food have been identified. For this reason, it is better for your health to depend on food to adequately nourish you rather than trust the contents of a capsule.

Many people will mistakenly depend on supplements for good health and won't worry about eating right or getting adequate exercise. They may be satisfied with a narrow nutrient diet erroneously depending on their supplement to make up for their nutritional carelessness.

It is possible that reliance on supplements may cause people to be deaf to important messages regarding the importance of physical activity, weight control, stopping smoking etc. People may come to think that the supplement they take will supply all their health needs.

The food supply in the United States is so rich and diverse that it is important for those involved in health evangelism to emphasizes a food-based diet to fulfill nutrient requirements and promote optimal health and to totally avoid any recommendation of dietary supplementation.

## Do Prescription Pills Work?

The scientific method has been highly developed to study this question. The pharmaceutical industry is regulated by the Food and Drug Administration (FDA). Rigorous requirements are imposed on any company that seeks official approval for a new drug. It can cost one billion dollars to bring a new drug to market. The expense is due to the rigorous scientific processes that must be applied to the study of new drugs.

If you wanted to prove that a certain chemical compound can cure or prevent some disease it would first be tested in an animal model. You would look for a species of animal that has a disease similar to that found in humans. If the mediation is shown to benefit diseased animals and did not injure or kill them from toxic side effects, then human trials may be done.

The first tests of a new drug in humans are done on a small group of healthy individuals to determine the optimum dose of a medication to achieve adequate blood and tissue levels. In the next phase of testing the drug is administered to a small group of sick individuals with the specific disease targeted by the drug.

There are many biases that can creep into studies that must be carefully controlled for. One way to do this is with a control group. A new drug is compared with the effectiveness of a placebo or another drug already approved for treatment of the same disease you are wanting to treat. In this later case you determine if your drug is less effective, as effective, or more effective than current standard therapy.

To be fair and balanced the placebo or standard therapy and the test drug need to be presented to test patients in the same shape, size, and color. Both the control group and the test group need to get the same number and same color of pills every day.

Another bias could result from doctors who know the difference between the test drug and the placebo. They could record favorable results for the test drug in their reports. For this reason, the doctors doing research need to be ignorant of what they are dispensing. If patients do not know what they are getting the study is said to be blinded. If the doctors also do not know for sure what they are dispensing, then the study is double blinded.

Another way to control for bias is to switch back and forth between the test drug and the standard therapy or placebo. When this element is added to a study, it is called a cross over study.

The best kind of study to prove the effectiveness of a new product is a double-blinded cross-over study. These kinds of studies take time, cost a lot of money, and have ethical implications. They are conducted under the continuously watchful eye of an Institutional Review Board

(IRB) that has ultimate authority over whether a researcher can initiate, continue, or needs to terminate a study.

## Side effects

Side effects can be temporary or long-term adverse outcomes produced by the ingestion or application of a product. Side effects may be mild, severe, or even fatal in some cases. Knowing the frequency and severity of adverse effects of a drug is important. Common side effects of a drug may include nausea, vomiting, diarrhea, skin rash, or itching. More severe side effects might include liver or kidney damage. The most extreme adverse effect is death.

When a drug is being studied, patients receiving the placebo and the test drug are given long questionnaires to complete at repeat intervals throughout the study. Symptoms that could be adverse effects are carefully documented.

In any human experimentation it is important to monitor symptoms the test medication produces and to measure possible adverse effects on various organ systems. For this reason, in drug trials, frequent blood tests are required to document any changes in liver, kidney or any other organ system. Most drugs will have side effects and it is important to establish that the benefit from the medication outweighs the risks.

## All Natural

Nutritional supplement packages do not usually list any side effects on the label or in promotional materials. This is because most supplements have never been tested for side effects. The usual claim is that because a product is "all natural" that there will be no side effects.

Tobacco is "all natural" and it prematurely kills over 450,000 U.S. citizens every year. Arsenic is natural and it will kill you too. Mercury is natural and it causes serious toxic effects. Salt is natural but can lead to high blood pressure. All food supplements cause some side effects in some people. The public does not know what the side effects are because the manufacturers of food supplements are not required to study or publish the side effects caused by their products.

# Safety

Safety is related to side effects. Side effects may disappear when a drug or supplement is stopped. Some drugs and supplements may cause more serious or even permanent damage to a person's health. Side effects of medications are discovered during the testing process before they are approved by the FDA for doctors to prescribe. But supplements are not tested and so not until wide public experience demonstrate that they cause sickness or death can the FDA step in and remove the supplement from the marketplace.

Ephedra was a component of several popular weight loss supplements that were sold over the counter. After several cardiac deaths with the use of Ephedra, the FDA stepped in and banned the use of this substance in supplements of all kinds.

On the other hand, many licensed drugs have safety issues. These are outweighed by the benefits that occur in critical situations. For example, the drugs that are used to cure lymphoma will cause a drop in your white blood cells, putting you at a risk of developing a variety of infections. Your hair will fall out and other serious problems can develop.

These are serious safety problems but are usually temporary and disappear after your cancer treatment is complete. On the other hand, you will die of lymphoma if it isn't treated. The serious safety problems associated with cancer drugs are acceptable because your life is at stake.

A health evangelists leave the recommendation of prescription medications to licensed practitioners. Also, do not recommend nutritional supplements. Focus on lifestyle changes, good food, exercise, avoiding toxic substances, and trusting God for the restoration and preservation of health.

# 22

# Narrowing the Field

AT THE PRESENT TIME THERE ARE MANY TYPES OF HEALTH PROGRAMS available to local churches. Many claim to be health evangelism programs. Some simply provide health information without monitoring or measuring any behavior change. Other programs screen for various risk factors for disease. Still other programs are interventional programs that aim to help people change harmful behaviors and learn to live a healthier lifestyle.

Some programs are short in duration and are completed in a day. Others run several days a week for up to a month. Some programs are free while others are expensive. Most health programs are privately owned. Some have a spiritual component and others are entirely secular. Most of these programs don't systematically evaluate the health evangelism variables that I advocate in this book.

The Seventh-day Church does not manage, control, or evaluate health programming. Health ministries need better organization and guidance than they have had in the past. Here are my suggestions.

There needs to be a body of consultants established to developed and agree upon on the essential elements of health evangelism. What is the difference between a health program and a health evangelism program? What spiritual elements need to be included in a health program for it to qualify as a health evangelism program?

These consultants should include individuals with diverse backgrounds. Experts are needed who can review the scientific validity of various programs to identify those that contain speculative health claims and/or questionable practices. The cost of programs should be evaluated to identify those that are excessively expensive. Theologians are needed to review the spiritual content of programs to see that they are true to scripture and the Spirit of Prophecy. Here are the primary elements that I feel need to be included in this process of evaluation.

**Health Variables.**

The health information provided in each program should be current, correct, and accurate. Is the behavior change advocated reasonable and can it be safely recommended? Are the interventions advocated appropriate to a local church setting? Are there interventions that should be limited to a more sophisticated health care institution where more supervision by health professionals would be more appropriate?

Are risk factors and changes in behavior being documented? Is the frequency of meetings and duration of the program appropriate? Programs in local churches should not presume to treat specific medical conditions and should not prescribe drugs or advocate, dispense, or sell supplements. As a person's health improves there will be a need to modify drug regimens. The church should enable people to live healthful lives but leave any required change in drug medication to the client's health care provider.

**Spiritual Variables.**

The most important feature of all health evangelism programs is to proclaim and explain how Jesus provides a person with the power to change. Health evangelism will provide for and measure Bible study. Health evangelism will advocate and explain prayer. The frequency of prayer can be measured. Health evangelism will be conducted in local Seventh-day Adventist Churches. Health evangelism will create a social/spiritual interface between church members and public participants.

Health evangelism programs will measure a person's changes in spiritual practices and beliefs that result from the program. Health evangelism will measure the steps a person takes toward baptism. Health evangelism will measure the susceptibility of a program participant to attend evangelistic meetings. Health evangelism will calculate baptism rates, involvement in church activities and retention rates.

**Social Variables.**

Church member involvement in health evangelism will be measured. What is the role of church members? Are church members passive observers? Do they model the advocated behavior? Are there small groups? Do church members facilitate small groups? Do church members contact program participants by phone, email, Facebook, or Twitter? Do church members socialize with participants outside of the health evangelism program? Do they go shopping with participants or share a meal with them at local restaurants? Is there in-home follow-up? How frequently and how often are follow-up activities carried out? How long are follow-up activities continued after a program?

**Educational Variables.**

Are the educational tools used to communicate with the public appropriate? Is the use of visuals appropriate? Is there a skilled presentation of information through PowerPoint or video presentations? Is there an appropriate use of printed materials? Is there a workbook for participants? Is there a guide for small group leaders? Is there an appropriate use of contracts where participants commit to perform new behaviors? Are the lecture materials appropriate for the audience? These are some of the educational variables that need to be evaluated.

**Ownership Variables**

Who owns or controls the health evangelism program? Is the program owned by an individual, group, corporation, or the church? If it is owned by the church at what administrative level is the program owned?

## Finance Variables

What does a program cost? What is the cost of attending a program for each participant? Where does the revenue stream go? Does the local church benefit? Does the revenue flow to the conference, union, or division? Does the profit flow to an individual or privately held corporation? What does the balance sheet of the corporation look like? What is the salary structure of the owners and employees?

## Evaluation Variables

What data are collected by the health evangelism program? Are demographic data collected? Is there an evaluation of pre- and post-program changes in knowledge, attitudes, and practices? Are risk factors and disease states documented? Are changes in risk factors and disease states evaluated? What is the duration of behavior changes? Are laboratory values measured and are changes documented over time? Are spiritual changes being documented? Are Bible study, prayer, and contacts with church members being documented? Is susceptibility to baptism, church activity, and resistance to apostasy being measured?

Is evaluation occurring just before the program begins? Are measurements taking place during and after the program? Are follow-up activities continuing at intervals of 3, 6, 9, months or a year?

## Audit Tool

Once these evaluation criteria are developed, an audit tool needs to be constructed. This will allow a standardized approach to evaluating existing programs. A systematic review of currently promoted materials should be subjected to scrutiny. See Appendix A for a list of proposed essential evaluation criteria and a numerical ranking system that could be used in an audit setting

# 23

# Proposed Audit Tool

IN APPENDIX B IS A PROPOSED AUDIT TOOL THAT WOULD BE USED TO evaluate programs that claim to be health evangelism programs and are seeking recognition and approval by the church or some organizational entity that assumes the prerogative to evaluate health programs. Initially, this tool could be sent directly to the program author(s) or owner(s) for completion.

Alternatively, a representative could visit the program's author or the corporate headquarters and conduct interviews to obtain the needed information. A third option would be for a representative to audit a program directly in some location as it was being conducted.

For the sake of fairness and transparency, the same audit tool should be used to evaluate every health evangelism program being appraised. In this way each program will be judged using the same standards as every other program.

Ideally, the reviewing organization would have representatives from the Health Ministry department of church administration at some level, medical experts, psychologists, educators, evangelists, and statisticians. It would be advisable to also include authors of one or more health evangelism programs on the review committee.

Once the evaluation tool has been completed, the results should be circulated to all the members of the reviewing organization. There should be a deadline for responses. A vote should be taken to confirm the final valuation and ranking of a program. Before the results are made known publicly, the program owner or author should be notified of the results of the audit and given time to respond, adjust, or appeal.

There should be an appeal process. Any appeal should be handled by at least two of the review committee members who were not involved in the original survey. If there is to be a change in the original evaluation, it should be discussed and voted on by the entire committee.

Requests to opt out of the evaluation process are honored but these programs should receive the **Not Recommended** label. Any program that is authored by a Seventh-day Adventist and is promoted to Seventh-day Adventist churches and institutions should be reviewed.

This proposed process for evaluating the quality of health evangelism does not exist at the present time. There should be a sponsoring organization. This might be a branch of the church administrative structure, a university, an independent organization that is currently a member of Adventist-laymen's Services & Industries organization, or a new entity that understands and is dedicated to the process of developing meaningful health evangelism.

# 24

# Networking and Marketing your Programs

NETWORKING IS THE PROCESS OF EXCHANGING IDEAS, DATA, AND EVEN program participants with other agencies, programs, or churches. Information about your health evangelism program needs to be communicated.

Communicate with church administrators. You should attend church sponsored meetings to share your success. You will want to publish your findings in appropriate journals. Do not forget to interface with the community as well. Secular service organizations and various governmental agencies need to know what you are doing. Voluntary organizations such the Heart Association, Lung Association, Cancer Society and Diabetes Association should know what you are doing in your health evangelism programs.

Once you have good data to share, make the rounds and share your success. This will result in referrals to your program from other agencies.

Take smoking cessation as an example. The Cancer Society, Lung Association and Heart Association, all encourage people to stop smoking. These organizations have films, literature and displays that discourage smoking. Some also conduct smoking cessation programs.

When you network with these organizations, you create an opportunity to use some of the excellent materials they have developed. Using good materials from other organizations helps legitimize your operations and shows a spirit of cooperation with outside agencies.

You may be invited to join a voluntary organization and participate in their activities. This is a good opportunity for you. I have served as a volunteer with the American Cancer Society, the American Heart Association, and the Texas Interagency Counsel on Smoking and Health. This was profitable for my health evangelism activities. It gave me access to great materials that I could use in my own programs and enhanced my credibility with my audience.

This is a two-way street. If you were to use some of the materials from the American Cancer Society in a smoking cessation program, they would want to know how many people attended and how much literature you distributed. The Cancer Society is anxious to document the utilization of their own materials. Your use of their materials makes them more successful as well.

This is more than advertising. You are developing relationships with community organizations. As your effectiveness and reputation grow, community agencies will be proud to affiliate with you and will refer individuals to your health evangelism programs.

So, reach outward and find organizations with similar goals. Use materials that have been developed by others when it is consistent with your own message. Receive program participants who are referred to you from other organizations.

## Referral

There will be individuals who attend your health evangelism programs who will need additional resources beyond those your program can provide. It is important to establish a roster of organizations to which you can refer problem participants.

*Your job is to change behaviors not to treat active disease.*

The clinically sick need the care of a medical professional. It is your function to change behaviors but not to treat active disease. Those who are ill need to be under the care of a physician in the local health care system. If a person does not have a doctor, you should know how to find one for them.

Those who might be offended by the spiritual content of your health evangelism program need a secular program to attend that omits the spiritual emphasis. You should have a list of behavior change programs in your region that address the problems your participants have--just in case they become upset with you and need a referral.

Then there will be those who simply fail to change their behaviors. These people may be successful for a short period of time but fail in the end. You have done all you can. Your church members have prayed for them and supported them, but they still failed. Such individuals usually need to be removed from their day-to-day environment to achieve success. Refer these difficult cases to lifestyle centers for more intensive behavior modification.

Most lifestyle programs enroll people for 7-28 days and control their diet, environment, sleep, and exercise. A person who has had trouble changing behavior at home is more likely to succeed in an institutional setting. These centers are relatively expensive to attend. Insurance programs usually do not cover the costs of behavior change programs. If there is a person from your church who would benefit from such a program and does not have sufficient resources to attend one, perhaps your church, or someone in your church, could help defray their expenses.

Lifestyle centers have operated as autonomous, self-supporting organizations for decades. They advertise widely to recruit their clients. Clients come directly from their homes, take the program, and then return home without any personalized follow-up. Not so with the clients you will refer to lifestyle centers.

A problem participant from your church who attends a live-in program will have friends back in the home church who know them, have helped them, and are praying for them. As soon as the live-in program is completed, these participants will be returning to your community. You can help them sustain their new behaviors.

## Do not Compromise

Your health evangelism program should be a spiritual program. Do not apologize for this. Do not make compromises with anyone to make yourself "more acceptable" or "more attractive" to, secular voluntary organizations or governmental agencies with whom you network.

Once I advised a local pastor who was wanting to run a Five-day Plan to Stop Smoking in his church to contact the American Cancer Society to obtain a couple of films and some literature I had recommended.

This pastor called me back a day or two later and was disappointed because the American Cancer Society would not share any of their materials with him. The reason was because he charged a nominal fee for his program and the Cancer Society didn't want their "free" material to be "sold." This of course was a misunderstanding by the American Cancer Society. The smoking cessation program was not operating for profit. The registration fee just covered the cost of the materials the pastor needed to purchase to conduct his program.

I contacted the Cancer Society and explained the situation to them and told them of my background in the field of smoking and health. As a result of my phone call, the Cancer Society delivered the films and brochures to the pastor's door. I was invited to become a member of the Help Smokers Quit Committee for the local chapter of the Cancer Society. A few weeks later I was invited to sit on the board of directors for the local chapter of the Cancer Society.

On the day of my first noontime board meeting, the staff of the Cancer Society called with the offer to get me a roast beef sandwich for lunch. I declined the offer stating that I was a vegetarian and would just grab a bite at the hospital cafeteria before I came to the meeting. They countered with an offer to get me chief's salad which I gratefully accepted.

I was early to the board meeting and instantly recognized my place at the table because there was a big, beautiful salad and thirteen roast beef sandwiches placed around the table. As board members came in everyone asked, "Who is he and how did he get a salad?" I explained that I was a vegetarian, a Seventh-day Adventist and was a new board member.

Of course, beef is a clean meat, and eating a beef sandwich once a month at a board meeting is a minimal compromise of my standards. No one would think less of me for eating a beef sandwich on a rare occasion. It would be a small compromise over a minor issue, but I chose not to compromise.

Board members were delighted to know that there were other options on the menu other than the traditional roast beef sandwich. Several months later at a subsequent board meeting, I was pleased to see 12 salads and only one roast beef sandwich at the table. The person who ate the beef sandwich apologized for not wanting to eat the "rabbit food" the rest of us were eating. He was a beef man and was not going to change.

The point is, do not compromise your standards in the process of networking. There will be many points at which you will have an opportunity to compromise. Do not do it. Others will want you to eliminate the spiritual emphasis in your program. Do not do it. There are plenty of Godless programs people can attend. Your programs are designed to be evangelistic. Your health evangelism activities involve church, church members and the gospel.

I ran across an outstanding example of compromise when I was promoting the Breathe Free Plan to Stop Smoking in Europe. At the time I was connected with the Health Ministries Department of the General Conference of Seventh-day Adventists. I was trying to get people to try the new Breathe Free Plan in place of the older Five-day Plan to Stop Smoking. I was also trying to get people to use their local churches as program locations. I stressed the importance of using church members as helpers in conducting the Breathe Free Program.

In certain European countries, the older Five-day Plan to Stop Smoking was given official recognition by the government. Those who conducted the Five-day Plan were employed by the government to conduct these programs for the public.

The Five-day Plan was conducted without any spiritual component. It was conducted in public places—not churches. And it was conducted by health educators—without the added benefit that would have come from the services of volunteer church members. This is a sad example of networking that resulted in a compromise of the basic principles of health evangelism. In my opinion this weakened the Five-day Plan to the point where it became relatively useless to the church.

The Seventh-day Adventist church doesn't need to be conducting health education programs that are totally secular. To do so represents a serious compromise of the principles of health evangelism which are put forth in this book. Networking is important, but not if you must compromise what you are doing. Compromise is a fine thing under many circumstances but not if it results in a diversion from the fundamentals of the gospel of health.

## Advertising

Health evangelism programs need advertising and promotion to get started. It has been my experience that as soon as a program becomes well established in the community, almost all advertising can be stopped. Usually, by the third or fourth program done in your church, you will be so well known that further advertising will not be needed.

It is important to have brochures that describe your program. You should schedule future programs 12 months in advance. Your brochures should have your yearly schedule printed in them. At the end of each health evangelism program, your audience wants to know when the next program is going to be held. Give each participant two or three brochures for them to hand out to their friends and neighbors. Most of your new participants will come from the word-of-mouth recommendations of previous participants.

Another good source of referrals is from health professionals in your community. The health professionals in your church and health professionals in the neighborhood should have a supply of brochures for their offices. They can refer patients who need the help you provide. A person referred by a health professional is more likely to attend a program than a referral from any other source.

Deliver a supply of brochures to health professionals in your community. Family practitioners, internal medicine doctors, pulmonary specialists, cardiologists, and cancer specialists will all be glad to refer their patients to your church for behavior change classes.

Other media can be useful as well. Regional newspapers will often run a feature story about your health evangelism program, especially if you purchase some advertising space at the same time. Radio and TV stations have community calendars where special events like your health evangelism program can be promoted.

Advertising on social media is particularly rewarding. Facebook is one of the best ways to advertise to your community. It is used by 71% of the United States regularly. The South Bay SDA Church in Chattanooga Tennessee has used this in connection with other advertisement forms and has found Facebook advertising to be the most effective and least costly way to advertise. It will take a little effort to set up your campaign, but once you have it, it will be very easy to do every time you run the program.

You will need to set up a Facebook Business account with a credit card in order to pay for the ads. There are many YouTube videos that show how to do this. Once that is set up you will need to develop your advertisements.

There are several ways to have potential participants register. On Facebook they will click a button to "Sign Up". It is best to have a registration page for them. This can be something on your website. Google Forms is the easiest way to set this up. You can target audiences in the vicinity of your church.

About one to two weeks before a program starts, I like to send a letter, text, or email to all previous participants to remind them that the new program is about to begin. Backsliders can come back and recycle themselves if they have slipped. Remind past participants to recommend your program to their family and friends. Many new participants come from notifications like this.

I also promote each program to participants who have attended other kinds of programs we have conducted in the church. Frequent reminders keep your church calendar fresh in the minds of the public. Participants who attended one program may very well be interested in other programs you conduct.

Posters may be useful when placed in local business and professional offices. Posters look best if done professionally but do the best you can with the talent and resources you have in your church.

# 25

# How to Deal with Special Issues

HEALTH EVANGELISM ACTIVITIES SOMETIMES RESULT IN SPECIAL problems that will cripple your programs if not handled properly. These problems tend to come up repeatedly. Handling these issues requires much prayer, tact, and counseling together. Here are ways I have dealt with these problems over the years. You may need to try different solutions depending on your circumstances.

## Dictatorial Leadership

When a health evangelism program becomes successful there is a tendency for the developer to become proud. You think the success of a program is largely due to your personal charisma, talent, and skill. There follows a dictatorial, controlling environment that hampers success.

It is best to develop and promote programs with the input of a committee. God blesses us when we work together to advance His cause. Making moves from a consensus developed when a group of workers have shared, studied, and prayed with one another, is superior to unilateral, dictatorial decisions.

## Health Fanatics

Health evangelism is given a bad name and is discredited by health fanatics. The devil has cleverly claimed the extremes of health. Health fanatics usually have no (or only a limited) education in the science of health matters. These people have come to believe one or more of thousands of bogus health theories that abound in our culture.

These fanatics go to extremes in drink and diet. Many are devout church members who think their actions are condoned by Scripture or Spirit of Prophecy. These fanatics will be quick to volunteer to help you with your health evangelism program. They will often want an opportunity to present their ideas or products to your audience. Kindly, but firmly avoid these people. They will only confuse your audience, taint your good reputation, and defame health evangelism.

The Covid-19 pandemic has brought on stage new types of health fanatics. It is settled science that vaccines are safe including all the ones licensed in the United States. Vaccines prevent infections and greatly reduce hospitalizations and deaths. The Seventh-day Adventist denomination favors vaccine use including the use of the Covid-19 vaccines. Those who conduct health evangelism programs should protect the public that comes to their programs by being in the best of health possible and fully vaccinated against communicable diseases. Anti-vaccination individuals should not direct the program or be small group facilitators.

The value of wearing masks to reduce (not eliminate) the transmission of respiratory viruses is also settled science. Mask mandates are viewed by many as an infringement on personal freedoms by governments and industry. They see in these mandates a foreshadowing of the extreme restrictions on freedom of worship that are predicted to come in the future.

The wearing of masks when mandated or otherwise prudent, protects the public that comes to your health evangelism programs from unnecessary exposure to respiratory pathogens. Anti-mask or anti-mandate individuals should not direct your program or be small group facilitators. The Seventh-day Adventist denomination is not against mask mandates when the need for them is indicated by pandemic conditions.

## Spiritual Zealots

These are devout church members. They have a zeal for God that can be useful, but may need to be tempered, especially in the early phases of a health evangelism program. The gospel presented in your health evangelism program should be problem-specific and free from religious jargon or distinctive doctrines.

These spiritual zealots may attempt to use your health program as an opportunity to introduce distinctive doctrines to your participants in an untimely manner. They will not confine their spiritual conversation to the health problems at hand. They do not bring just the milk of the Word but the meat as well. This will result in confusion and alienation of otherwise susceptible participants.

Do not necessarily give up on this group. They do want to help, but they bring too much with them. If they can be convinced to go slow and to confine a discussion of God's help to the behavioral problem at hand, they can be useful.

## Spiritual Novices

These church members set a bad example. They do not particularly believe in the health message. They do not practice the health message. When someone who wants to live a healthier life gets to know one of these people, they will become discouraged. In the estimation of these babes in the word, how you live is secondary to trust in God.

These church members, when it comes right down to it, think that most health evangelism is a form of salvation by works. They live degenerate lives. These church members often wake up when they develop diabetes, have a heart attack, or a stroke. These members are then willing to help you.

Do not give up on these members. If you have an obese church member who wants to help in a weight control program you can do one of two things. You can request that they take the program along with public members to demonstrate that they are serious about weight control. Once these church members have developed a measure of control over their habits and have a new or deeper relationship with God, they are ready to be a helper in the next program.

On the other hand, you can take a chance and plug them into your program. I have used obese church members as helpers in small groups in a weight management program. These people were always the ones to lose the most weight. They were making painful adjustments to their own lives at each step of the way just like others in their group. Their lives were literally on the line. Most did well. Those who did not do well usually did not want to help in the next program.

## Nutritional Supplements

The nutritional supplement business is a multi-billion-dollar industry in the United States. In every church I have visited or been a member, there are well intentioned but misguided members who are distributors of vitamins, minerals, or herbal products. Avoid these people and their products.

It is especially distressing to me when I see poorly informed pastors and their wives promoting and selling these products among their congregation and in the community. Many of these people feel that the use of these nutritional pills or potions will help keep you off "drug" medication and are consistent with the writings of Ellen White. This is not the case as clearly made in Dr. Mervyn G. Hardinge's book, *A Physician Explains Ellen White's Counsel on Drugs, Herbs, & Natural Remedies* published by the Review and Herald Publishing Association. (2001)

Do not advocate or promote any nutritional or vitamin supplement in any health evangelism program. God made food. Man extracts small chemical components out of plants and promotes them as being better than the original food. Food is wonderful. Food is adequate. Stick with good food and skip the pills, capsules, and powders.

## Food Demonstrations

Food demonstrations present special issues. For everyone to see a demonstration clearly, an overhead mirror or projection will be required. If the group is small, all participants can crowd around a table.

If you are going to serve food samples, this should be done in proximity to a regular meal so as to not be eating between meals. Food served as part of a food demonstration may substitute for a meal if sufficient samples are served to constitute an adequate meal.

Measure out all ingredients so that the recipe can be put together rapidly. If baking or prolonged cooking is required, have a batch completed and ready to serve so there will not be additional delay in cooking food.

Recipes are important and should be provided to the attendees. Ideally, they should be low in saturated fat and cholesterol and should have a limited sugar content. We should only demonstrate recipes that represent good nutrition. Recipes must pass the "taste test." The food should look good and taste good as well!

Importantly, those demonstrating a recipe should be familiar with the recipe they are presenting. Not just having fixed it a few times at home to get used to the recipe, but it should be a recipe that has been in regular use by the presenter for years at home.

Church members are usually so truthful that if they do not eat the food they are demonstrating at home, they will confess that they have been trying all week to get the recipe just right. I have been asked if a certain concoction looked OK right in the middle of a demonstration. These small errors suggest that the members of your church do not eat this food and are unfamiliar with it.

Experience with a recipe is important in selling it to an audience. I had a sweet little old Italian lady in one program demonstrate a soup recipe that had been in her family for generations. She had learned the recipe from her mother. It had a couple of "secret" ingredients that made the soup "special." This lady with her strong accent just won the audience over. Everyone loved her soup. Everyone took the recipe home. The evening was a great success.

You should screen recipes to see that they are appropriate from a nutritional point of view, but it is so important to be authentic that I would rather use family recipes that may be a bit suspect but have been in constant use, rather than some recipe a nutritionist hands out for you to try.

## Organic Foods

Organic foods are more expensive than ordinary foods. The nutritional value of organic foods is not significantly different from regular foods. In a health evangelism program about nutrition, it is better to focus on the big problems in diet and leave "organic" arguments for later programs in which the topic can be explored in detail and where it can receive a proper balance.

## Genetically Modified Foods

Virtually all foods have been genetically modified in one way or another over the past couple of hundreds of years. Plants that are disease resistant are superior to those that are not. Plants producing a greater yield will produce a larger crop for the farmer and will feed more people than older cultivars. Without genetic modification the current world population could not be sustained on the plants commonly grown 100 years ago. Without genetically modified foods the world would be starving much more than it is today.

On the other hand, scientists have been able to insert genes in plants to produce compounds that are toxic to insects that try to eat the plants. This results in larger and healthier crops, but the impact on humans has not been studied.

Scientists have also created some plants that are resistant to weed control chemicals. This makes weed control much easier and greatly increases crop yield, but the results of these plant modifications on human health have not been established.

In Genesis, God promises us, that until the end of the world there will be "seedtime and harvest." I do not think it is wise to make a large issue out of GMO foods until there is sound science on one side or the other.

We need to eat healthfully of the abundance that is available to us. What we eat is certainly able to put the weight on us. Obesity is an epidemic that speaks to the availability of excess calories. GMO foods do not appear to be causing starvation or unusual diseases based on the evidence available at present.

## Supplements of Vitamins, Minerals, Herbs, and Micronutrients.

Carefully conducted studies of the nutrient content of foods widely available for all of us, indicate that the foods we eat today are nutritious and contain all the elements needed for good health.

The use of supplements of any kind is a statement of distrust of our creator and sustainer. Those who use supplements and believe in them should stop thanking God at mealtime because in their estimation the foods of God's design, grown on God's good earth are so deficient that a man-made supplement is needed to correct the deficit God has allowed to become established in the food we buy in the grocery store.

Trust in God and the food he provides. You do not need supplementation of any kind for the preservation of health. There is good science, Scripture, and Spirit of Prophecy counsel that these supplements are not needed in the human diet. Do not use, endorse, promote, or sell supplements of any kind in any health evangelism program.

## Stick to Science and Scripture

Much of the public and many church members are suspicious of science. The scientific method is an extremely valuable tool in proving the validity of many things. Population studies in which hundreds of millions of dollars have been invested have proven the truth of the dietary principles contained in Scripture and Spirit of Prophecy writings. The use of these data, combined with Bible texts and selected quotes from the writings of Ellen G. White, represent the most powerful argument you can make for changes in behavior. Do not criticize science or Scripture in your presentations.

## Cures for Disease

Those who are sick are looking for a cure. In many churches there are laypersons who believe in simple cures for complex diseases. These people have an extremely limited understanding of physiology, and the pathology of disease. But they have extreme confidence in grape juice, charcoal, or some diet to cure disease. Do not let these people express their opinion in your programs or privately counsel your participants.

Let the sick go to doctors and hospitals. Health evangelism is about prevention not about cures. Living right may make your diabetes, weight, and blood pressure better. Exercise may reduce your risk of a heart attack but the sick need to be under the care of health care professionals.

Your health evangelism program should be about preventing disease by controlling harmful behaviors not curing people of their diseases. You should not be in the business of practicing medicine without a license. Do not promise to cure anything.

You can prevent or reduce the risk of cancer, you can prevent or reduce the risk of a stroke or heart attack, but you cannot cure cancer, cure a stroke, or cure a heart attack. The modern medical system works on those who have become sick. This is the work for hospitals and doctors. You must not pretend to do their work for them.

Hospitals and doctors spend little or no time on prevention. Prevention requires behavior change which is so difficult and usually impossible without God's help. Stick to behavior change issues and stay away from cures.

# Independence

As your health evangelism program becomes increasingly successful, attempts may be made by individuals or organizations to assume control or manage your program. This will happen if your program attracts wide interest in the community and baptisms result. This is especially true if your program generates significant income from fees collected or from donations.

Successful health evangelism programs will come to the attention of other churches. As this occurs, church administrators or others will want to have some involvement or control of your program. What should be done?

Program details, data, and financial records should be open for any responsible individual or organization to inspect. You should be open with church administrators who make inquiry. The blessing and endorsement of local churches and church administrators will go a long way to legitimize your work and will help open doors to other churches.

Cooperation, however, should not result in loss of control. Pray for wisdom on how to approach this. Relinquish management and promotion of your health evangelism program, only if it appears that it is the best interest of God's work.

A successful health evangelism program is not an opportunity for you to become famous or rich. Successful health evangelism's sole purpose is to advance God's work. The whole process should be controlled by God. Your role may need to diminish so the church and God's work can get the credit for the success of health evangelism.

On the other hand, God may need you to keep a steady hand on the health evangelism program(s) you have developed. You may need to stay connected with your programs to preserve them. God will guide. Do not be selfish when success comes.

## Copyright

All materials you develop should be copyrighted in your name. This is not to guarantee recognition or profit for you, but to protect your materials from being stolen and misappropriated by others who may not understand health evangelism as you do.

I have known people who developed useful health educational materials but left their product in the public domain only to have it stolen by someone else who then copyrighted that material. Those who copyrighted the stolen material then turned around and prohibited the original developer from promoting or using their own material. What a sad lesson.

Your goal should be to see health evangelism spread far and wide. Copyright the materials you develop and then generously allow others to use them and even modify them. Do not copyright materials to restrict health evangelism or to make a profit, although making a living from the work you do is appropriate.

Your copyright may be transferred to a church entity if you are satisfied that official recognition and endorsement by the church will result in a wider use for your program. Make sure the program you transfer retains its soul-winning elements.

## Commercialism

Some health evangelism programs become commercially successful. If you are an employee of the church at some level of administration, I would expect that you shouldn't make any profit from a health evangelism program you develop or promote. The church is paying your salary and providing you with benefits. Any product you develop while working for the church ought to be the property of the church organization.

The situation is different if you earn a living for yourself. If a health evangelism program you develop and copyright becomes a commercial success, you need to be careful in the choices you make. It is appropriate for you to make a living wage from the work of your hands. Profits from any health evangelism program, however, should largely be used to advance health evangelism among local churches. The local church that uses your program should realize enough profit to offset all expenses and provide that church with enough margin to promote other health evangelism activities.

There are opportunities to develop and sell products that promote your program. These products should be selected carefully. Tee shirts, ball caps, bookmarks, and refrigerator magnets, may help create name recognition for your program but if not done carefully may cheapen your message that it is God who changes behavior for the good.

Good health comes from a plant-based diet, exercise, and avoiding toxic substances. Do not distribute or sell health supplements, protein bars, special lines of prepared foods, vitamins, or minerals. These are contrary to the Seventh-day Adventist health message and an undesirable way to create a profit in a church-based program.

# 26

# Health Evangelism Revitalized

SEVENTH-DAY ADVENTISTS ARE CERTAIN ABOUT SEVERAL THINGS. THE seventh day is the Sabbath of the Lord our God. Jesus is coming soon. This gospel will be preached in all the earth and then the end will come.

We have a health message. Those who live it are the healthiest people in the world. Healthful living will be a prominent component of the restoration promised to those who trust Jesus as their Lord and Savior.

We are challenged by this quote of Ellen White.

> "I wish to tell you that soon there will be no work done in ministerial lines but medical missionary work." **General Conference Bulletin, April 12, 1901 par. 21**

Troublous time are upon us now and we anticipate that things will be getting worse in the future. Some envision health evangelism as being the last limited avenue of service open to us at some time in the future when other avenues of witnessing are closed.

I prefer to think of health evangelism as a superior form of witnessing. Health evangelism has a practical health producing quality that demonstrates that what we say works. Health evangelism reveals Jesus as the power who saves physically, mentally, and spiritually.

Health evangelism is **scientifically accurate** when wisely using data from studies done in populations from around the world. Health evangelism rejects false methods of healing.

Natural science operates within the limits of intrinsic human capabilities. Health evangelism goes beyond an individual's capacity for behavior change. It **adds evangelism to science**. It points to the Creator of science who has power over all the elements of nature and power over His submissive needy creatures who reach beyond themselves for help.

Health evangelism **offends human pride**. It takes the frustrated, unsatisfied, failing person away from the modern, shining towers of science and places him in the often-mundane local church. The church which in the end is the only home Christians have in this world. The church that is the theater of God's grace.

Health evangelism utilizes **unlikely practitioners** for behavioral intervention, church members who themselves suffer from the same habits, and addictions as those who come for help. But these examples prove the effectiveness of the offered cure.

If God is effectively changing those who are as weak and prone to failure as I am, then there is hope for me too. Every church member has something to do, encouragement to give, prayers to offer, availability when needed, friends to make, love to share, but most of all an example of righteous living to live.

Health evangelism works by **simple means**. God's methods are always simple. **Prayer** works. There is a flood of assurances in **God's word** not found in all the self-help books. Divine behavioral therapy is a more effective tool than cognitive behavioral therapy. There is more help outside yourself than you will ever find by looking for power within yourself.

Health evangelism requires **individual effort**. Success is not found in a pill a practitioner prescribes for you, or in surgery performed on you. You need to be the one to act in your own behalf. The steps that always stumbled before will now step successfully toward your goal. God will enable you to achieve not fail.

Health evangelism **really works**. The testimonies of victory day by day and week by week encourage all others in the struggle. The success of one becomes the success of another.

Health evangelism results in **new convictions**. That the God of health evangelism is the only God. Old prejudices are abandoned, old creeds forsaken. It is not reasoning, it is not teaching, but experience that creates these new convictions. I now know for certain what transforms and what doesn't, what saves and what doesn't.

Health evangelism generates **gratitude**. You are thankful because you have received and continue to receive God's help. You have received help you could find nowhere else. The profound gift prompts profound gratitude.

Health evangelism inspires **worship**. Your whole being is so flooded with gratitude to God. It prompts questions, "What do you believe in your church?" which is code for "I want to know more about this God who changes me."

Health evangelism is an **economical** enterprise. It changes more lives for less money than any other form of witnessing. Health evangelism purifies the church. Church members shape-up or ship-out.

Health evangelism will be realized for the evangelistic powerhouse it is when **data collection** and analysis are valued. We are members of a skeptical church power structure that is data driven but is also responsive to the leading of the Holy Spirit especially when bolstered by supporting numbers.

Health evangelism has many proponents but has suffered from limited success or outright failure when the vision was flawed, and essential elements were missing.

I believe that health evangelism will be the last viable witnessing modality remaining when the church is limited in its witnessing by governmental restraint. But I believe that health evangelism can rather immediately become the superior form of evangelistic endeavor. This will occur once it is organized and implemented in the way that it was intended to be conducted.

May God help us work for ourselves and others in the ways He intended. Even so come Lord Jesus.

# Appendix A. Essential Elements in Health Evangelism

These are the elements that optimize the evangelistic potential of a health program

1. Church location.
2. Utilization of a pastor's services.
3. Utilizing church members in a one-to-one relationship with participants.
4. Small group activities.
5. Spiritual approach to behavior change.
6. Utilization of prayer as part of the program and daily home assignments.
7. Utilization of Scripture as part of the program and daily home assignments.
8. Designed to put people in a path leading to baptism and church membership
9. Data collection and analysis that track spiritual variables as well as scientific variables.
10. Scientifically sound.
11. Up to date
12. Follow-up at intervals over a year
13. Low cost per session, No commercialization of the program.

**Proposed value of each essential element expressed numerically.**

| Program Element: | Numeric Value |
| --- | ---: |
| **Program Location** | |
| All programs held at the local church | 10 |
| Programs may be held in the local church, but this is optional | 5 |
| Most program are conducted in a secular setting | 0 |
| | |
| **Pastor Involvement** | |
| Pastor involved in all sessions | 10 |
| Pastor occasionally involved or participation is optional | 5 |
| No pastor involvement | 0 |
| | |
| **Church Member Involvement** | |
| Church members personally involved in each session | 10 |
| Church members modestly or minimally involved | 5 |
| Church member involvement is not required | 0 |
| | |
| **Small Group Activities** | |
| Church members lead small groups each session | 10 |
| Church members involved in some groups | 5 |
| Small groups but not lead by church members | 2 |
| No small group activities in the program | 0 |
| | |
| **Follow-up Activities** | |
| Follow-up activities for a period of one year | 5 |
| Follow-up activities done by church members | 5 |
| Follow-up activities done in participants' homes | 5 |
| Follow-up activities centralized at the church | 3 |
| Follow-up centralized but not at the church | 2 |

| | |
|---|---|
| Follow-up by mail or phone only | 1 |
| No follow-up activities | 0 |

## Spiritual Behavior Change

| | |
|---|---|
| Jesus proclaimed as agent of change in each session | 10 |
| Jesus referred to in less than 50% of sessions | 5 |
| Program limited to "Higher Power" or vague "God" references | 2 |
| Only psychological measures for behavior change | 1 |
| No behavior change advocated | 0 |

## Prayer

| | |
|---|---|
| Prayer planned for daily and tracked | 10 |
| Prayer recommended daily but not tracked | 7 |
| Prayer offered publicly and frequently during the program | 5 |
| Prayer in private before the program begins by leaders | 3 |
| Prayer is not designed into the program | 0 |

## Scripture Assignments

| | |
|---|---|
| Scripture assigned for daily study and tracked | 10 |
| Scripture assigned but not tracked | 7 |
| Scriptures used during the program | 5 |
| No scriptures during the program | 0 |

## Scientifically Sound

| | |
|---|---|
| Data presented from sound peer reviewed literature | 10 |
| Some good data but some speculative or unsubstantiated data | 5 |
| Program based on anecdotal evidence or speculation | 0 |

## Commercialization

| | |
|---|---|
| Non-profit or church operated program | 10 |
| Profit margin 10% or less of the cost | 8 |

| | |
|---|---|
| Profit margin more than 10% of the cost | 3 |
| Supplements advocated or sold during the program | 0 |
| Devices advocated or sold during the program | 0 |

Data Collection

| | |
|---|---|
| Data collected before, during, and after program | 10 |
| Data collected before and at last session only | 7 |
| Only registration data collected | 3 |
| No data collection | 0 |

Cost to each participant (Excluding lab work)

| | |
|---|---|
| No cost to the participant | 10 |
| Cost less than $5.00 per person for the entire program | 8 |
| Cost $5.00 to $10 per person for the entire program | 4 |
| Cost more than $10 per person for the entire program | 0 |

**Possible Scores**

The maximum possible score is 125 if a program is optimized for evangelism. The minimum possible is 0 for a purely secular program conducted in a public setting.

The next step is to systematically evaluate all the health programs that are currently being used or promoted among Seventh-day Adventist churches. This survey would be conducted by distributing the standardized audit tool by mail to each of the health programs that are used by churches. If a program failed to respond to the request for information, a site visit could be conducted to corporate headquarters or to a locally conducted program to obtain information regarding the program

Once this evaluation has occurred and an analysis has been performed, a ranking can be developed. The detailed analysis of each program should be made available to churches on request, but a simple ranking system could be used. This simple ranking of programs should be published so that churches that are considering conducting health evangelism can make a more informed decision about what kind of programs should be selected for their local church. An example of a simplified ranking system is presented here.

**Final General Ranking Categories:**

> **Excellent** – Incorporates all recommended elements that promote evangelism
>
> **Acceptable** – Incorporates most recommended elements.
>
> **Primarily Secular** – Contains excellent information but minimal evangelistic elements
>
> **Not recommended** – Not good science – minimal evangelistic elements

This process of evaluation and ranking should be performed regularly on an annual or biannual basis. Some programs will be modified by their authors/owners to better fit a more ideal health evangelism model, and this should be recognized by a change in the ranking of these upgraded programs. New programs will be designed, tested, and deployed. These should be promptly evaluated as they become available. Churches should be encouraged to conduct health evangelism program that have been optimized for their evangelistic impact.

# Appendix B. Proposed Audit Tool

This is the suggested worksheet that would be used in evaluating a health program that was being used in local churches or suggested for use in local churches.

## 1. Program Description:

Name of the program: _____

Program purpose: _____

Duration of the program: _____

Number of sessions: _____

Frequency of sessions: (weekly, daily, etc.) _____

Program author/owner: _____

Program distributor(s): _____

Cost for a participant to attend an entire program: _____

Year Program was developed: _____

Number of programs conducted each year: _____

Scope/number of states/countries where program is available: _____

## 2. Program Location:

Where is the typical or ideal location for the program to be conducted?

_____

Is a local church utilized as a location for conducting a program?

    ____ Yes. Required or highly recommended.
    ____ Yes. Preferable but not essential to program success.
    ____ No. Not recommended or required.


## 3. Materials:

Please check the types of materials that have been developed for this program.


## 3A. Promotional Materials: Indicate Y for yes and N for no.

    ____ Media package.
    ____ Letters promoting the program.
    ____ Posters
    ____ Handouts/Flyers
    ____ Radio Spots
    ____ TV Spots
    ____ Newspaper articles
    ____ Newspaper advertisements.
    ____ Social Media: Please be specific_____
    ____ Other. _____


## 3B. Program Materials: Indicate Y for yes and N for no.

____ Directors manual? Instruction on how to organize and conduct a program?

____ Lecture materials.

    ____ Health emphasis materials. How many lectures? _____

    ____ Psychological emphasis materials. How many lectures? ____

    ____ Spiritual emphasis materials. How many lectures? _____

    ____ Printed. What types? _____

    ____ PowerPoint. What types? _____

    ____ Video/DVD of presentations. Types? _____

    ____ Other _____

____ Helpers Materials.

    ____ Do helpers have instructional material?

    ____ Are there social activities?

    ____ Are there spiritual activities?

    ____ Are scriptures used in these activities?

    ____ Are there scientific activities?

    ____ Are there behavioral modification activities?

____ Small Group Materials.

    ____ How many small group sessions are there? _____

    ____ Social activity materials? In how many sessions? _____

    ____ Spiritual activity materials? In how many sessions? _____

    ____ Scientific activity materials? In how many sessions? _____

    ____ Behavioral modification materials? In how many sessions? _

    ____ Other. _____

____ Workbook/Take home materials for participants.

    ____ How many sessions have take-home materials? _____

    ____ Social activity take home materials? How many sessions? _

    ____ Spiritual take home materials? How many sessions? _____

    ____ Scientific take home materials? How many sessions? _____

    ____ Behavior modification take home materials? How many? _

Other Materials that have been developed._____

_____

## 4. Personnel:

What personnel are required to conduct a program? Give a brief job description of each.

_____
_____
_____
_____
_____
_____
_____
_____

Does this program utilize any of the following personnel?

Physician level health professional?

    \_\_\_\_ Yes. Required or highly recommended.
    \_\_\_\_ Yes. Preferable but not essential to program success.
    \_\_\_\_ No. Not recommended or required.

Nurse: RN, LVN, MS?

    \_\_\_\_ Yes. Required or highly recommended.
    \_\_\_\_ Yes. Preferable but not essential to program success.
    \_\_\_\_ No. Not recommended or required.

Auxiliary Health Professional: PT, OT, Lab, X-ray, Social Worker, etc.

    \_\_\_\_ Yes. Required or highly recommended.
    \_\_\_\_ Yes. Preferable but not essential to program success.
    \_\_\_\_ No. Not recommended or required.

Lay persons without formal medical training.

    \_\_\_\_ Yes. Required or highly recommended.
    \_\_\_\_ Yes. Preferable but not essential to program success.
    \_\_\_\_ No. Not recommended or required.

Pastors

    \_\_\_\_ Yes. Required or highly recommended.
    \_\_\_\_ Yes. Preferable but not essential to program success.
    \_\_\_\_ No. Not recommended or required.

## 5. Science.

Give a brief description of the science behind this program. What is the scientific evidence to support the purpose and the techniques advocated or promoted in this program?

_____

_____

_____

## 6. Behavior Change.

What specific behavior changes are recommended in this program?

Are participants' unhealthy behaviors before the program identified? _____

How is this done? (Questionnaire, laboratory test, measurements?) _____

Are participants' changing behaviors monitored during the program? _____

How is this done? (Questionnaire, laboratory test, measurements?) _____

Are participants' changes in behaviors monitored at the end of the program? _____

How is this done? (Questionnaire, laboratory test, measurements?) _____

Are participants' changed behaviors monitored after the program? _____

If yes, at what intervals and for how long? _____

## 7. Use of Evangelism Variables:

Do you use the Non-Adventist Person Visit (**NAPV**)? _____

      Do you use **Scripture** in the program? _____

      Do you evaluate the use of Scripture in the Program?

      How frequently? _____

      Are there daily Scripture reading assignments? _____

      Do you evaluate how many are doing the scripture assignments? _____

         If yes, how do you evaluate this? _____

Do you use **Prayer** in the Program? _____

      How frequently is prayer used in your program? _____

      Are there daily prayer assignments? _____

      Do you evaluate how often participants pray? _____

      If yes, how do you evaluate this? _____

Do you have participants **contact Seventh-day Adventist** church members for help? _____

If yes, how often do you recommend contact?_____

Do you evaluate the number of contacts that are made? _____

If yes, how do you evaluate this? _____

Do you evaluate the number of participants who request **Bible studies**? _____

Do you evaluate the **susceptibility** of participants to attend **evangelistic meetings**? _____

Do you evaluate the number of participants who are eventually **baptized**? _____

Do you evaluate the number of participants who become **active SDA members**? _____

Do you evaluate the **retention** of participants by the church? _____

## 8. Small Group Activities:

Does the program contain small group activities? ____ No. (Go to section **9**) ____ Yes.

Do you provide leaders for small group activity? ____ No. ____ Yes.

Are small group leaders church members? ____ No. ____ Yes.

How many leaders are there in each group? ____ (Typically, what do you aim for?)

How many program participants are there in each group? _____

How many sessions have small group activity?

    ____ All sessions.
    ____ More than half the sessions.

_____ Less than half the sessions.
_____ None.

In a typical meeting how much time is spent in small group activity?

_____ 5-14 minutes
_____ 15-29 minutes
_____ 30 minutes or more

What percentage of a program session is spent in small groups?

_____ 5-25% of a session is spent in small group activity.
_____ 25-32%
_____ 33-49%
_____ about 50% or a bit more?

Does each small group session have a specific agenda?

_____ Yes. Activities are structured and are patterned after the day's lecture.
_____ Yes. Guidelines are general in nature and activities vary from group to group.
_____ No. This is social time unrelated to the topic for the session. This is time to build friendships.

**9. Follow-up Activities:** Indicate Y for yes and N for no.

_____ There is no specific follow-up.

_____ There is at least one follow-up meeting at a central location where all participants are invited.

_____ How many follow-up meetings of this type are there? _____

_____ Follow-up is done primarily by mail or online.

____ How many follow-up contacts of this type are made? _____
____ Follow-up is done in the participant's home. _____
____ How many follow-up contacts of this type are attempted? ____
____ Follow-up questions focus on maintenance of behavior change?

____ Follow-up questions inquire about the use of a person's spiritual resources in maintaining their new behaviors?

    ____ Inquiry is made as to the use of prayer.
    ____ Inquiry is made as to the use of scripture.
    ____ Inquiry is made as to interest in Bible studies.
    ____ Inquiry is made as to church attendance.

____ Follow-up questions include questions about attitude or mental state.

Other features of your follow-up activities. _____
_____
_____

**10. Data Collection and Analysis:** Indicate Y for yes and N for no.

    ____ Registration Form? Basic demographic data?
    ____ First Session Questionnaire? Documenting initial behaviors?
    ____ Questionnaire or progress cards utilized during the program?

        ____ Each session?
        ____ Other? _____

    ____ Last Session Questionnaire? Document changes during the program?
    ____ Three-month follow-up questionnaire?

____ Data collected in personal visit?

    ____ Data collected by mail or email?

_____ Six-month follow-up questionnaire?

_____ Data collected in personal visit?

_____ Data collected by mail or email?

_____ Twelve-month follow-up questionnaire?

_____ Data collected in personal visit?

_____ Data collected by mail or email?

_____ Other. Please describe? _____

_____ Data entry and analysis.

_____ We only keep paper copies.

_____ Analysis consists of totals added up directly from paper copies.

_____ Data is entered into a database maintained on site.

_____ What type of software do you use? _____

_____ Have you analyzed the data? _____

_____ Data is entered into a remote/online database.

_____ What site maintains your data? _____

_____ Have you analyzed the data? _____

Please describe the results of your scientific data analysis. _____
_____
_____

Please describe the results of your spiritual/evangelistic data analysis.
_____

# Appendix C. Best Weigh

Best Weigh is a 10-week program designed to help people lose weight, learn the principles of good nutrition, and experience God as the agent of lasting behavior change in the human life. Best Weigh is a health evangelism program developed by Dr. Elvin Adams in 1974. Since then, it has been used around the world and helped thousands of people experience the power that a connection with God brings to practical health issues.

Best Weigh is designed to follow the principles outlined in this book. It is designed to be conducted in Seventh-day Adventist churches. It utilizes church members as small group leaders. It contains not only correct scientific lectures for health professional presentation, but spiritual messages for presentation by the pastoral staff.

Best Weigh uses Bible verses for daily inspirational reading. Best Weigh teaches people to pray. These spiritual components have been shown to significantly improve the successful weight loss of the participants who take the Best Weigh program. Best Weigh incorporates these principles in an easy-to-use format and gives a systems-based solution to those seeking to implement a health evangelism program that is "out of the box."

Best Weigh LV is available on a thumb drive and includes digital copies of a Director's Manual, Helper's Guide, participant Best Weigh Workbook, nutritional PowerPoint slides ready with notes for presentation, spiritual outlines for a pastor's segment, and the forms and documents for ease of presentation, public relations efforts, etc.

Dr. Adams updated the program to its latest iteration, Best Weigh LV, in 2022. This program is available by contacting Dr. Eric Nelson. Email: enelson06m@gmail.com or mail: 1128 Boy Scout Rd, Hixson, TN, 37343.

# Appendix D. Jesus Was Thin, So You Can Be Thin Too

This book is a valuable tool for people wanting to lose weight. It utilizes 150 scripture verses that can be applied to weight management. The most common comment I have received from those reading the book is that confronting obesity from a spiritual point of view is "sobering and true."

The title is not sacrilegious. Psalm 22 is a very remarkable and specific prophecy of the sufferings of Jesus. We see the scene of the crucifixion clearly in the words, "A company of evildoers encircles me; they have pierced my hands and feet—**I can count all my bones**—they stare and gloat over me; they divide my garments among them, and for my clothing they cast lots." This psalm comes to its fullest realization in Jesus.

Jesus first became emaciated during the 40 days of fasting in the wilderness at the beginning of his ministry. This was a lesson for us on appetite control. During His lifetime he walked hundreds of miles. He ate a sparce diet and often shared his meals with those in need.

Jesus was thin. This prophecy in Psalms indicates that "all his bones" were visible. His ribs were not covered with a layer of fat. Jesus is our example in all things. We need to strive to be thin like He was. We will be healthier for it.

This book is for anyone struggling with appetite control and can be used as accessory reading material for those taking the Best Weigh program. It is available at any online book distributor.

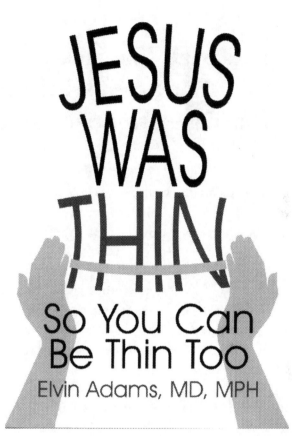

JESUS WAS THIN

So You Can Be Thin Too

Elvin Adams, MD, MPH

# Appendix E. The Healthiest People. The Science behind Seventh-day Adventist Success

Seventh-day Adventists are the healthiest people in the world. In every country where they have been studied, they emerge having the longest life expectancy, less cancer, less cardiovascular disease, and the lowest mortality rate of any segment of the population.

Seventh-day Adventists have been studies most extensively in the United States. They have been investigated for over 70 years. The current cohort study enrolled nearly 100,000 subjects at the onset. Hundreds of peer-reviewed scientific papers have been published using Seventh-day Adventist data.

This book contains the most concise distillation of the most important of these studies. The book is crammed with graphs that accurately portray the Seventh-day Adventist health advantages. The Adventist lifestyle is examined in detail.

The references to the articles quoted in this book fill 22 pages. There is not a more comprehensive document published today summarizing the Seventh-day Adventist Health advantage.

This is the book you need to prove you know what you are talking about when advocating specific dietary and exercise recommendations for the public.

The Healthiest People is available from any online bookstore.

# Appendix F. Total Health Spokane

If Jesus were on the earth today,
how would HE reach the people?

Christ's method alone will give true success in reaching the people.

The Saviour mingled with men as one who desired their good.

He showed His sympathy for them, ministered to their needs, and won their confidence.

Then He bade them, "Follow Me" MH 143

# TOTAL HEALTH SPOKANE

A Volunteer Missionary Experience and Field School in Gospel Medical Evangelism

## Positions Available for August 2022 Team

Contact John Torquato, MD
208-699-2136 (cell/txt)
JTorquato1@gmail.com
Review program and application at THSvolunteer.com

## Mission Responsibilities & Activities

- A full-time commitment of 9 months to Volunteer Missionary Work with Field School Training.
- Participate in 6 week Gospel Medical Evangelism Field School and ongoing training through the year.
- Be trained to provide health education and health coaching/health partnering to interests
- Receive training and practice the principles of Company Evangelism.  (aka Team Evangelism)
- Work in teams with other missionaries and local church members to:
  - teach health classes and/or cooking classes
  - develop and run at least one weekly small group per volunteer
  - minister to community members regarding felt needs (aka Beneficent Work)
  - develop and guide at least two community based beneficent projects per class
  - participate in colporteur work and door to door health work
  - actively engage and disciple church members in community-based outreach ministry
- Teach Bible studies to interested individuals including all 28 fundamental doctrines of the SDA church.
- Personally live and teach patients the health message, including a vegetarian diet
- Attend and integrate into your assigned church for Sabbath School, Church and Prayer meeting.
- Participate in the THS mentorship program with your chosen/assigned mentor
- Participate in 1 day per week vocational activity to provide for personal needs and self-support.
- A host home will be provided where you will share a room with at least one other volunteer.
- Participate 4 hours per week in chores for your host home.

For information regarding mission activities, housing and finances
Contact John Torquato at jtorquato1@gmail.com, 208-699-2136 (cell/txt)

Near the end of Ellen White's life, God communicated through her the need for a different type of evangelism....

"During the night of February 27 (1910), a representation was given me in which the unworked cities were presented before me as a living reality, and I was plainly instructed that there should be a decided change from past methods of working. For months the situation has been impressed on my mind, and I urged that companies be organized and diligently trained to labor in our important cities."[1]

"There should be companies organized and educated most thoroughly to work as nurses, as evangelists, as ministers, as canvassers, as gospel students, to perfect a character after the divine similitude."[2]

*"Company Evangelism"*

Soon after, in 1910, a team in Loma Linda, California led by evangelist John Tindall took this vision and ran with it. It soon became one of the most effective methods of evangelism the church had ever seen.

The results spoke for themselves. Over the course of twelve years almost every effort resulted in at least 100 – 200 baptisms. Churches were revived and remained so years after the close of the initial effort.

Churches saw an astounding 75% – 90% retention rate of converts. "People come flocking into the church," one physician put it, "and a large number are converted, not to a man or a few doctrines, but to Jesus and His message."[3]

Before the campaigns closed more money was brought into the treasury than had been expended. The effort more than paid for itself by the time it finished.

Most importantly, it highlighted the loving ministry of Jesus and put Seventh-day Adventists in a new light before the world. Out of curiosity, the secular editor of a three-county newspaper interviewed the team individually to get to the bottom of the ministry. Her article concluded with these words: *"We have heard of Adventists, but we have never seen Adventists like these. This is the most beautiful representation of the life of Jesus in His loving ministry that we have ever seen."*[4]

John Tindall

The results and testimonies go on and on. However, one of the most impactful statements comes from Willie White, Ellen White's own son. In remarking on what he saw in these efforts, he was reported to have said, *"I wish my mother could have seen this! This was the type of work she was calling for and believed in."*[5]

So what was it that touched people's hearts and attracted so much attention? The secret was that they employed Christ's method of ministry. They came close to people in Christian kindness and helped them in practical, tangible ways to a new life, all the while pointing their new-found friends to Jesus, the Great Physician, and His love.

They changed people's lives by touching their hearts.

Here is a brief synopsis of their work.

The team provided large meetings for the public each week that touched on healthful diet, disease, and the message of God for this time. The positive and practical were stressed.

[1] White, E.G., Manuscript 21, 1910
[2] White, E.G., *Counsels on Health*, pg. 396.5
[3] Campbell, Lenore D., "A New Evangelism," *The Medical Evangelist* (1920), pg. 3
[4] Gulley, Norman R., *Gospel-Medical Evangelism*, pg. 77
[5] Pierson, Robert H., *The Wildwood Story*, pg. 5

Wanting to come close to the people, classes and community small groups were set up during the week where interested individuals could come and receive more personal, hands-on instruction.

Not content with expecting the people to come to them, this team went to the people! Daily they could be found ministering at the bedside of the sick, encouraging the tempted, praying with the discouraged, and empowering the interested.

The results and spirit of the work spoke for themselves.

*Experiment in Hayden, Idaho*

**Total Health Spokane**, a ministry co-founded by Dr. John Torquato and Pastor Wayne Kablanow, is trying to bring back this crucial, yet forgotten, ministry of our past.

In the year 2014 we began this process and saw the exciting beginning of similar results.

Six young people sacrificially committed seven weeks to participate in an intensive health initiative in Hayden, Idaho. Inspired by Tindall's work, they became health evangelists. Twenty-four patients were selected from Dr. Torquato's office. Each worker was assigned four patients. They teamed up with local church members and conducted an in-home lifestyle change program with a religious foundation.

Dr. John Torquato

These energetic medical ministers showed these patients how to cook healthfully. They exercised with them, took them shopping, and prayed with them. An additional 36 guests from the community joined in weekly health classes at the church. The work was done under the guidance of a physician (Dr. Torquato) and the spiritual direction of a pastor (Pastor Kablanow).

All the while, local church members joined in the visits and built relationships. At the end of just seven weeks, six of the patients made a commitment to the Sabbath truth. It was truly a revolutionary experience for everyone involved.

Pastor Wayne Kablanow

*A Vision Born*

God worked mightily in Hayden. In 2017 we wanted to take it to the next level. We wanted to bring back this lost ministry. We wanted to put Christ's method on full display, and unleash its power to change lives. We wanted to show that health ministry is not just a temporary event or program, but a way of life.

The positive results in Hayden led us to develop a much larger health evangelism initiative in nearby Spokane, Washington. With strong support from the North View Seventh-day Adventist Church, we laid ground work to conduct a two-year medical ministry field school.

Here is a brief explanation of the work.

From September 2017 to August 2019, THS recruited 5 self-supporting students who practiced health outreach. Several steps were used. Under the direction of a licensed physician, they conducted in-home lifestyle programs. Working with local church members, they also held Bible studies. In addition, the local church will provided service projects for the community.

For two years this team held multiple health programs and outreach efforts, each following the basic pattern of ministry in health, spirituality, and benevolence.

A ministry-minded clinic was part of the foundation of the effort, seeing patients every day and coordinating their care with the medical minister students. The medical ministers helped in any way help was needed, whether cooking, exercise, shopping, accountability, praying, opening God's Word, or just plain being a friend. The goal was to empower the interested parties to transition into a life of wholeness and freedom.

These dedicated self-sacrificing volunteers finished their commitment working hard for the salvation of souls. As a result of their two year sacrificial effort there are now individuals who are members of the Seventh-day Adventist Church. Praise God! By the blessing of God and through God's divine power, fruit came from the sacrificial labors of these dedicated volunteers, working in conjunction with missionary minded church members who have now stepped up to disciple the new believers..

*A New Generation*

In 2020 we had a year of changes and challenges. First we had the retirement of one of our cofounders of THS, Pastor Wayne Kablanow. Although Pastor Kablanow retired, he has stayed on as a mentor and advisor for Total Health Spokane. As Pastor Kablanow retired we received a new pastor and co-director for THS, Pastor Joe Reeves. Pastor Reeves has picked up the torch and has run with it since starting in his new position as the pastor of Mead, Washington and Spirit Lake, Washington church district, and new co-director of Total Health Spokane. Also in 2020, we started our second group of 5 missionaries. Immediately upon starting our mission year, the CoVid-19 pandemic struck. Although we had to shift-on-the-fly, we immediately made the transition to an on-line health coaching program that continued the efforts of meeting the needs in the community with the principles of ministry we have been experimenting with, and at the same time following state mandated guidelines for safety and social distancing. Again, as a result of the sacrificial service of these dedicated volunteers there are individuals who are in various stages of spiritual growth and development. Praise God!

Pastor Joe Reeves

We continue to develop yearly groups of THS volunteers and as we work we feel we are ready to hit our stride. With plans to continue saturating the community with the message of hope which we have to share we are stepping forth in faith that God will provide resources and volunteers to finish this work.

We desire to respond to the gospel commission and lead many community members to a full commitment to Jesus through baptism into the Seventh-day Adventist Church. Our plan is to organize new members into small home groups. They will be trained to reach out in the same way they were reached. Ultimately, the model that is developing will be shared with others as one example for city evangelism based on the inspired counsel. We believe the model given to the church from Ellen White's 1910 vision has the potential to transform the way city evangelism is done across North America, and even around the world.

This is our desire. We want to bring back this lost ministry. We want "jets of light" to shine forth from Spokane and from every city where such sacrifices for the Lord are made. We want the work which the Lord has inspired the church to do to be a "memorial" for God.[6]

*A Step of Faith*

Our volunteers support themselves by working one day per week and by fundraising. Their goal is to earn approximately $650/month for their own support for the duration of the 9 month program. We believe once this ministry gets started, it will support itself. However, initially our volunteers fundraise and work in various fields of tentmaking to provide themselves with:

- Housing
- Food
- Toiletries
- Communication
- Transportation
- Short term "Travel insurance" for the year

We believe God is leading in this health initiative. We continue to step out in faith and invite as many as have a heart to serve and partner with us in this adventure to stand beside us and our self-sacrificing volunteers. You can participate by praying that the work will go forward unimpeded. You can participate by joining us for our next 9 month training and service cycle. You can participate by providing a sacrificial gift to support someone else who is serving when you are not able. Your sacrificial participation and/or gift, whatever it may be, will bring people to Christ through earnest prayers and dedicated volunteer work which using a holistic approach to evangelism.

[6] White, E.G., *Testimonies for the Church*, VOL 9, pg. 28, par. 4

When a boulder gets going, it keeps rolling, but often it needs a push to get started. This is how we view this work. At the outset it requires our heaviest sacrificial investment, but once it gets going, we believe God will keep it rolling because it is the work He is calling for and that is near to His heart.

These are the last days. We want the right arm of the third angel's message to go forward with power, to be vindicated, and to open the doors and hearts that God intended it to before His soon return. Friend, will you prayerfully join us in bringing back this lost ministry of Jesus?

*"When the cities are worked as God would have them, the result will be the setting in operation of a mighty movement such as we have not yet witnessed."[7]*

Reaching bodies and hearts for Christ,

John Torquato, MD
Co-Director, Total Health Spokane,
President, Family Medical Care Clinics Corp
(208) 699-2136

Pastor Joe Reeves
Co-Director, Total Health Spokane
Pastor, North View Seventh-day
Adventist Church, (509) 368-4032

P.S. Our greatest need is prayer. Please pray for our hearts. Pray for the hearts of the people we will work with. Pray for our plans and needs. And please pray as we minister to the City of Spokane as an example of the many cities that need this type of ministry across our nation. God bless you!

---

*Stay Updated*

- Email updates— Send request to registrar@totalhealthspokane.com
- Website— www.totalhealthspokane.com
- To join our next class in training and service — www.THSvolunteer.com

*Mail Your Tax-Deductible Donations to Support Our Volunteers*

Total Health Spokane
PO Box 970
Mead, WA 99021

*Memo:* "Total Health Spokane"

---

[7] White, E.G., *Medical Ministry*, pg. 304

Printed in the United States
by Baker & Taylor Publisher Services